W9-CMF-832

ISBN 0-8223-3374-0

9 780822 333159

THE CONTROL OF

GLOBAL RESOURCES

JAMES RIDGEWAY

It's All

for Sale

Duke University Press

Durham & London

2004

© 2004 JAMES RIDGEWAY
All rights reserved
Printed in the United States of
America on acid-free paper ∞
Designed by Rebecca Giménez.
Typeset in Adobe Minion by
Keystone Typesetting, Inc. Library
of Congress Cataloging-in-
Publication Data appear on the
last printed page of this book.

Contents

ACKNOWLEDGMENTS

I wish to thank Jean Casella for all her help throughout this project; Judy Davis who kept tabs on preparation of the manuscript; and my wonderful interns who worked years on this book: Gabrielle Jackson, Cassandra Lewis, Rouven Guissaz, Kate Cortesi, Ariston Lizabeth Anderson, Sandra Bisin, Joanna Khenkine, Phoebe St John, Sarah Park, Meritxell Mir, Michael Ridley, Josh Hersh, Caroline Ragon, Josh Saltzman, Rebecca Winsor, and Adrian Brune. I am also grateful to Curtis Lang, Phillip Levy and Bridge Street Books, Adrienne Fugh-Berman, Alpha Diallo, Jeffrey St. Clair, Camelia Fard, Bo Eddy, Cindy Mellon, Alysa Zeltzer, Mark Ritchie, Al Krebs, Charlie Arnot, Kris Jacobs, Rob Weissman, John Richard and the Center for Study of Responsive Law, Public Citizen, Tyson Slocum, Ronnie Cummins, Russell Mokhiber, David Ridgeway, Mike McCarthy. I want to thank Valerie Millholland, Mark Mastromarino, and the most helpful staff at the Duke University Press. And I am especially grateful to Patricia Ridgeway.

INTRODUCTION

Commodities seldom draw much attention in the interpretation of today's world events. And yet they have played an important role in the evolution of colonialism and empire, and in the waging of small and large wars. They have influenced the flow of migration and emigration. People were enslaved to exploit commodities. They have always been at the heart of things.

The earliest known trade routes across the world, which brought distant and disparate cultures into contact, were created in order to obtain and transport new commodities. The ancient Silk Road from Japan to the Mediterranean was one. Another was the route to trade pepper, which in some places was treated as money. Marco Polo and Columbus are famous as explorers, but they were also businessmen—pushed on perhaps by their adventurous spirits, but also by the quest for new sources and routes for the trade of valuable commodities. (So too were the Chinese, great traders of the times, who it now seems may have beat out the Europeans in the "discovery" of the Americas.)

Colonialism was justified by Western ideas of racial, religious, and civil superiority, but it was often driven by the quest for natural resources, the raw materials of the Industrial Revolution. Slavery was supported by a system that turned human beings into commodities, to be handled no differently from the molasses and rum that completed the famous eighteenth-century "triangle trade" route. In the nineteenth century, the British manufactured textiles and sent them to India, then refilled the ships with opium and dispatched them to China. The money they received for opium was used to buy tea, which was sent to England. A hundred years later, the United States supported Pinochet's coup against Salvador Allende in Chile in part because of his nationalization of the nation's big copper deposits. While a determination to "contain" communism and Soviet power was certainly the paramount motivation behind America's wars and covert actions in the developing world during the cold war years, such motivations were often closely intertwined with issues of resource control. The Cuban revolution, for example, reduced America's supply of nickel, forcing the United States to quickly find other sources of this crucial metal. The same event was used to justify enormous subsidies to the American sugar industry, as sugar was deemed a commodity necessary to "national security," too precious to justify reliance upon volatile Caribbean and Latin American suppliers.

The linkage of commodities to national security has been used to justify military interventions and deployments to protect essential routes of trade, as well as supplies of commodities. In the 1980s the U.S. military began to talk about protecting certain "strategic" trade routes around the world, the most prominent running from the Persian Gulf around the Horn of Africa to North America. The Strait of Malacca, through which oil tankers passed from the Middle East to Southeast Asia and Japan, was another. The American invasion of Panama in 1989 was based on the determination of the United States to control a pivotal trade route. And at the beginning of the twenty-first century, military planners were studying how to protect the Northwest Passage—stretching from the North Atlantic across the Arctic to the Pacific Ocean—which connects Europe to Asia more directly than those trade routes leading through the Panama Canal or around the tip of South America. Global warming and melting glaciers have opened up the Northwest Passage throughout the year.

The struggle for control of resources took a new turn with the end of the cold war. During the cold war the United States and the old Soviet Union had supported opposing groups of "freedom fighters" struggling to control nations in Africa, Latin America, and Asia. These groups vied for control of a country's government—and by implication its resources—in the interests of nation building. Today the situation is quite different. Many contemporary conflicts in the developing world take place below or outside the level of nation states. A study by the United Nations in 2002 revealed networks of rogue army officers and so-called warlords, errant forces on the loose and allied with cynical politicians and transnational corporations to control and exploit forests, as well as diamonds, copper, and other minerals. In many cases, formal political considerations have been virtually removed from the equation, or they take a back seat to the bald fight over lucrative commodities. In American terms, the situation harks back to the days of the nineteenth-century robber barons and their henchmen, who were a law unto themselves in the timber and gold-mining camps of the West.

When regional strife in seven African states brought their armies together in the Congo, the elite officers of the Zimbabwean army began profiting from the mineral trade there. When that army withdrew, the officers signed a secret deal with politicians in the Congo to continue the exploitation of diamonds.

As they did so the revolutionary quarrels of the cold war were replaced by non-ideological mercenary armies whose main interest was making money. An investigation by the Center for Public Integrity in Washington found more than 90 military companies operating in 110 countries. These armies for hire are to some extent the modern equivalent of the French Foreign Legion.

"These corporate armies, providing services normally carried out by a national military force, offer specialized skills in high-tech warfare, including communications and signals intelligence and aerial surveillance, as well as pilots, logistical support, battlefield planning and training. They have been hired both by the governments and multinational corporations to further their policies or protect their interests."[1] Indeed, one large corporation owns a private military company as a subsidiary. These military companies thrive below the radar in the worldwide small-arms bazaar, where a firm can outfit itself with secondhand Russian gear or pirated arms from one of the former Soviet-bloc nations in central and eastern Europe. Small arms do not amount to much in terms of the overall arms market—perhaps 10 percent of the total—but they do the work in most of the wars and are responsible for virtually all the killing. In real terms, these are the true weapons of mass destruction.

The U.S. government, which during the cold war years was thought to have excellent programs to track the arms trade, lost interest just as the private armies were taking off and stores of Soviet small arms had begun to flood the market. Today, in fact, the United States is a prime customer for suppliers of the privatized military. According to the Center for Public Integrity, the government since 1994 has signed 3,061 contracts with 12 of the 24 American-based private military companies. The business was lucrative, valued at $300 billion. British mercenaries also have worked for American governmental agencies.[2]

Traditional notions of sovereignty and ownership are subverted in other ways as well in today's world. Throughout the nineteenth century and early twentieth, colonialism was the way in which Western powers controlled various vital commodities. To own the commodities, they "owned" the nations in which they were located. It would appear that in the anticolonial struggles of the mid-twentieth century, the third world nations regained ownership of their own resources. But outright ownership of a commodity does not necessarily spell control of the business—or its profits. In the petroleum industry, for example, the oil-producing countries have a much greater stake in ownership of their oil than ever before. Yet the international business still is controlled by a handful of big oil companies that process, transport, and distribute the end products. In post-Independence India, to cite another example, the auctions at which farmers sold their raw tea were supposedly free and aboveboard, while, in fact, Indian officials claimed, they were rigged so that a small number of companies actually controlled the business from London.

A trend toward the globalization of business has been accompanied by a continuing trend toward concentration. The result is that a surprisingly small number of large companies control many of the basic commodities we use in everyday life. While we are led to believe that foreign trade in raw materials involves many thousands of different producers, traders, and purchasers, in fact the trade is most often governed by a few companies. Despite the rise of OPEC, five major international oil companies still dominate the worldwide petroleum industry. Four private corporations control the world trade in grain; four in meatpacking; three in timber; one in tea; one in coffee. Two are fighting it out for fresh water, and one company sells much of the world's cigarettes. One company has a monopoly on diamonds. And on and on.

If there is one thing the trade in resources does not do, it is to follow the mythical free-market precepts still so passionately argued by the academic economists and politicians. In fact, since the Industrial Revolution trade in raw materials has generally been shaped by a handful of individual entrepreneurs and corporations, and today on occasion by a combination of corporations and nations. An example of the latter type of combination was the creation of a cartel that included representatives of the Australian and French governments along with executives of the Rio Tinto Zinc company, a firm that plays a significant role in mining uranium. For a time in the early 1970s the cartel held sway over world uranium prices.

The business of commodities is controlled in part by surplus and scarcity. The energy crisis of the early 1970s conditioned us to think in terms of shortage—a shortage of oil for gasoline, of cobalt for aircraft parts, of coffee, or of rice. But history instructs that the opposite has also been the case. Surplus, not shortage, has been the driving force in building markets, creating supply, and determining price. Indeed, it can be argued that a central concern of the modern world economic system during the twentieth century has been to organize and promote markets so that they are protected from ruinous surplus.

Two important cases illustrate the point. The first concerns food. Perhaps the single most important problem for American foreign policy since the building of the railroads and the opening of prairie agriculture in the middle of the nineteenth century has been how to dispose of farm surplus, notably grain. While many farmers left the land for the city in the early twentieth century, mechanization enabled the surplus to keep on growing. The surplus was reduced and farmers saved from deep depression by two world wars and the Korean and Vietnam conflicts. After the Second World War, conservatives and liberals in the United States found agreement in a new approach to getting rid of the surplus in the form of the Food for Peace program. Under it the government oversaw the disposal of the surplus to American allies abroad. In short, food became a weapon in foreign policy. At the same time, during the Nixon administration, the government formally encouraged a concept of agribusiness that supported management of the surplus by the private sector, not by government agencies. As a practical matter, this meant that disposal of the surplus was increasingly the job of the major grain-trading companies, not the government.

Ironic as it may seem, the recent humanitarian concerns for making the food surplus available to millions of poor, undernourished people must be viewed as almost incidental to the overall march of American agricultural policy, which has sought over the last century to win a profitable and stable market for the surplus. For example, cancellation by the United States of grain sales to the Soviet Union in 1979 was a setback to long-term American policy, throwing the grain markets into temporary panic and raising the specter to farmers of future surplus.

Surplus, not shortage, has also governed the oil industry since its inception. Prospectors in western Pennsylvania in 1859 feared that an uncontrolled flood of oil would cause prices to fall and destroy their markets. Through the Standard Oil Trust, John D. Rockefeller sought to organize the industry so that it would not be overwhelmed by unbridled competition fed by surplus. After the First World War major international companies formed an international petroleum cartel in Mesopotamia (now Iraq) to prevent the vast new supplies of oil entering into world markets from making unmanageable their control of those markets. That cartel, enlarged to include other producing areas, endured past the end of the Second World War and survived until the rise of OPEC in the 1960s. One reason why the oil companies moved into the coal industry was their fear that this abundant resource might be turned into a devastating, uncontrollable river of synthetic oil.

The war in Iraq was never primarily about terrorism or even weapons of mass destruction. Like so many other conflicts throughout history, it was driven in large part by the American superpower's struggle to control valuable commodities. The current map of the Middle East was set in place by the Western powers to facilitate the expropriation of oil. The roots of American involvement in Iraq are intertwined with the history of British colonialism and empire in the region, reaching back to the early twentieth century. In a certain sense, the United States today finds itself in a similar situation, with raw materials as the driving force for forging its own postcolonial worldwide political empire.

In anticipation of the First World War, Winston Churchill, then lord of the admiralty, decided to take the British navy's advice and switch its main fuel source from coal to oil, so as to make the battleship, the chief naval weapon of the time, a more supple weapon. To obtain the oil, the navy had been quietly backing various prospectors who had discovered oil in the Mesopotamian desert and had asserted control over both oil and territory.

By the early 1920s the British governed much of present-day Iraq, Iran, and Jordan, under a mandate from the newly formed League of Nations. They found themselves sitting on a great trove of oil, and British companies proceeded to use their growing surplus to attack the American market. They set up shop and started underselling the American oil companies, whose operations were then still limited to North America and controlled primarily by the Rockefeller family.

In fending off the British, the American government, through the U.S. Geological Survey, issued reports warning of a grave shortage of oil in the United States. The threat of shortage was the basis upon which the United States began to push for its own involvement in the Middle East. With the sun setting on its empire, the British cut the Americans into the oil business by including them in a so-called cooperative venture known as the Iraq Petroleum Company. This venture was the predecessor to the Seven Sisters cartel—a consortium of one British, one Anglo-Dutch, and five American firms—that came to dominate the oil business beyond the Second World War and the cold war and into the early years of OPEC. The power of the big companies today remains enormous, although it has shifted away from production to distribution.

Middle Eastern oil did not mean much to the West until after the Second World War, when because of its low cost it came to play a greater role in the world oil business. (In the mid-1950s, the price of Middle Eastern oil ran between 5 and 15 cents a barrel, while the world market price was around $2.25.) The increasing price of oil coincided with the rise of nationalism in the area and the overall decline of British and French colonial power. To maintain their grip on oil, the big companies kept their hand in the game by playing the countries off against one another. When the nationalist Mohammad Mosaddeq came to power in Iran in 1951, the CIA fomented a coup that replaced him with the Shah. In 1961, when Iraq sought to regain control over its own immense reserves, it ran head-on into a Western embargo. Then the Seven Sisters got Kuwait and Iran to increase their output to make up the shortfall on the world market. Iraq was punished with reduced production and hence lower revenues.

The Persian Gulf War of 1991 was fought over oil, and Iraq's production subsequently was sharply cut back and placed under sanctions. Even so, the United States bought large quantities of Iraqi oil, so much so that it was the fifth-largest supplier to the U.S. market. By 2002 Saddam's saber rattling threatened neighboring oil countries, in particular Saudi Arabia, where the royal family's position was under attack.

Even a cursory reading of history would seem to demonstrate that Western policies toward Iraq have long been framed by oil. But to read American press accounts of the last decade, oil distantly trails a range of other factors—

from Kuwaiti national sovereignty, to the rise of Muslim fundamentalism, to threats to Israel, and lately to the vaguely defined war on terror.

As the environmentalists have pointed out, this long history of battling surplus in the petroleum industry cannot continue forever. There is disagreement over when the world will exhaust its supplies of oil and natural gas. And while the oil supply of the world evidently is immense, as indicated most recently by finds in the Arctic, western Africa, and central Asia, not to mention the uncharted areas of Iraq, different pressures may well combine to bring on alternative energy sources, whether those be solar or nuclear power, or even synthetic fuels made from coals and shales. Unfortunately this has never happened. (Even during and after the energy crisis of the 1970s, there was little movement toward alternatives.) If history is any guide, alternative energy sources will be a long time in coming.

Moving beyond the questions of control and surplus, a survey of the world commodities industry is startling in other respects. What businessmen take for granted, an outsider finds astounding—namely, how useless or deleterious many of the principal components of trade are. For instance, in terms of dollars, the worldwide trade in heroin and cocaine ranks with that in grain or metals. Tobacco, which causes cancer, remains a significant commodity in world trade and, until recently, was vigorously supported in its export by the U.S. government. Tea, a plant of minimal nutritional value, consumes land and labor in Asia that might otherwise be employed in growing food. Ever since sugar first appeared in the Middle East before Christ's time, it has hop-skipped its way from one Mediterranean island to another, finally crossing the Atlantic to the Caribbean and thence going on to the North American continent. Wherever it was grown sugar scarred the land and made the people subservient to a monoculture economy. Its demand by royalty eliminated the possibility of agricultural diversity in the Mediterranean. Later the sugar crop formed the industrial base for slavery in the New World. And all this for a product that nutritionally does more harm than good.

As time goes on and both science and globalization advance, the list of commodities grows. Things never before considered commodities—things that were free, unlimited, or beyond the pale of human commerce—have become commodities today. The world's shortage of fresh drinking water has not led to substantial exploration of new sources, but rather to greater exploitation of current ones, making the provisioning of fresh water a good business opportunity. Businesses are keen to snap up supplies and barter water in international commerce. Turning water into a privately traded commodity is often undertaken in the name of efficiency. The oceans are being commodified, as oil drilling pushes further and further from the coasts. Offshore fishing rights are auctioned for territorial waters around the globe, and in the shallow seas adjacent to land the water is divided up and transformed into private fish farms. The sky—the earth's inner and outer atmosphere—is fast becoming a commodity, bought and sold in bits and pieces. It is already a crowded transportation highway for the commercial airlines, and also a garbage dump for polluting industries on earth. Today, companies can participate in federal programs to buy and sell air pollution rights—in effect purchasing space in the atmosphere. The human being, as a slave, has been a commodity for thousands of years. This trade continues in pockets of the world today—but now, parts of human bodies are commodities as well, from blood to eyes, kidneys, and hair. As the twenty-first century hits its stride, efforts are being made to commodify not only living things, but also, in a sense, life itself, with biotech companies making ownership claims to genetically engineered life forms.

It's All for Sale

Fresh Water

Clean drinking water is the one commodity we cannot do without. Yet it is also, perhaps, the commodity that we most take for granted. Like the air we breathe, it can appear not to be a commodity at all, but rather a free, limitless, natural phenomenon. The amount of the earth's water totals 330 million cubic miles, but only a smidgen of this vast supply, 2.6 percent, is fresh water, mostly from rainfall. Households and municipalities consume 10 percent of this water, and industry 20 to 25 percent. Irrigation accounts for around 65 to 70 percent.[1]

From the early twentieth century on, clean drinking water has been provided by local government, and in the United States sometimes through massive projects such as the numerous Colorado River diversion schemes that have been financed by state and federal governments. But that is not the way it has always been. In the early part of the nation's history, private companies supplied water. The mid-nineteenth century saw the development of modern sanitation practices, spurred by concerns for public health. In the early twentieth century, towns and cities in the United States wrested control of drinking water from private companies and made it a function of municipal government.[2]

But industrialization and especially development of modern agriculture have taken a toll on the American water supply. Today municipal water supplies are frequently polluted with heavy metals, pesticides, and other toxic substances. People unwilling to trust governments to guarantee the safety of the water supply are turning back to the days of privately supplied drinking water, in the form of bottled water. At the same time, cities and towns sometimes contract out with a private company to manage their water supplies. The consumer pays indirectly through taxes or in certain cases directly to the company.

Around the world water consumption is growing rapidly, and is expected to double every twenty years, a rate that is more than twice that of human population growth. More than one billion people cannot obtain fresh drinking water; projections suggest that at the quarter-century mark the demand for water will have outstripped overall supply.

An analysis of the world's water supply issued in October 2000 by the World Resources Institute states that overall the system is so degraded that "its ability to support human, plant and animal life is greatly in peril." Four out of every ten people live in river basins which already are experiencing water scarcity. "By 2025, at least 3.5 billion people or nearly 50 percent of the world's population will face water scarcity." In addition "more than 20 percent of the world's known 10,000 freshwater fish species have become extinct, been threatened or endangered in recent decades." The report points out that dams, canals, and other types of diversions have been built on 60 percent of the world's largest 227 rivers. These have contributed to the degradation of the world's freshwater systems, as have pollution, over-exploitation, the introduction of nonnative species, and habitat destruction. The introduction of nonnative fish in Europe, North America, and Australia and New Zealand, for example, has ended up destroying many species of native fish. "In North America, alone, 27 species and 13 subspecies of native fish became extinct in the last century largely due to the introduction of non-native fish." Polluted water continues to be a major cause of illness in the developing world.[3]

The most dangerous cases of pollution and overexploitation of the water supply are invisible because they take place underground. About 97 percent of the earth's liquid fresh water is stored in underground aquifers. Some of these aquifers are enormous. The Ogallala aquifer in the United States, for example, touches eight midwestern states and covers 453,000 square kilometers. Aquifers have been increasingly tapped as water sources as populations and croplands have grown. Today they are the source of drinking water for 1.2 to 2 billion people.

Asia draws one-third of its water from groundwater; Europe, 75 percent; Latin America, 29 percent; and the United States, 51 percent. One aquifer underlying eastern China provides water for 160 million people. Some of the world's largest cities—including Djakarta, Lima, and Mexico City—depend entirely on underground aquifers for water. In rural areas groundwater is often the only water source. In the United States it supplies 99 percent of the rural population.[4]

Among the most striking examples of groundwater abuse occurs in Bangladesh. Over 35 million Bangladeshis are drinking water contaminated with arsenic, and anywhere from 1 to 5 million are expected to die from that often slow-acting but deadly poison. The World Health Organization calls it the "largest mass poisoning of a population in history." Bangladesh is the eighth most populous nation in the world, with 135 million people living in an area the size of the state of Wisconsin. In the last two decades of the twentieth century, government and international groups such as UNICEF sought to persuade people to stop drinking pond water and tap into underground aquifers with wells.

DEPENDENT ON IRRIGATION, today's agriculture is draining groundwater supplies around the world. India is the third largest grain producer in the world and leads in total irrigated acreage. More than half of India's agricultural land gets water from underground aquifers, and the number of wells that draw groundwater increased from 3,000 in 1950 to 6 million in 1990.

Agriculture is also a leading cause of water pollution, affecting both underground sources as well as rivers, lakes, and other bodies of surface water. Nitrogen fertilizers, such an important component of the 1960s Green Revolution that introduced hybrid crops and newly developed pesticides and fertilizers, are a major cause of water pollution. As it turns out, less than half the nitrogen in these fertilizers is profitably used by crops, and much of the rest flows into underground water. The U.S. National Research Council estimates that "in the United States between a third and a half of nitrogen fertilizer applied to plants is wasted," because so much of it is just spread over the ground, and little reaches the actual plant.[5]

Ever since publication of Rachel Carson's 1962 book, *Silent Spring*, there has been a campaign to regulate pesticides. But it has made little progress. More than forty years after she sounded the alarm, there still are no safety standards for many pesticides. Standards exist for only thirty-three chemical compounds. In March 2002 the U.S. Geological Survey reported that 22 different antibiotics, as well as other prescription drugs, veterinary drugs, hormones, steroids, and fire retardants, have been found in 48 percent of 139 streams in 30 states. Traces of antibiotics used in animal agriculture were discovered downstream from various farm operations. In recent years public organizations have raised alarms because of increased use of antibiotics in animals to promote growth. Enormous quantities of feces from livestock farming also drain into the water system.

In addition, there is, of course, urban sewage. Nitrates drain from lawns and golf-course fertilizers and leak from landfills. These nitrates not only contaminate drinking water, but also destroy aquatic life, in part by spurring the growth of algae that covers the water and cuts off the oxygen supply.

Petroleum and various chemical additives called Volatile Organic Compounds (vocs) dribbling from old underground storage tanks are the most common form of groundwater contamination. In 1993 the EPA estimated there were some 100,000 tanks, many of them two or three decades old. To get rid of chemical residues that they knew were dangerous, companies for decades simply poured them into the water and into the earth—down drains, into septic tanks, into deep wells—or buried them. In the United States there are thousands of Superfund sites, where pollutants have been buried and are leaking into the surrounding groundwater. Groundwater in parts of the developing world, which sometimes depends on it as a sole source of drinking water, is widely being poisoned as chemical use continues to grow dramatically. World Watch reports, "In India, for example, the Central Pollution Control Board surveyed 22 major industrial zones and found that groundwater in every one of them was unfit for drinking."[6] The Aral Sea is a stark example of how a large body of water simply gets used up.

The earth now faces the volatile confluence of two major trends: a continuing, exponential growth in population, especially in the developing world, and a reduction in the supplies of clean, fresh water. As the demand for water increases and supply wanes, international companies sensing a profitable opportunity have jumped into the water business.

In the developing countries, where access to clean water is hard to come by, the World Bank has encouraged water privatization, but often at full cost, without any subsidy or support. This means that the governments of these nations must stretch their already strained budgets, or else pass on the high costs of this life-sustaining commodity to sometimes desperately poor consumers. This policy, along with the trade liberalization policies of the North American Free Trade Association and the World Trade Organization, provides an underpinning for private corporations anxious to make money from the provisioning of water.

Bechtel Enterprises of San Francisco, part of the Bechtel Group, contracted to manage the water system of Cochabamba, Bolivia, after the World Bank told Bolivia to privatize. The company pushed up the price of water, but the city rebelled. The military was called in. After four months of struggle, Bechtel quit the city, and the World Bank gave up its privatization program. The company is now under contract to help San Francisco upgrade its water system. Monsanto, the St. Louis-based agribusiness firm, also sees profits in water. At the beginning of the twenty-first century it was in the water business in Mexico and India. Water supplies in Mexico City already were in dire straits.[7]

In the United States, Lee County, Florida, took back control of its water system following an audit that showed that the private company contracted to run the system was not maintaining equipment properly, and the county's utility director estimated privatization had cost the citizens an extra $8 million. In Atlanta, the scene of the nation's largest water-privatization program, an audit in 2001 indicated that the private company was lagging in maintenance while at the same time asking the city for more money.[8]

ESTIMATES OF THE world market for water range anywhere from $300 to $800 billion annually, with 300 to 500 million people already getting their water from private corporations. This trend is by no means limited to the developing world. Most water systems in Great Britain were privatized under Margaret Thatcher's Conservative government, and more than three-quarters of the French draw water from private sources, including two French-based companies, Vivendi Universal and Suez. Maude Barlow and Tony Clarke write in *Blue Gold* that these two firms accounted for 70 percent of the existing water market at the end of the twentieth century. "Suez operates in 130 countries and Vivendi in well over 90. While Vivendi is the larger of the two water giants, posting bigger annual sales than its rival mainly because of its diverse operations and large customer base in France, Suez serves far more people (approximately 100 million) around the world. Of the 30 water contracts awarded by big cities since the mid-1990s, 20 went to Suez."[9]

Four other firms follow close behind these two leaders: Bouygues SAUR, RWE-Thames Water, Bechtel-United Utilities, and Enron-Azurix. These large corporations are transnational conglomerates with a sprawl of interests ranging from construction to entertainment. Most importantly, because they own natural gas production and pipelines as well as electricity, they are well positioned to become wide-reaching utility holding companies. Because of deregulation in the United States, major oil companies, which also produce most of the world's natural gas, have gone into the pipeline business, and now are positioning themselves to expand these utility holdings into water and even handling wastewater. This is of considerable significance because, with the coming water shortage, countries and private companies increasingly are looking at the prospect of hauling water from faraway areas (i.e., Canada and Alaska to the lower forty-eight states) by supertanker or huge bobbing plastic water bottles towed by a tugboat, and by pipelines. (One Canadian company made a deal to transport water from Sitka, Alaska, to China, where, taking advantage of cheap labor, it will be turned into bottled water.) These water pipelines would lie close by existing gas and oil pipelines.

The remaining, much smaller, companies specialize only in providing water. Three British firms got a boost when Thatcher privatized water: Severn Trent, Anglian Water, and the Kelda Group. There is also an American company, the American Water Works Company, which was purchased in 2003 by the German conglomerate RWE. With some 50 million American customers, it is the largest private water company operating in the United States. Also, "in 1999, Vivendi purchased U.S. Filter Corp. for $6 billion in cash. The same year, Suez—which built the Suez Canal in the 1860s—paid $1 billion for United Water Resources and bought two major U.S. water treatment chemical producers, Nalco and Calgon, for $4.5 billion."[10]

The United States may indeed be "the biggest, most underexploited water market on Earth, . . . with estimated annual revenues of $90 billion. About 86 percent of the municipal water in the United States is delivered by public utilities, while only 13 percent is delivered by private companies. But water companies are swiftly expanding their foothold in the United States through operations and maintenance contracts for water delivery and wastewater treatment services, or by assuming temporary or permanent ownership of water utilities."[11]

In 2002 legislation was proposed in the U.S. Senate (the Water Investment

Act of 2002) to require municipalities seeking federal aid for their water infrastructure to "consider" privatization as a means of cutting costs.[12]

IN THE INDUSTRIALIZED world those citizens who can afford to do so have already abandoned municipal water supplies as a source of drinking water, and instead get their water in bottles. As an alternative to tap water, bottled water is purchased in large jugs for water coolers, in smaller jugs or bottles, or in single-serving containers as a beverage in competition with such products as coffee, tea, and soft drinks.

Bottled water is regulated in the United States by the federal Food and Drug Administration, which sets standards. By definition, bottled water is sealed in a sanitary container; it cannot contain sweeteners or chemical additives (other than flavors, extracts, or essences, which must not exceed 1 percent of the final product) and must be calorie free and sodium free (or very low in sodium); and it may contain natural or added carbonation.

There are basically three types of bottled water. The biggest-selling category is water from a specific natural spring, such as Poland Springs and Evian. Some of it, like Coca-Cola's Dannon, comes from natural springs in different locations, and some of it, like another Coca-Cola product, Dasani, is "manufactured" water—municipal water which has undergone an elaborate purification process. Sparkling water—mineral water with natural or added fizz—is a fast-growing, prestige segment of the market, dominated by Perrier and Pellegrino. Its poor relation, seltzer—carbonated municipal water—has also grown in popularity.

When the bottled-water phenomenon began in the 1980s, it was perceived as a stylish, prestigious product, but since then, health concerns have outstripped image as a motivation for purchase (though few people over sixty buy bottled water). Prices have been reduced, and domestic brands now outsell foreign brands. By the end of the twentieth century, bottled water had become the single fastest-growing segment of the beverage industry in the United States, growing at a rate of 9 percent a year.

Individual bottles are the fastest growing part of the business. The largest chunks of the U.S. market lie on the Pacific Coast, with 21 percent, and in the Southwest, with 16 percent. Nationally, annual per-capita consumption stands at 12 gallons.

The market is so large that Pepsi and Coca-Cola have jumped into the business. The entrance of the large beverage firms with elaborate distribution systems makes it difficult for the smaller companies to compete. The business has become concentrated, with a handful of international companies accounting for 65 percent of the market, which in 1998 had total revenues of nearly $4 billion, almost double its level in 1990. Perrier alone accounts for one-quarter of the entire bottled-water market.

Despite public protests privatized water appears to be the future trend. Even the United Nations has gone in that direction. At a March 1998 conference in Paris, a UN Commission on Sustainable Development proposed that governments turn to "large multinational companies" for capital and expertise, and it called for an "open market" in water rights and an enlarged role for the private sector.

The future course seems depressingly obvious. Everyone knows the world's water is polluted. We more or less have given up on doing anything about it. Instead of attempting to put a stop to pollution through governmental regulation, we will just switch to bottled water. We look forward to a future in which the commodity most necessary to sustaining life ends up in the hands of private corporations.

Fuels

COAL ▸ Coal fired the Industrial Revolution. In fact it was not until 1912, the year that Winston Churchill, then first lord of the admiralty, ordered the British Navy to switch from coal to oil, that petroleum rose to paramount importance.

When energy shortages occurred toward the end of the twentieth century coal once again became prominent, as both government and industry studied the feasibility of turning the fuel into a synthetic gas that could supplement what were then thought to be dwindling reserves of natural gas. As a result, during the energy crisis of the 1970s the coal industry briefly became entangled with the petroleum business.

The earth is well endowed with coal. Most of it lies in North America, Asia, and Europe. The U.S. Department of Energy estimates that there are over 1,000 billion recoverable tons of coal under the surface of the planet. The United States and China are the leading producers of bituminous (and subbituminous) coal—the most common coals in the United States, with a moisture content less than 20 percent and used for electrical production— each accounting for some 1 billion tons. The two nations produce more than half of the world's coal. Far behind come India, South Africa, Australia,

Russia, and Poland. According to the U.S. government, coal resources ought to last 210 years—assuming that consumption continues at current levels.

Coal accounts for about 35 percent of U.S. energy production. Nearly all of it fires the boilers of utilities to make electricity. The industry has been busily opening up the vast coal resources in the Powder River Basin of Wyoming and Montana and the Colorado plateau of Colorado and Utah. Still the highest-quality low-sulfur coal continues to come from deep underground mines in West Virginia, eastern Kentucky, and western Virginia.[1]

Eastern coal is generally older than western coal, and the additional years of compression result in a higher quality. The highest rank of coal is anthracite, and is found principally in Pennsylvania and Alaska. Bituminous coal, the next-best grade, is located in the Appalachian and central states, Colorado, Utah, Alaska, Wyoming, New Mexico, Missouri, and Texas. While more than half of the remaining coal reserves in the United States are west of the Mississippi, these deposits are of a lower quality than those in the East and more likely to cause serious air pollution. Western coal often can be strip-mined, which makes it cheap, but because it is of a lower grade, more coal has to be burned to generate energy, which in turn produces more pollutants.

The coal resources of the United States are immense, totaling some 4 billion tons, according to the U.S. Geological Survey, and accounting for 25 percent of the world's estimated recoverable reserves. Most of the coal comes from twenty-five different identifiable beds.[2]

THROUGH MUCH OF the twentieth century, the American coal industry was a medieval enterprise. Over the years, the mines have claimed the lives of thousands of men. The mountains of Appalachia, which ought to be so rich because of the fuel, are instead poor, with many people sick from disease and injured by accidents.

In its early days the coal industry consisted of hundreds of small, barely profitable mines. Like the early oil industry coal depended on railroads to open up markets. In the anthracite fields of Pennsylvania, the mines were controlled by the railroads. And through the end of the twentieth century railroads such as the Burlington Northern and Norfolk & Western exercised an important influence through control of both foreign and domestic markets.

In an atmosphere of ruinous competition, John L. Lewis built the United Mine Workers into a powerful labor force. After repeated strikes resulted in government seizure of the mines during and after the Second World War, Lewis and the mine operators, led by George Love, then president of Consolidation Coal came to terms in 1950. Their agreement was an important juncture in the coal industry, for it established a long period of labor calm during which the industry reorganized: Mechanization was introduced, employment was reduced, small companies were consolidated into larger ones, and the spot market was replaced by long-term contracts.[3]

Throughout this period, the military played an important role in the structuring of the coal business. During the height of the cold war, the Pentagon was building up its supply of nuclear bombs. To manufacture them, uranium-enrichment facilities in Kentucky required vast amounts of electricity, which were provided by the Tennessee Valley Authority. The TVA previously supplied electricity from hydroelectric projects, but increased demand by the military caused the Authority to build new electric plants fired by coal. In procuring this coal, the TVA helped to reorganize the industry into large companies, encouraging them to mechanize. Eventually, as the largest purchaser of coal in the nation, the TVA became a dominant factor in the coal industry.[4]

Throughout the 1960s, coal was a major preoccupation of the big international oil corporations. (They had toyed with developing synthetic oil from coal back in the 1920s, when the two groups—Standard Oil of New Jersey and I. G. Farben in Germany—actually formed a cartel to organize the markets for synthetic fuels.) The growing tide of nationalism in the Middle East, with its implicit threat to their continued hegemony over oil, made them think once more about the future prospects for coal. The international oil concerns looked to the electric utilities as an immediate market for their coal. But they had a wider vision as well. Coal could become the feedstock for a new synthetic fuels industry, which could eventually produce petrochemicals and coal gas to replace dwindling supplies of natural gas. The setting for the new industry would be the sparsely populated northern prairies, beneath which lies the Fort Union formation, an enormous block of coal comprising 20 percent of the world's supply and 40 percent of total U.S. reserves. Fort Union coal can be strip-mined with ease. The seams run from seventy-five to one hundred feet deep.

In the early 1960s the coal business was tightly concentrated into a handful of big companies. It was then that oil companies moved in. First, Exxon quietly obtained major reserves in southern Illinois. Conoco, Inc., bought Consolidation Coal Company, which was then the leading coal firm, and was reported to be on the verge of producing a coal gasoline at prices competitive with gasoline made from oil. (Consolidation Coal became CONSOL Energy, Inc., in 1991, and Conoco merged with Phillips Petroleum Company in 2002 to become ConocoPhillips.) By 1970 five of the fifteen largest coal companies were owned by oil firms, producing 16 percent of all production and, more importantly, holding 40 percent of the nation's coal reserves. Railroads, the Burlington Northern in particular, held immense amounts of coal reserves as well.

But the economics of synthetic fuels never worked out. As environmentalists applied more and more pressure to have coal-fired power plants clean up their polluting emissions and as natural gas came into its own as a cleaner fuel for producing electricity, the petroleum industry backed out of the coal business. However, companies like Exxon, continued to have large holdings.

The American industry at the beginning of the twenty-first century is overshadowed by a handful of big corporations. Peabody Energy, a publicly owned firm, is the largest coal company in the world. Second is Arch Coal, Inc., formed in 1997 through the merger of Ashland Coal, Inc., and Arch Mineral Corporation. Its value was enhanced through the purchase of Atlantic Richfield Corp. holdings in the West. Another major producer is Kennecott Energy Company, a subsidiary of the Rio Tinto mining group with holdings around the world. Based in Wyoming, Kennecott Energy has operations in Wyoming, Colorado, and Montana. CONSOL Energy continues as another large coal producer.

Consolidation Coal, now Consol Energy and a historically dominant player in the American industry, was long the biggest producer of underground bituminous coal. In 1966 it was bought out by Conoco. Then in 1981 DuPont bought Conoco and its subsidiary Consolidation Coal. During the 1990s the German energy company, RWE Group bought into CONSOL, at first taking a 50 percent holding and sharing it with DuPont. In 1998 it increased its holdings to 94 percent, with DuPont continuing to hold 6 percent. RWE derives much of its income from managing European electric utilities (it is the largest provider of electricity in Germany) along with providing natural gas and oil. It is the third largest provider of water in the world, with operations in many different nations. The company claims to provide 43 million people with water and wastewater services, a growing field, and it is keeping pace with major acquisitions in the United Kingdom and the United States. In 2003 it purchased the American Water Works Company, which included holdings of Enron, which at that point was becoming more and more active in the wastewater business. The company seeks to be positioned as the principal utility provider, supplying electricity, gas, water, and wastewater management for large cities around the world. And as Enron collapsed, RWE stepped up its energy-trading operation, seeking to become a large and viable international energy broker.[5]

It is worth noting that, because it lacks any ready access to oil and gas, Germany long has relied on its coal resources. During the Second World War Hitler mobilized the German chemical industry to develop a process for changing coal into synthetic petrol that was used to power the German *Luftwaffe*. This history of coal and synthetic fuels places RWE in a unique position in the United States, where the future may well include synthetics.

Massey Energy Company lags somewhat behind these firms (it ranked seventh in the United States in the Energy Information Administration's 2001 annual coal report). Another major player in the industry is a second German company called RAG American Coal Holding, Incorporated. A subsidiary of the German RAG Coal International, it operates two Powder River Basin mines in Wyoming.

The world trade in coal is not large (some 12 percent of all coal consumed is involved in international trading). The exporters by rank in 2003 were Australia, China, South Africa, and Indonesia. Unlike the United States, which has dropped far behind, other countries are hotly competing with China, Indonesia, and Australia for the Japanese coal business. Colombia has become a major supplier of coal for the European continent. The Russians, as part of the Soviet Union, were one of the world's largest coal producers, but now put out only a modest tonnage. South Africa is not only a major exporter of coal, but also the top producer of coal-based synthetic fuel.

OIL ▶ The story of how oil was found and won is one of the great events of the modern age. A decade after the California gold rush, Edward L. Drake, a former railway conductor, drilled a well and hit a gusher of oil at Titusville, a town on Oil Creek in northwestern Pennsylvania. At twenty dollars a barrel the oil was like "liquid gold." Soon prospectors were crawling all over northwestern Pennsylvania.[6]

Just as the oil rush hit Pennsylvania, the thrifty young John D. Rockefeller was running a flourishing produce commission firm on the Cleveland docks. He and his partner invested some of the profits from their business in an oil refinery. That enterprise burgeoned, and Rockefeller sold out the produce business to concentrate on oil. He opened another refinery along with an office in New York City. Rockefeller was the head of all these firms, which he merged in June 1870 into the Standard Oil Company.

Rockefeller built up the refinery business by obtaining secret rebates on oil shipped by the railroads. He reinvested all profits in the company, and when other firms went under, he had enough money on hand not only to survive, but to buy out the competition. He cajoled, fought, and outsmarted his competitors until they joined him. When independent oilmen sought to make an end run around Standard Oil by laying pipelines to the East Coast, Rockefeller bought the refineries to which they intended to sell their oil, then laid his own pipeline.

By 1879 Standard Oil had a monopoly on the oil business. As the only buyer, it controlled all the shipping and the refining of almost all oil in the United States. The revenues of Standard Oil grew dramatically. In setting up the Standard Oil Trust in 1882, the company became a bank for the entire industry. Beyond that, Standard Oil participated in the great financial deals of the time: the construction of the western railroads, the electric light companies, the copper and iron and steel industries, and so on.

Rockefeller built his empire through control of refining and marketing. Other firms not part of the Standard group, like the Texas Company, which was to become Texaco and Gulf, imitated Standard Oil, incorporating production, transportation, refining, and marketing under one roof.

In 1911–12 two events dramatically changed the nature of the oil-refining industry. First the courts broke up the Standard Trust into thirty-three different companies. These firms, like the Trust's competitors, proceeded to integrate themselves from top to bottom. Standard Oil of New Jersey was by far the largest of the spin-offs; as Exxon Mobil, it is today's industry leader. Other spin-offs included Standard Oil of California, Standard Oil of Ohio, Standard Oil of Indiana, and Socony-Vacuum (the Mobil in Exxon Mobil). All in all the offshoots of the Rockefeller empire controlled half the oil reserves of the nation.

The second important event occurred in Great Britain, where the government, adopting the Admiralty's plans, decided to fuel the navy with oil, not coal. In anticipation of the change in fuels, during the last quarter of the nineteenth century, the British Navy had been encouraging different oil prospectors in the Middle East. With the navy firmly committed to oil, and hence a large market assured, the British oil ventures were drawn together into the Anglo-Persian Oil Company, predecessor to British Petroleum. The government sent troops to protect the operations in Persia and signed long-term contracts for the supply of oil. In seeking Middle Eastern oil, Winston Churchill argued that it would free the navy from dependence on Standard Oil and Shell, the two firms that then dominated the international oil trade.[7]

As the petroleum industry in the United States grew, the major companies established understandings with state and federal governments, allowing these governments to directly participate in organizing the industry. Such state regulatory bodies as the Texas Railroad Commission limited production, as a "conservation" measure, to stave off an oil glut. The theory of conservation, as propounded by the industry, achieved a signal victory during the New Deal with passage of the Connally "hot oil act," which gave federal sanction to state pro-rationing laws. These state laws, heavily influenced by industry, set production limits.

After the First World War Standard Oil and other American companies became alarmed at the British incursion into oil. They feared a foreign monopoly, and also foresaw the end of cheap oil as U.S. reserves ran down. These fears were bolstered by reports from the U.S. Geological Survey of an imminent shortage. The industry therefore encouraged the U.S. government to exert pressure on the British to allow American participation in the oil fields of Mesopotamia. A series of meetings between American and British interests ensued, which resulted in the creation of a new company owned by the major international oil corporations. That company was called the Iraq Petroleum Company, and it was, in effect, a cooperative, invidiously known as a cartel, through which the different major companies organized the production and distribution of oil in different parts of the world by regulating production. The shape and operations of the cartel changed over time, but the overall scheme was kept in place through the end of the Second World War and into the early stages of the cold war. Then, abruptly, the fortunes of the international oil industry changed.

As the cold war developed in the 1950s, the Middle East became the center of the first serious confrontation between the Soviet Union and the United States, with oil playing a significant role. The Soviets were threatening along a line extending from Greece through Turkey to Iran, where they sought oil concessions. The governments of the Middle East were feeble, not to say fickle, allies—petty, corrupt, and cloaked in unfathomable culture and religion, all of which, in the view of American diplomats, made the region easy prey for uprising. It was not so much the spread of communism, but a nationalist leader that the United States feared. As it turned out this was a real fear, taking form in the rise of Egypt's Nasser.

The oil concessions themselves were worth fighting for. In the words of one senior diplomat of the era, Middle Eastern oil reserves constituted the world oil "jackpot," and the United States could not afford to let them go.

In these circumstances, the international oil companies became an important vehicle of U.S. foreign policy. They upped the prices they paid to the Middle Eastern oil-producing governments, and in return the United States granted the companies special tax breaks. More important, President Eisenhower formally quashed an antitrust investigation into the cartel, and instead strongly backed the companies and the existing arrangements on national security grounds.

Then, in March 1951, the government of Iranian nationalist premier Mohammad Mosaddeq took over the assets of the Anglo-Iranian Oil Company (BP). For a brief time, American interests sought an accommodation with Mosaddeq, hoping to replace the British as the major concessionaires. When these efforts failed, the Central Intelligence Agency fomented a coup. The Shah dismissed Mosaddeq, and when the premier refused to go, rioting broke out. The government fell, and the Shah took full control. The next step was for President Eisenhower's personal envoy, Herbert Hoover Jr. to rearrange the oil concessions.[8]

The coup against Mosaddeq was a turning point in the fortunes of the industry. It set off fresh nationalist fervor in Iran, gradually leading toward a profound change in the structure of the oil industry.

Hoover's reorganization of the Iranian oil concessions contained what proved to be a fatal flaw for American oil interests. The new concession arrangement divided up Iranian oil among British, French, Dutch, and, for the first time, American interests. But it did not include the Italians, who entirely depended on imports of fuel. At the time, the Italian state company was headed by Enrico Mattei. Infuriated at being cut out of Iran, Mattei fought the companies. Following the battle of Suez in 1956 he successfully persuaded the Iranian parliament to revise the petroleum law to allow for a new production system of joint ventures. Before then the foreign companies had been paying a royalty for every barrel of oil taken from the concession. Until the first joint venture the Italian state company put up the capital, and the Iranians got the jobs. If oil were found, Italy got first crack at it, but the Iranians got the profits.

The joint venture between Italy and Iran became a model for later "participation" agreements. Mattei's ideas were adopted by younger and more-militant Arabs in other oil states.

Matters came to a head in the late 1950s, when the United States erected oil-import quotas to keep out foreign oil in order to maintain a high domestic price. With the world already enjoying a great surplus of oil, prices outside the United States declined, and the income to the producing nations dwindled. Faced with this situation the Arab oil producers, together with Venezuela and Iran, met in Baghdad to work out some form of collective action in defense of their nations' economic interests. The result was the formation of the Organization of Petroleum Exporting Countries (OPEC). The tide of nationalism in the Middle East was a major factor in persuading the oil companies to diversify their holdings. On the one hand the big international companies spread their search for oil into Southeast Asia, in the shallow seas off Indonesia, near Indochina, and down to Australia. They moved actively into Alaska and from there into the Canadian Arctic. In the United States, they stepped up the campaign for increased drilling on the outer continental shelf. More important, they turned back into the North American continent and began to buy up other energy sources—coal and uranium. The oil industry began to be called the energy industry.

In the early 1970s OPEC countries combined in a boycott that strangled the U.S. economy, causing severe shortages and giant price hikes in fuels. But the boycott was short lived, and in the subsequent arrangement worked out between the companies and producing countries, OPEC's influence was reduced.

By the early twenty-first century the Middle East was more important than ever as a supplier of the world's oil. Two-thirds of the known world oil reserves are in that region. The Middle East accounts for some 30 percent of actual production. And by 2020, according to a Bush administration estimate, 37 percent of the world's exports will come from the area. Saudi Arabia is the largest single producer and sits atop one-quarter of the world's oil reserves.

Iraq is a potentially key player. With a modernized industry it could produce quantities of oil sufficient to rival Saudi Arabia. It has large known reserves, and reportedly there are portions of the country yet to be mapped geologically. U.S. control of Iraqi oil would open up a larger reservoir of oil for the United States—where it is anticipated that imports will provide two-thirds of the total oil.

Direct U.S. involvement in Iraq has other repercussions. Control of Iraqi oil allows the United States to wield a major counterweight to OPEC, placing it eventually in a position to use Iraqi oil as leverage in controlling prices. It could lessen the importance of Saudi Arabia, and give the United States added clout in its dealings with Russia and Venezuela, and in West Africa, where there has been strife over the terms of oil production. It would put the United States in a position of controlling the rates and terms of production. For example an American-instigated price decline would force out small companies and countries which had wanted to prospect in Iraq. A falling price would make such exploration unprofitable. On the other hand American control over Iraqi oil also means a degree of protection for domestic American producers, who also need a high world price to stay in business. And last but not least it gives the big international oil companies a chance to recover oil resources they lost with the creation of OPEC. These companies, which control refining and distribution, but own a declining amount of reserves, can now jump back into the business of amassing huge reserves. In the minds of Iraq invasion planners, a takeover of the country might also buoy the dollar, which in 2003 had dropped below the euro. That in turn would give the United States added clout in its dealings with the European Union and much of the world.

Keeping a grip on Iraqi oil means U.S. hegemony in the region and military presence in central Asia. American dominance entails maintaining a network of military bases, ships, and planes to protect shipping lanes from the Persian Gulf around the tip of Africa back to the United States. Oil plays a large part in extending U.S. hegemony over trade routes worldwide. During the Iraqi crisis of 2003, the U.S. also was considering military outposts along the West African coast, so as to be able to project American power from the Gulf of Guinea south along the coast, where considerable gas and oil will be produced in the future. Achieving a degree of stability in Liberia became important because continuing unrest there endangered America's longstanding use of the country as a central staging area in Africa for intelligence and propaganda. In West Africa the U.S. oil companies confronted the entrenched French oil interests in France's former colonies. But the region held an allure for the American companies because it was just a stone's throw across the Atlantic to East Coast markets, especially the growing East Coast natural gas markets, which might be serviced in the future with liquefied natural gas drawn from the Gulf of Guinea.

The United States must watch over the routes carrying oil from Indonesia to Japan and elsewhere in Asia. The continental United States provides a large market for all this oil. And American companies will play a role in supplying the world's biggest energy consumer—China—which is soon to become America's economic competitor. All in all, seizure of Iraq may allow the United States to reverse the tides of nationalism which gave rise to OPEC, and effectively establish what amounts to a latter-day economic colony.

The world markets for energy are shifting eastward toward China, which is snapping up ever-greater supplies of oil. By the beginning of the twenty-first century much of China's imported oil came from the Middle East. But looking ahead it also had its eyes on the Caspian fields. The trade routes from the Persian Gulf down through the Indian Ocean and across the Strait of Malacca to the South China Sea became more important, at times raising political tensions between China and the United States over who controls these vital South Asian sea lanes.[9]

China's burgeoning need for energy raises new questions for both diplomacy and the industry. How will Chinese modernization, with its heavy reliance on fossil fuels, affect global energy markets? Will China abide by international environmental standards, and who ultimately will control the sea lanes? Though the country is increasingly looking to hydroelectric and nuclear power, in the near future easy access to oil remains the key for China's move into the global economy.

China is the world's second-largest energy consumer—soon to become the largest. A net importer since 1993, by 2020 the communist nation will be importing up to two-thirds of its oil. Eighty percent of those supplies will come from the Middle East. The main exporters now are Oman and Yemen, but China is hoping to obtain supplies from Saudi Arabia as well. It even sought ties with Saddam Hussein in Iraq, providing aid in building missile defense systems to curry favor for oil. Along with oil China will be importing substantial amounts of natural gas, in the form of liquefied natural gas from the Middle East and Australia, and possibly importing it via pipeline from as far away as the Caspian Sea area.

By the year 2000 China had become more active in exercising control over energy supply lines. But, as it did so, the United States also placed more emphasis on its own military operations in the area. The U.S. bases in the Persian Gulf and Indian Ocean enabled it to project force across South Asian waters. Taiwan became an ever-more-important foundation post, and the United States built up a new port for operations in Singapore. Other nations situated along the routes are the Philippines, Malaysia, and Thailand.

All this activity suddenly brought a whole new set of factors into play. When the U.S. spy plane was forced down over China in 2001, Beijing claimed the United States had invaded its waters. The United States dismissed this claim, insisting the plane was seventeen miles offshore—well outside the recognized territorial limit of twelve miles. Facts tended to back up the American position. However, it is worth noting that under the Law of the Sea Treaty signed by all other coastal nations except the United States and Germany, coastal states can claim territory out to 200 miles to protect their economic interests (like oil and gas and fishing.) While the United States did not sign the treaty, it nonetheless cited the 200-mile limit as a rationale for throwing out Soviet, Japanese, and Scandinavian factory ships fishing off the American coast. Under the treaty there is a right to overfly the 200-mile limit, except when it interferes with the economic interests below. It is almost certain that future territorial claims over minerals, especially oil and gas, in South Asia will invoke the 200-mile limit, contained in the Law of the Sea Treaty. The means for enforcing the 200-mile limit will be through the United Nations, where China is a major player.

By the end of the twentieth century the West was placing undue hope in increasing its energy resources by taking oil from the Caspian Sea area in central Asia. Once a part of the Soviet Union the region was broken up into half a dozen small nations. Nearly a dozen U.S. companies were engaged in forty oil projects in Kazakhstan and Azerbaijan along with twenty-four other western oil firms and two from Russia. Oil revenues will be crucial to the health of countries in the Caspian area as well as in the Transcaucasian region over the next twenty years. The central Asian states involved are Kazakhstan, Turkmenistan, Azerbaijan, and Uzbekistan. Proven reserves are about equal to those of the North Sea, somewhat less than those of the United States, and far less than the Middle East's reserves.[10]

Along with oil there is natural gas in substantial amounts, so much so that the former Soviet republic of Turkmenistan is listed as one of the top gas producers in the world. Overall, the region's proven reserves appear to be about equal to those of the United States. The biggest gas deposit appears to be in Turkmenistan and Uzbekistan.

Still the Caspian region actually produced but 4 percent of the world's oil in the late 1990s and an infinitesimal amount of gas. Most of its oil and gas was consumed within the former Soviet Union.

A major challenge in the Caspian play is to organize pipelines that can take oil and gas to markets. Building a pipeline, however, not only costs large sums of money, but also involves intricate negotiations. To date, only one successful pipeline carries gas from western Turkmenistan to northern Iran.

In the past most oil and gas from the Caspian passed through Russia, the oil going northwestward into Europe by means of a well-established pipeline system. The Chechnya conflict put the pipeline at risk, with both sides attacking it, and the Chechens setting in over 100 taps to suck oil out for their local refineries. The broken pipeline was rerouted to the Black Sea and thence to the Dardanelles and the Mediterranean.

The Russians have dominated the Caspian play for over a century, finding the oil and building the pipelines and refineries. Today Russia obtains substantial revenues from Caspian oil, which it sells outright and on which it collects royalties. The *Military Review* points out that the combined revenues yield over 40 percent of all exports. Even though its outright control is gone, Russia exercises enormous power over oil, for example, forcing the consortia run by Chevron and Kazakhstan to build a new pipeline from the Tengiz oil field through Russia to Novorossiysk, thereby maintaining control over the oil.

While the Caspian play nominally must take account of drifting political winds in the newly created former Soviet republics of central Asia, it boils down to a struggle between Russia and the United States, with Russia especially looking to exact a high price for transporting oil and gas through its sphere of influence. And just below these two competitors is Iran to the south, which the United States has been trying to isolate. America's staunch ally, expansionist-minded Turkey is on the west, and America's long-time ally Pakistan, on the east. But Pakistan is highly unstable and dangerous, if only because of its nuclear aspirations. And looming just over the horizon is China, whose territory extends down into central Asia.

Other projects include building a corridor pipeline carrying oil from Azerbaijan through Georgia and the Caucasus to a port on Turkey's Mediterranean coast. The United States at one point sought to persuade Turkmenistan to build a gas pipeline under the Caspian Sea to carry gas to Europe, and the Americans wanted to get Kazakhstan to build a similar oil pipeline under the Caspian to Turkish ports. Kazakhstan had a plan to run a pipeline from the Caspian to the Russian port of Novorossiysk on the Black Sea.

The most-direct route would be a north-south pipeline from the Caspian straight down through Iran to Iran's Gulf ports. Iran has the world's second largest gas reserves, along with substantial oil resources. Such a pipeline was reckoned in 2000 to cost a fraction of the $3 billion estimated cost of going to Turkey. But the U.S. foreign policy determinedly aimed at isolating Iran and doing business with the country was complicated, and there was always the possibility that right-wing religious fundamentalists would seize the pipeline. So, while the United States stubbornly refused to permit business with Iran, various European companies, along with Chinese, Russian, and Indian ones, were all negotiating deals with Iran at the beginning of the twenty-first century. The other route would go from the Caspian through Afghanistan down through Pakistan to ports on the Arabian Sea, possibly with another segment going into India. But the Taliban made dealing improbable. Finally there was the possibility China would try to create a Caspian route through Xinjiang province to the rapidly expanding markets there.

Among the seldom-noticed regions of the world that could play a larger role in providing oil is the Arctic, that vast expanse, thousands of square miles around the globe within the Arctic circle. Alaska is just at the edge of the Arctic play, which could involve hundreds of offshore oil and gas wells. Their output would be processed and then shipped by sea or through pipelines down into the continental United States or into Europe. In addition to oil and gas there are large reserves of coal in Alaska. Siberia runs 4,000 miles from the Urals to the Pacific and is said to possess half the earth's hydrocarbon reserves. It is rich in oil and gas and has great reserves of diamonds, gold, platinum metals of all sorts, and uranium. Russian natural gas from Siberia has played a major role in converting much of the energy base of western Europe from coal and oil to gas.[11]

Canada historically has been viewed as a sort of energy bin for the United States. NAFTA has pushed Canada, Mexico, and the United States into a tighter hemispheric trading zone.

North American trade ties, especially when it comes to natural resources, have a lengthy history. During the nineteenth century Canada's major dealings were with Great Britain, which provided much of the investment and bought staples—furs, breadstuffs, and lumber. But by the mid-twentieth century all this had dramatically changed, and most of all foreign investment in Canada came from the United States. Almost three-quarters of Canada's imports came from the United States, and in 1963, by one count, American corporations controlled two-thirds of all the oil and gas in the country. The United States provided some two-thirds of all the capital investment in the oil and gas business, and the ten leading producers were American companies. An oil company owned the sole west-east pipeline. U.S. companies had staked out oil and gas reserves in the Mackenzie delta in the north, as well as resources in the East around Ellesmere Island and in the Arctic itself.

As the twenty-first century opened efforts by the United States to tie

Canada ever tighter to American markets through hemispheric trade arrangements appeared to be redundant. U.S. companies already owned the industry. And it was a fact that, as President George Bush said, U.S. energy needs were linked to Canadian resources. (Oil and gas were complemented by hydroelectric power from James Bay and tied to the export of another of Canada's crucial resources, fresh drinking water. The water was to be carried through pipelines and aqueducts that lay alongside oil and gas pipelines.)

Through NAFTA Mexico also becomes part of the U.S. resource bin. It is the eighth-largest producer of oil in the world, and every time OPEC raises prices, Mexico gets more money. The industry is state owned, and, while it represents less of the nation's export revenue than it did during the OPEC days of the 1970s, oil money actually represents a greater percentage of tax funds which run the country. That is in part because Mexico is unable to collect more than 15 percent of the taxes owed it.

There is periodic discussion about privatizing Pemex, the state company, or at least some aspects of it, and there are private openings in the natural gas business.[12]

Although the politics of oil during the twentieth century often have been strongly influenced by predictions of scarcity, they, in fact, have been driven by surplus, that is, how to keep the business alive and profitable amidst glut.

All through the latter part of the twentieth century and on into the twenty-first, the experts argued about the size of the world's petroleum resources. In 1956 M. King Hubbert, a famed geophysicist who worked first for Shell and later at the U.S. Geological Survey predicted U.S. oil production would peak in the early 1970s. Initially these predictions were rejected, but in 1970 production began to fall. At the beginning of the twenty-first century another group of analysts, applying Hubbert's methods, estimated that the peak year for world oil production would come between 2004 and 2008, at which point 1.8 trillion barrels of oil will have been produced. All the oil was produced within a 100-year span. Kenneth S. Deffeyes, a Princeton professor with lengthy firsthand experience in the industry, in his book *Hubbert's Peak: The Impending World Oil Shortage,* believes there are no new advances to be found in technology and that we have gone as deep as we can to drill for oil. Nor is there any place new to drill, with the exception of the South China Sea, where a dispute over boundaries hinders any progress. But even here, Deffeyes says, there is no bonanza to be had. "Whether it is Iraq or Iran, the undiscovered oil in the Middle East is very likely the largest untapped supply in the world," writes Deffeyes.[13]

The government's central reporting agency on the subject, the U.S. Geological Survey, reported an increase in the world's oil resources to 1.574 billion barrels in 1993, with most of it coming from already known oil fields. As for undiscovered oil, the Survey sets that figure at 649 billion barrels, with one-third of the total coming from the nations of the former Soviet Union, and almost another third from North Africa and the Middle East.

The oil industry itself looks to a changing future. The CEOs of the major companies are anticipating the end of the hydrocarbon age, envisioning a general shift from coal to natural gas, and then to renewable sources. In that context some have predicted that petroleum's 40 percent share of the global energy market will decline to 25 percent by 2050. Meanwhile the natural gas market will grow until gas accounts for 20 percent of the world market. The rest would come from nuclear and various renewables. The other possibility is that fossil fuels will give way to hydrogen, with fuel cells becoming a commercial reality by 2025. Within the United States itself, government and industry argue that there is more oil to be drilled in the Gulf of Mexico, along the West Coast—principally off California—and in the Alaskan Arctic. There also is interest in oil in the Great Lakes area.[14]

NATURAL GAS ▶ The desire to clean up the nation's dirty oil and coal-fired power plants has led the United States to zero in on natural gas as a clean fuel, one that can overnight fix the growing pollution problem. Much of America's natural gas is discovered during the search for oil, and, for many years, oil companies simply discarded the gas, burning it off at the wellhead. Today, however, they instead capture the gas, and sell it to pipelines that carry it to local firms, which distribute it in cities and towns across the country. Up until the last quarter of the twentieth century the use of gas was determined by the existence of pipelines.

Natural gas has a topsy-turvy history, determined in large part by a lengthy struggle between private companies that produce and transport gas on one side and the federal government on the other. Over many years the federal government sought to devise some scheme for regulating gas. The industry fought it every inch of the way. As part of trust-busting reform, the federal government took steps to separate the actual production of gas from its transport and final distribution. There was another reason for government interest. Much of the gas and oil produced in the United States comes from public-domain territories, that is, from wells lying below the waters off the continental shelf and from other lands administered by the Interior Department.

In certain respects the battle over natural gas has been a pivotal issue in the American economy: It costs so much and involves so many players in producing and transporting gas through pipeline systems. Moreover the fuel causes little pollution, thus directly addressing environmental concerns.

Two of the keys to this debate are fixing the amount of gas known to reside under the ground and then estimating future resources that will be recovered in the process of future exploration. While much of the gas is produced from public-domain territories, the federal government, which administers them, has no independent knowledge of how much gas is located there. Instead it depends on the industry's data.[15]

In the three decades between the Truman administration and Jimmy Carter's term as president, the gas industry, which is to say the petroleum industry, was anxious to end federal regulation. The petroleum companies thought the government's policy ended up setting prices too low to make a profit. Low prices would never inspire wildcatters to go out and search for more gas. Unless things changed, the industry warned, there would be a gas shortage. Of course there were critics who claimed the industry had devised the possibility of shortage as a gimmick, to scare politicians into raising the price. But these were few and far between.

In *Phillips Petroleum v. Wisconsin* (347 U.S. 672 [1954]) the U.S. Supreme Court had ruled that the government must regulate the wellhead price of gas—that is, the price paid to the oil companies by the interstate pipeline companies. Fearful of government regulation, the industry retaliated by seeking to deregulate the price through legislation in Congress and by threatening a gas shortage if prices were held down.

During the Eisenhower and early Kennedy administrations, there was little effort to bring gas under price control. But then the Federal Power Commission (eventually superseded by the Federal Energy Regulatory Commission), gradually developed a scheme for area pricing. The industry fought it. Finally, in 1968, the Supreme Court once again upheld the right of the FPC to control prices. In its decision the court said the FPC could allow producers to increase the price of their gas whenever the gas association's figures showed that the rate of new discoveries had decreased. Until then there had been no slowdown in new discoveries, and the reserves had been steadily increasing. After the court decision the industry spoke of an alarming "energy crisis," which it warned could occur because of a shortage of natural gas. This shortage would arise because the government had denied producers adequate profit for gas exploration and production. Accordingly the gas association's reserve figures began to decline. During the 1960s and 1970s several different inquiries suggested that the industry withheld gas to drive up prices. Thus, in the late 1960s, economists for the utilities industry told Congress they had discovered various wells in the Gulf of Mexico that had been shut off from market. In 1971 staff economists from the Federal Power Commission noted what they thought to be a 50 percent under-reporting by the companies. These economists asked the full commission for permission to conduct an independent investigation, but the commission refused.

More inquiries followed, eventually leading to a major investigation by Congressman John Moss's subcommittee. Moss discovered that the gas estimates were put together by the largest-producing companies. These firms chose the geologists who served on the gas association's committee, and the geologists admitted to the committee that they pretty much provided the estimates their employers wanted to give. One geologist listed the reserves of a gas field as "zero," not because he knew that to be the case, but because his company gave him no idea of what the field contained. Other geologists said they simply guessed at the amounts of gas or made estimates based on tidbits of information they saw in the trade press. Moss found one field containing 400 billion cubic feet of gas that had not been listed for two years, even though it had two platforms and thirteen wells. If this single field had been included in the gas association's 1974 figures, it would have increased that year's national estimate by 23 percent.[16]

All in all, Moss found that the gas association had missed 8.8 trillion cubic feet—a substantial amount.

In part, of course, the underreporting of reserves is a device to increase prices. But there are other subtle forces at play here. During this period the oil companies that produce most of the gas were acquiring substantial holdings in coal, especially in those fields along the eastern slope of the Rockies. They looked forward to the day when that coal could be turned into a synthetic gas. But coal gas has always been an expensive proposition. As prices rose the industry discovered more and more natural gas. The need for a synthetic equivalent subsided and by 2000 had generally disappeared.

Natural gas became a factor in the European energy market in the last part of the twentieth century. Since then it has steadily increased in importance as an energy source across western Europe and in Great Britain.

Much of the gas in western Europe during the late 1900s came from the North Sea. The primary source—50 percent—has been the Groningen field in the Netherlands. The big international oil companies played a major role in transporting this gas to consumers. Imports from Algeria and the Soviet Union provided other sources.

During the cold war the Soviet Union set about constructing a pipeline system that could transport gas from Siberia and the Far East to Moscow and then into western Europe. The Soviets hoped natural gas could turn into a major source of foreign exchange.

As a rule natural gas has been piped from the wellhead, where it often has been discovered with oil, to markets across landmasses. Transporting gas across large bodies of water appeared neither practicable nor necessary. Thus, while gas in the United States was captured and transported by pipeline for use, it generally was regarded as useless elsewhere and burned off as it came out of the ground. In North Africa and the Middle East, trillions of cubic feet of gas were wasted in this manner.

Then, in the early 1960s, the leaders of the newly independent Algeria were confronted with a crisis. The French, their departing colonial masters, had kept for themselves control of the valuable oil deposits. But they allowed the Algerians to take the natural gas, which they viewed as worthless. To begin with, the Algerians captured the heretofore worthless gas, made it into a liquid by freezing it, and then loaded the liquefied gas into tankers and shipped it across the Mediterranean to markets just opening in Europe. The European market grew, but the Algerians could not take advantage of the opportunity because its ally, the Soviet Union, was trying to sell its own gas. During the 1960s an American firm, El Paso Natural Gas Company, worked out an arrangement for importing Algerian gas in its frozen form to the East Coast of the United States.[17]

This was a grand plan, conceived amidst the supposed shortage, and its proponents eventually looked forward to the day when Algeria would be supplying as much as 15 percent of the entire American gas supply. Some argued that a nation which had long been a French colony now would become an economic appendage of the United States.

It was clear that a new industry with limitless possibilities had been born. With the onset of the OPEC oil embargo and the worldwide hysterical search for fuel, frozen gas, transported in tankers just like oil, appeared to be a solution and opened possibilities for a burgeoning market for years to come.

As the Algerian deal with El Paso was being worked out, a British company, Burmah Oil, was devising a similar scheme for carrying huge amounts of liquefied gas from Indonesia to Japan. The Japanese economy is entirely dependent on shipments of oil from abroad, mostly from the Persian Gulf. At the same time the country has been under strong pressure to clean up its environment. For that reason alone, LNG was a temptation. The prospect of importing a major fuel from nearby Indonesia, with which Japan had close business ties, was doubly appealing. And, of course, the specter of the oil boycott made the Japanese want to hurry up and find a fuel source outside the Middle East.

Starting with Richard Nixon and continuing through to Jimmy Carter's administration, natural gas regulation became toothless, and it was lifted altogether during the Reagan administration. Prices rose, and the hysteria over natural gas shortages disappeared. Soon the industry which had claimed the world was running out of gas, reported a surplus, and began to advertise it for uses in ways that had hitherto been considered foolish. During the energy crisis of the 1970s, environmental activists argued against using scarce gas for such things as producing electricity. However, by the late 1980s, environmentalists were clamoring to burn gas for electricity in order to reduce pollution. And the industry was ready to supply it from a now-bottomless supply.

One of the temporary fallouts of the gas glut was LNG. Once a panacea, it now appeared superfluous, and the industry temporarily lost interest. At the same time petroleum companies abandoned dreams for a synthetic gas made from coal. They sold off the coal companies they had snatched up only a few years before. However, the petroleum industry in certain cases retained large coal reserves against an uncertain future. Amidst the glut the gas business in the United States was changing. Most natural gas currently consumed comes from North America, where BP is the single largest producer and reserve holder. In the United States gas mostly comes from the Southwest, with future reserves in the Rocky Mountains and additional Gulf fields.[18]

Natural gas has been used as a fuel more in the United States than anywhere else. But the prospect is fast changing as gas is carried over longer and longer distances by pipeline and ship. Most of the future gas will come from the former Soviet Union and the Middle East, where 70 percent of all reserves are based. Russia has more reserves than any other country, followed by Iran. Russia is also the world's largest gas producer and the largest exporter. Gazprom, the Russian State monopoly, dominated the market at the beginning of the twenty-first century, but its market share was expected to decline over time. The largest single gas field in the world is located in Qatar. Saudi Arabia also has substantial gas resources, ranking it fourth in world proven gas reserves.

Because of its demand as a relatively clean fuel for the production of electricity, the U.S. Department of Energy in December 2003 predicted that gas use for electricity generation will double, from 5.3 trillion cubic feet in 2001 to 10.6 trillion cubic feet in 2025. Total natural gas consumption is expected to rise from 22.6 trillion cubic feet in 2001 to somewhere between 31.8 and 37.5 trillion cubic feet in 2025 (depending on economic growth during that period). By the end of the period (2025) electric generation is expected to consume 33 percent of all natural gas produced.[19]

The *Oil and Gas Journal* estimates that total 2003 gas reserves amount to 5,501 trillion cubic feet, with the largest increases coming from Central and South America and the Middle East.

Because gas is worthless without a means to transport it from the producing fields to consumer markets, pipelines are a crucial cog in this industry. In the United States a partially interconnected maze of pipelines brings gas from wells in the South and Southwest as well as from Canada to big consumer markets on both coasts and the Chicago area. Gas was unused in western Europe until the discovery of oil in the North Sea yielded supplies of gas for that market. The Soviet Union's immense pipeline from Siberia to Moscow and western Europe has already been mentioned. But big gas finds in the Persian Gulf and Southeast Asia were largely wasted. In recent years the producing states in the Persian Gulf have begun to lay out plans for gas pipelines interconnecting their fields, and there are hopes of bringing gas along with oil from the distant Caspian Sea area of central Asia to western Europe and China. In Southeast Asia there have been long-term plans for an intricate pipe network that would bring gas from Indonesia, the region's largest producer, to Thailand, Malaysia, Vietnam, and eventually the Philippines. Southeast Asia now uses gas to make 40 percent of its electricity.[20]

The North American market is increasingly interconnected. By the end of the twentieth century new pipelines ran from Canada to Montana and South Dakota and on into the Midwest. Canadian gas from the nation's Maritime Provinces and Sable Island is piped to the U.S. Northeast. The biggest increase in gas trade has been between Mexico and the United States, however, with Mexican gas flowing northward to American markets along the Texas and California borders. The gas trade between the United States and Mexico goes both ways, depending on regional needs.[21]

The electric industry demand also has meant a recovery in the LNG business. The United States currently imports LNG into only a few ports. The gas originally came from Algeria, but now comes from Tobago and Trinidad, where it is collected from the Middle East, Nigeria, and Australia. The danger of a terrorist attack on LNG tankers or LNG plants where the frozen liquid is turned back into gas has lent a note of caution to the business.

Within the United States gas markets are tied together in a web of pipelines throughout the nation. There are 175 interstate pipelines covering 300,000 miles, with key lines running from producing fields in the Gulf states up the East and West coasts. Lines from Canada reach down into California and to the east. The pipelines do not form a real grid, so that any breakage can lead to sometimes-severe disruption of the entire system. There were eight major accidents during the 1990s. Pipes made before the 1970s are riddled with weak points, where the welding of seams was flawed. The newer, stronger pipelines, on the other hand, are often poorly managed, with water getting into the pipes and corroding them. What makes the pipeline system especially vulnerable to accidents (and terrorists) is the inadequate monitoring system. As of September 11 monitoring amounted to a few undermanned stations to oversee thousands of miles of pipeline. The control station for the Bellingham, Washington pipeline is in Salt Lake City, separated by thousands of miles and running through America's two highest mountain ranges. Salt Lake City, Tulsa, Oklahoma, and Houston, Texas are major hubs for controlling pipelines throughout the country. But distance is not the only problem. Even when controllers spot a problem they have a hard time figuring out what caused it, and it can take hours to reach the nearest major valve and turn it off.

Consumer groups have long complained about weak federal statutes controlling the pipeline business. It is up to each individual company to design its own system. Weak regulations, in the words of one expert means that "each individual company is up to its own devices. Some of them let their pipelines go until something pops." Between 1986 and 1999 popping natural gas pipelines killed 296 people and injured 1,357 others. In August 2000 10 members of a family were killed in southern New Mexico by a pipeline explosion that left a crater 86 feet long, 46 feet wide, and 20 feet deep. The explosion also shot 600 feet high, melted tents and camping gear, and transformed sand into glass.

Until now, most natural gas has been consumed inside national borders. But the rapidly expanding market for gas as a way to make electricity without violating pollution standards has caused the industry to once more seriously consider an international trade with LNG. Higher prices and lower production costs make LNG more attractive than it once was. China, which consumes large amounts of energy and will consume even more in the near future, provides an example of how pipelines and ships will transport gas in international trade. In 2002 China outlined an ambitious plan to purchase gas in frozen liquid form from three different international combines. Organized with the assistance of Merrill Lynch, the Chinese company, CNOOC Limited, itself 70.6 percent owned by the government, called for bids from three international consortia, each of which included a major participation by one or another of the big international oil companies: They included a combine led by BP and the Indonesian government for gas to be exported as LNG from Irian Jaya; Shell and BHP Billiton, a huge metals company, in a deal to transport gas from the Northwest shelf in Australia; and Exxon Mobil which would obtain gas from Qatar. The whole deal was valued at $450 million, representing some 3 percent of all internationally traded LNG. Similar deals were expected to follow. The gas is to go to Shenzhen, some twenty miles from Hong Kong, and represents a major effort to switch the energy base from coal to gas for numerous factories in Guangdong Province, on the Pearl River above Hong Kong. Embarrassed by the filthy air pollution around its prized city, the government is building a pipeline from west to east, but it will not hold enough gas for this area. In addition coal also was clogging up the industrial system. The transportation of and storage capacity for coal compete with industrial capacity that could be used to bring in foreign currency, said Mark Qiu, CNOOC's chief financial officer.[22]

At the same time China in 2002 was engaged in the final stages of lengthy negotiations that would create an international consortia to build a 2,500-mile pipeline from central Asia in Xinjiang Province—where Kazakhstan, Kyrgyzstan and China come together—all the way across China to Shanghai. The pipeline venture is made up of China's state company, China National Petroleum Corporation, Shell, Hong Kong China Gas, Exxon Mobil, and Gazprom, the Russian gas giant. The entire project, developing the gas fields in a remote corner of central Asia and building the extraordinarily long pipeline, was estimated to run $9 billion or more. This project will help

China reduce its reliance on coal, widely used as fuel in electric utilities. But it also is of considerable political importance, tying the westernmost Chinese region, which is Moslem and quasi-independent, to the rest of the country.

As part of the effort to move gas processing out of the United States to south of the border, the United States and Mexico have been looking at plans to turn the Sea of Cortez side of Baja California into a vacation Mecca, while at the same time planning five LNG terminals along the peninsula's Pacific coast, providing one network to shunt Mexican gas into the United States. The industry hoped that this route would bypass U.S. regulatory red tape.

Two American oil and gas companies (Phillips Petroleum and El Paso Natural Gas) in 2001 signed a letter of intent covering the construction of an LNG plant in Darwin, Australia, that could supply gas to southern California and the Baja peninsula from 2005.[23] And in the Gulf of Mexico American companies laid plans for an LNG facility that could provide gas to Mexican markets; additionally there were plans for replacing dwindling stocks of Gulf of Mexico gas with an infusion of Mexican gas pumped through the American-owned offshore infrastructure, which in turn is hooked up to several interstate pipelines in the United States. These deals suggest how Mexico will become both a source of gas for North America and a way station for transmission of Pacific basin gas northward.

In yet another development that augurs for a wider acceptance of LNG is the plan by Norway to build an LNG plant on the shores of the Barents Sea in the Arctic. It would produce gas for Europe.

Natural gas has been growing in popularity as a fuel for making electricity. While two decades ago the oil producers said the world was running out of gas, they now look to a comfortable surplus. And, because gas is cleaner than coal, they are boosting it as a pollution-free fuel for the future.

Indeed, gas is thought by some to usher in an entirely new phase of the electrical industry. Here the thinking is that small, local power plants are the way to go in the new free market. These small plants, so the argument goes, are especially appealing because they do not lose a lot of juice when sending it to consumers, and they often also produce surplus heat that can warm nearby buildings. (Heat generated from a big utility plant sitting in the middle of the desert is wasted.)

Micropower has other attractions. Its output, unlike the filthy coal-fired plants, is clean and can meet stiffening environmental standards. The local plants burn natural gas, which is a comparatively clean fuel, and in the future planners want to employ hydrogen and solar energy. And gas's advocates believe that these local power stations will provide a reliable and uninterrupted stream of electricity, whereas the big old behemoths deliver brownouts and blackouts. *The Economist*, one of the world's foremost proponents of deregulation, rhapsodized in 2002: "In time, micropower may also change the way electricity grids themselves operate—turning them from dictatorial monopolies into democratic marketplaces. Add a bit of information technology to a micro generator and it will be able both to monitor itself and to talk to other plants on the grid. Visionaries see a future in which dozens, even hundreds, of disparate micropower units are linked together in so-called 'microgrids'. These networks could be made up of all sorts of power units, from solar cells to micro turbines to fuel cells, depending on the needs of individual users." Critics of micropower think its possibilities are vastly overstated.[24]

Over the short term there has been concern that, because of the abandonment of regulation over both natural gas and electricity, a monopolistic situation exists in which the producers can call the tune—precisely what the New Deal regulators of the 1930s sought to avoid in establishing their regulatory system over energy pricing.

In California, as elsewhere in the United States, privately owned suppliers of electricity are intertwined through long-term contracts and outright ownership with several large out-of-state gas producers, certain of them in the Southwest. During the autumn of 2000, with the state facing an energy shortage, there were accusations that these producers had withheld gas supplies to run up the price.[25]

Although power in California is distributed by big systems like Pacific Gas and Electric (PG&E) and Southern California Edison, the actual production of electricity in certain key areas comes from out-of-state providers in Nevada and elsewhere in the intermountain West, and from hydroelectric projects in Oregon and Washington.

The usual practice has been for hydroelectric producers up the coast to swap power with California, sending huge blocks south to help out with air conditioning during the summer. During the winter, when Oregon and Washington experience peak demands, California returns the favor. But this process has changed. Because of reduced snow and rain in the north, the amounts of electricity being sent south have declined, and because the output of old, polluting plants in California has been reduced, the amounts going north have also gone down. This situation may have worsened the crisis, but it does not go very far in explaining its origins. The Washington, D.C.–based group Public Citizen issued a report charging that demand for electricity in California has declined—not increased—over six months. At the same time state data reveals that a huge block of power—11,000 mega-watts—is not being used. "Power producers are inappropriately citing in-creased demand to justify building new plants," states the report, "and they are hoping to speed the process by suspending California's environment-friendly standards."[26]

The city of San Francisco subsequently filed suit against energy com-panies, charging market manipulation. Public Citizen released a study sug-gesting the companies have cooked the books, holding large blocks of elec-tricity off the market when demand is less than it was a year ago—all part of a grand scheme to rig the market. Peter Navarro, an economics professor at the University of California at Irvine who follows deregulation, wrote in the *Los Angeles Times* that California utilities had been bled to death by conspir-ing energy producers based in Texas. With PG&E and Southern California Edison facing growing liabilities, he argued, the big utilities decided to force the state into a quick bailout. To achieve this Edison paid a huge dividend to its shareholders, thus ridding itself of any excess cash to buy power. PG&E and Edison also moved assets over to their unregulated subsidiaries so that these assets could not be used as credit to purchase electricity.

As the Enron scandal deepened in 2002, the California energy crisis became entangled in the affairs of the bankrupt Enron Company. Enron had been a key player in California, and, as information leaked out, it became clear that the state's alleged shortage probably played a role in Enron's des-perate last efforts to save itself. The company seems to have used California to manipulate prices and hence its own earnings. And in doing so it also sought to influence federal energy policy to bolster its own interests.

An internal company memo prepared by Enron attorneys on 6 December 2000 describes a series of subterfuges with Hollywood names, in which the firm sought to make money by screwing up the market, then getting the state to pay it billions for straightening out the fake mess. At the heart of this operation was a unit called Enron Energy Services, run at the time by Thomas White, who later became Bush's secretary of the army. In December 2000, of course, he did not yet hold that post, because Bush had not been sworn in. Amidst a controversy over White's past dealings he resigned in April 2003.[27]

Meanwhile in Washington, according to disclosure forms on file with Congress, the company paid Quinn Gillespie and Associates, a Washington lobby operation, more than $500,000 to lobby the "Executive Office of the President" on the "California electric crisis." The firm's cofounder Ed Gillespie had worked at the Republican National Committee as communications director and had been a top Bush advisor during the presidential campaign. Quinn Gillespie was lobbying to prevent the federal government from delving into the crisis and re-regulating electricity.[28]

By this time Bush himself insinuated that the people of California would just have to face up to the crisis of their own making. On 29 January 2001 the new president sought to distance his administration from the California energy crisis, arguing that his energy task force would seek long-term remedies, not short-term fixes. Bush suggested California's energy deregulation plan was to blame for the state's problem, which "is going to be best remedied in California by Californians." Bush then tried to change the subject by pushing Enron's interests in another area, the petroleum reserves of the Arctic National Wildlife Refuge. "How do we encourage conservation on the one hand, and bring more energy into the marketplace? And a good place to look is going to be ANWR," said Bush. "And I campaigned hard on the notion of having an environmentally sensitive exploration to ANWR, and I think we can do so."[29]

What politicians in Washington have known for years is that the Alaska debate is code for the more-serious efforts by the oil and gas industry to find a way to transport Alaskan natural gas to the lower forty-eight, eventually through a pipeline across Canada and into the Midwest. As the leading broker in natural gas and owner of the nation's largest natural gas pipeline, Enron's future was closely tied to such gas imports.

Behind the scenes Enron CEO Ken Lay himself was twisting arms. Curtis Hebert Jr., head of the Federal Energy Regulatory Commission, told the *New York Times* that he had received a phone call from Ken Lay early in 2001. Hebert knew Lay was a friend of the Bush family and a heavy contributor to the Bush campaign. Lay asked him to push for faster and deeper deregulation in electricity. If he did so, Hebert recalled, Lay said he would continue to back him within the administration; if not, the implication was there would be a new chairman. "I was offended," Hebert told the *Times*. Lay subsequently denied he was trying to force out Hebert, who was replaced by Pat Wood. All through these early days of the Bush administration Lay and other Enron executives were consulting on policy matters with Vice President Dick Cheney's energy task force.[30]

URANIUM ▶ Uranium mining remains an appendage of the military industrial complex that took shape during the Second World War. Attempts at recasting the business as part of a fuels industry supplying nuclear power plants have been frustrated by one problem after another.

Uranium is usually discovered in conjunction with other metals, and, in part, its cost depends on just how hard it is to separate out the uranium. Up to now, most U.S. uranium has been discovered in sandstone formations. Once the rock is dug up, it is hauled to a mill and there processed into uranium concentrate, or yellowcake. From the mill yellowcake goes to a plant where it is changed into a gas and enriched. After enrichment the fuel is fabricated into a usable form.

Uranium contains the fissionable isotope U-235, which is used to fuel the most prevalent type of nuclear power plant, the light-water reactor. The first important source for uranium was pitchblende deposits found in Czechoslovakia before the beginning of the twentieth century. Pitchblende containing high-grade uraninite was later discovered in the Belgian Congo (Zaire), Canada, and the United States. Uranium from the Great Bear Lake mines in Canada and domestic mines on the Colorado Plateau in the United States supplied the nuclear material for the Manhattan Project during the Second World War.

Most developed uranium resources have been found in four principal forms: pitchblende (the massive form of uraninite); conglomeration with important minerals (thorium, gold, silver, copper, etc.); sandstone, conglomerate sands, and related strata; and uraniferous shales and phosphate rocks. Most exploration has focused on sandstone-type deposits that can be crushed and then subjected to a chemical process in the milling stage so as to extract usable uranium. The domestic industry was developed largely through the impetus of the U.S. military. Following the Second World War a struggle developed between military and civilians over control of nuclear research and development. The civilians subsequently succeeded in creating the civilian-run Atomic Energy Commission with a military oversight committee attached.[31]

The first action of the AEC in the 1950s was to launch a major uranium exploration program with guaranteed price schedules, haulage allowances, production bonuses, and technical assistance to mining companies. Due to the strategic importance of uranium at that time, the AEC remained the only legal buyer. It also controlled key stages of the nuclear fuel cycle.

The Eisenhower administration emphasized putting the nuclear industry into private hands, and subsidies were gradually scaled down. In 1972 the AEC altogether stopped buying uranium. More recently the government began to eliminate on a gradual basis the prohibition against uranium purchases from abroad. The International Atomic Energy Agency (IAEA) estimates that world uranium resources of 4 million tons should last for 65 years. In addition, there are thought to be some 16 million tons buried in undiscovered resources, which would stretch the time period out to 300 years. Nearly one-third of known recoverable resources are in Australia. Other major deposits include: Kazakhstan, 15 percent; Canada, 14 percent; South Africa, 10 percent; and Namibia, 8 percent. U.S. reserves amount to a bare 3 percent of the world total. (Within the United States, there are proven reserves in the Powder River Basin of Wyoming and in Nebraska. American mining is concentrated at these sites. Reserves in other states, including New Mexico, have not been exploited so far.

Total world production is roughly 35,000 metric tons annually, with 50 percent of the total coming from Canada and Australia. Canada alone produces one-third of the world's total supply. Together Australia and Canada are expected to provide most of the world's uranium over the next decade. Actual mining of uranium will soon be surpassed by stashed defense stocks of both the United States and Russia.[32]

The mining end of the uranium business is highly concentrated, with eight companies accounting for 80 percent of world production. Among them, as ranked by the World Nuclear Association in 2002, are COGEMA Resources, Incorporated; Cameco; Energy Resources of Australia (ERA), Limited; Kazatomprom Company (Kazakhstan); WMC Resources, Limited; and Rössing Uranium Mine (owned by Rio Tinto Zinc).[33]

At the beginning of the twenty-first century three companies stood out as major players in the industry:

— COGEMA, a subsidiary of the French government-owned holding company AREVA Group, maintains substantial mining operations in Canada and also in the northern areas of Niger. It also has an exploration program targeting Canada, Niger, and central Asia. COGEMA companies are involved in other stages of nuclear power production, including conversion and enrichment, and spent fuels reprocessing and recycling, with products going to electric utilities worldwide. COGEMA accounted for as much as 20 percent of world uranium mine production in 2002.[34]

— Cameco, a Canadian firm originally owned by the Saskatchewan provincial government, was privatized in the early 1990s, and by 2002 had become a publicly held corporation. It owns and controls the world's largest uranium mines and mills, which are located in Saskatchewan. The company produced about 17 percent of the world's mined uranium in 2002. Cameco also obtains uranium from mines owned by U.S. subsidiaries in Wyoming and Nebraska. Its customers are electric utilities scattered around the world. Cameco also is owner and operator of one-third of the sizable Kumtor gold mine in Kyrgyzstan in central Asia.[35]

— Energy Resources of Australia was the third-largest uranium producer in the world in 2002, accounting for some 10 percent of uranium output. It operates the massive Ranger mine in Australia's Northern Territory, selling uranium oxide along with uranium concentrates to nuclear energy utilities in North America, Japan, South Korea, and Europe. The firm is also developing mines in Jabiluka, Australia, a project that is highly controversial due to the ties of aboriginal peoples to the land and the proximity of the surrounding Kakadu National Park. The parent firm, Rio Tinto Group, has a 68.4 percent stake in ERA. Rio Tinto is among the largest of international mining conglomerates, operating in Australia, New Zealand, and the Americas.[36]

In addition to the military the main market for uranium has been electric utilities. In 2002 there were 441 generating units around the world with a capacity of over 350 gigawatts, with a quarter of the amount in the United States. Sixteen percent of the world's electricity comes from nuclear energy, with reactors in the United States, France, Japan, Russia, Sweden, the United Kingdom, Germany, South Korea, and Canada. The U.S. utilities import close to 90 percent of their uranium needs. Canada provides some 33 percent; Russia, 12 percent; Kazakhstan, 10 percent; and Uzbekistan, 7 percent.

With the end of the cold war the hope of the uranium industry lay in an expansion of nuclear power plants. But nuclear power has a tough road ahead. Over the last quarter of the twentieth century cost has held back nuclear power. Coal-fired electricity has been much cheaper, and to make nuclear power even competitive with other forms of energy, the government has had to provide subsidies in terms of cheap mining rights and insurance among various others. Even when costs come down, the safety issue always looms in the background, with Three Mile Island and Chernobyl uppermost in many people's minds. In the early days of the Bush administration, with the president's emphasis on solving an energy crisis with more oil and gas development, nuclear power got a lift, and several reactors were put in the planning stages.

But the terrorist attacks on the World Trade Center in New York and on the Pentagon in Washington on 11 September 2001 raised new obstacles. Unexpectedly the scant security around the nuclear power plants along with the difficulty of ever ensuring their safety became issues of major concern.

Then there was the question of what to do with nuclear wastes. Efforts to find a politically acceptable waste disposal site caused a furor in the U.S. Congress, and it was only after bitter and protracted debate that the Bush administration was able to move forward with a scheme to deposit spent nuclear fuel deep within the Yucca Mountain site in Nevada. Studies raised questions about the danger of earthquakes and pollution from radioactive materials leaking into underground aquifers. In early July 2002 the U.S. Senate passed the Yucca Mountain plan over the "veto" of the Republican governor of Nevada, Kenny Guinn. (The Congress had set up special rules to govern what turned out to be a twenty-year battle, by giving the Nevada governor a veto and then establishing procedures for overturning it.) The House had passed the plan in May 2002. The Senate vote was a big step forward for the Yucca Mountain project, but it faced numerous other regulatory hurdles and lawsuits before it could actually be implemented. Meanwhile some congressional members became concerned when they learned the actual route of the waste shipments went through cities and towns in their districts and states, including, for example, the transportation of spent fuel across Lake Michigan. Even so the nuclear industry viewed passage of the legislation as crucial to keeping itself alive; no new reactors have been built since 1973.[37]

Finally the emergence of natural gas as a clean fuel competitor to nuclear reduced even further nuclear power's appeal. Instead of the old-fashioned huge power plants necessitated by burning fossil fuels and uranium, natural gas envisions a decentralized industry of small generating facilities. For all these reasons the future of nuclear power remains murky.

In addition to military and nuclear power uses, uranium is employed in numerous ways by the medical industry and in various other industries: for example, in inertial guidance devices, in gyrocompasses, as counterweights for aircraft control surfaces, as ballast for missile reentry vehicles, and as a shielding material. Uranium metal is used for x-ray targets for production of high-energy x-rays. Its nitrate has been used as a photographic toner, and the acetate is used in analytical chemistry. These uses by some 35 DOE facilities and 20,000 commercial users result in large amounts of low-level nuclear wastes.

Furthermore the U.S. War on Terror highlights the little-noticed military fallout from nuclear development, such things as the unfettered trade in plutonium. The main plutonium trade at the beginning of the twenty-first century consisted of shipping spent fuel from Japan to reprocessing plants in France and the United Kingdom, where the plutonium was separated and stored to be later mixed with uranium to make new fuel that could be shipped back to Japan. In 2002 Japan had thirty-three tons of separated plutonium stored on the European continent, which it wants European companies to make into a mixed fuel called Mox. After September 11 the transoceanic trade between France and Great Britain and Japan was questioned by nations along the route, like South Korea, due to the increased fears of attacks. The United States warned to be on the lookout for small, fast boats of terrorists who might strike these slow-moving, lightly armed ships. If one of the ships were blown up, the explosion would amount to a dirty radioactive bomb exploded at sea, with its fallout floating about the world's atmosphere.[38]

Terrorists provide another real market for uranium. "[A] lack of control over the thousands of radioactive sources worldwide makes their acquisition and use by terrorists a real possibility," according to Mohamed El Baradei, director general of the International Atomic Energy Agency, writing in the *Washington Post*.[39]

And more mundane are aspects of what amounts to military garbage, such things as the dozen or more Russian nuclear submarines that sunk off the coasts of the old Soviet Union. The problem of waste disposal grew all around the world, with the United States and other nations seeking nuclear dumps in the old Soviet Union, as well as in seemingly remote spots, such as the former U.S. trusteeship of the Marshall Islands in the central Pacific.

Metals

COPPER ▶ While copper is one of the earliest metals people used for making tools, its recent history and current usage are closely tied to electricity. It played a crucial role in the Industrial Revolution, making possible the transfer of solid fuel to electric power. Copper has been called the metal of the electrical age.

Primitive peoples found copper stones as early as 8000 B.C. and hammered them into crude tools and weapons. By 4000 B.C. North Africans and Arabs are thought to have traded copper on the western shores of the Gulf of 'Aqaba. Over time people learned how to melt and cast copper, then how to smelt the metal. Thousands of years went by between these different steps. Since deposits of copper and tin often are located near one another, it was not surprising that the two were combined into bronze, a hard metal employed in weaponry.

Antiquity is strewn with evidence of copper's important role in civilization: copper nails from the second city of Troy, Chinese cauldrons, classical statues of the Hellenic period, water pipes, swords, ornaments, roofing, and domestic articles of every variety. The use of copper spread with the Romans and could be found wherever they obtained supplies, such as on the island of Cyprus. They made brass coins by mixing copper and zinc.

During the Middle Ages in Great Britain, foundries were established for making brass bells. These foundries later provided the techniques for constructing cannon. By the sixteenth century London had become a great center for the manufacture of copper-based armaments.

In 1800 most of the world's supply of copper came from mines in Britain and from the Hartz Mountains in Germany. About 16,000 tons of copper were produced each year, about as much as one of today's great mines provides in one month. By the mid-nineteenth century Britain was supplying half of the world's copper. The metal also came from Japan, China, and Russia.

Before the introduction of mass manufacturing the copper industry was taken up with producing buttons and pins and providing basic materials for sculpture and other fine arts. The metal's uses expanded as the result of the Industrial Revolution. Introduction of steam power created a sizable market for cylinders, valves, taps, and flanges as well as other engine parts made from copper or brass.

The market continued to grow as new uses were found for copper. It was discovered that silver could be overlaid upon a copper base, and thus began the manufacture of Sheffield silver. The introduction of modern sanitation in the middle of the nineteenth century brought with it the beginnings of indoor plumbing and the wide use of copper pipes. Copper was also used for roofing, and in cannon for warfare. Ship bottoms were sheathed with copper. Finally came the development of electricity. Copper played a major part in all the early electrical experiments. The demand for copper began to increase sharply as the electrical business took off. Consider, for example, that the armature of Faraday's dynamo required less than eight pounds of copper in the mid-1800s. Compare that with the 15 tons of copper used in the components of a modern 500-megawatt turbo generator.[1]

Copper wires and bars also were used in transmitting electricity, over greater and greater distances. By the last quarter of the nineteenth century copper wire was employed in a growing range of uses from electric lights to telephones to railroads, and its demand increased.

In 1882 the rich Anaconda copper mine in Montana began to ship ore to the world market, and annual production jumped from under 50,000 to 250,000 tons in three years. While world demand was indeed increasing, supply outran it. In an effort to limit surplus Pierre Secretan, manager of a leading French metals company, put together a syndicate of wealthy individuals and set out to corner the market in the hope of stabilizing copper prices. As word of Secretan's corner spread, others jumped in, and the price of copper, which had been sagging, picked up. Secretan then went to producers in Chile, America, and Spain and promised them a minimum price for three years if they agreed to restrict production. Meanwhile his syndicate continued to buy up surplus supplies, but all to no avail. Stocks of copper kept flooding into the market. As the syndicate bought more and more, the corner crumbled. The Banque de France stepped in to take possession of the surplus, satisfying Europe for nine months. Fortunately the demand for electricity in 1889 was growing, and the surplus eventually was eaten up in the expanding market.

The next try at a cartel came in the 1920s. By then U.S. copper production accounted for over half the world's total output. Production in Chile, mostly controlled by a few American groups, accounted for another 25 percent. The only additional source of copper at the time was the Belgian Congo (now Zaire), but most of that metal was smelted in the United States. In all, the U.S. copper groups controlled 75 percent of the world's copper.

Most of the U.S. mines were high-cost, compared to the very-low-cost copper deposits available in such places as Chile and Africa. During the First World War the high-cost U.S. operations were kept going because of military demands, but after the war the market slumped. In 1926 the American groups formed Copper Exporters, Inc., a cartel with the purpose of stabilizing copper prices. As had happened with the Secretan corner thirty years earlier, prices were temporarily forced up. Even in the 1929 crash the cartel stubbornly held to its price-fixing scheme.

By 1930 copper scrap dealers were frantically trying to get rid of their inventory at any price. Demand was falling, and, worse yet, producers outside the control of the cartel in southern Africa (what is now Zambia) were working to increase production to take advantage of higher prices. In fact African producers were contributing to the surplus that was pushing prices down. The cartel broke up, and by 1932, with U.S. production cut to one-quarter of its 1929 levels, low-cost copper was flooding into the United States from Chile and Canada. After that the market broke up, and the U.S. copper industry sought protection behind tariff barriers. Only the Second World War put the copper industry solidly back on its feet.

During that war and the Korean War the U.S. government controlled and stabilized the copper business by organizing production and establishing stockpiles. These stockpiles proved important in meeting the demands of the Vietnam War. But by the end of the 1960s the U.S. stockpiles were exhausted, and the importance of the government as a regulator of the copper markets declined.

The copper business experienced a traumatic jolt right after the Korean War. Prices then were so high that industrial users switched to the much-less-expensive aluminum. Because the changeover had involved high capital costs, it was expensive to change back to copper once prices declined.

During the 1960s the copper industry went through periods of glut and shortage, with the African nations beginning to demand a higher percentage of return. In Chile between 1964 and 1970 the Frei regime initiated a policy of gradual nationalization. The government bought a 51-percent stake in the mines from their U.S. owners, to be paid for over a future period. In both Peru and Zambia similar plans were set into motion, and in the Congo the government took over the mines. Key links to former companies remained, however. In Zaire the management of the actual mining enterprise remained Belgian, as did the sales company. Processing also remained in Belgian hands.

When Allende came to power in Chile he interceded in the Frei arrangement and, rather than wait for gradual turnover, expropriated the mines outright. He made promises about compensation to the mine owners, but it never was clear how much the Chilean government would pay or when.

The copper companies fought back, successfully attaching supplies of metal Allende attempted to sell in international trade. More importantly they prevented the refinancing of Chile's foreign debt. Inability to refinance foreign debt holdings contributed to the government's fall. Allende was killed in a coup, and the rightist government of Pinochet was installed.

Allende's demise came in the midst of a nationalist surge among the other copper-exporting nations. Late in the 1960s four major copper producers (Chile, Zaire, Zambia, and Peru) had joined to form CIPEC (Conseil Inter-gouvernements des Pays Exportateurs de Cuivre). Its member nations depended to a considerable extent on the export of copper for foreign exchange, and CIPEC was heralded as their potential cartel organization. But, as history instructs, copper is not an easy commodity to control. CIPEC members controlled only 25 percent of the world's copper. To enforce minimum price levels through production cutbacks was not easy, especially since these nations were under continual pressure from international banks to expand, not contract, production, no matter the price, so as to pay their debt. Moreover the economies of these countries were for the most part marginal, leaving little room to establish stockpiles. And while these traditional suppliers were attempting to pull themselves together, new nations were emerging as major producers, among them New Guinea, the Philippines, Indonesia, and Canada. The Japanese, who then were purchasing sizeable amounts of copper, were influential in establishing these additional producers, since they were anxious to diversify and find stable, long-term supplies of copper.

Meanwhile CIPEC's efforts to reduce the flow of copper had little effect. No one wanted to repeat Allende's experience, and in other nations participation agreements were worked out by which the governments were accorded policy control while financial incentives existed for the prospective mine developers.

Chile became the prime example of this trend. Allende had been anxious to move the nation away from reliance on copper as a source of foreign exchange, and to this end he had begun to develop agriculture. The new military junta, eager to increase foreign exchange to meet the bank debt, reverted to prior policies and sought to generate funds by selling off reserves of copper and other minerals to foreign investors. Meanwhile the African members of CIPEC were seeking to reduce production of copper with a view of shoring up the falling prices occasioned both by the 1974 recession and over-production. Chile plunged on, however, selling off copper reserves to foreign bidders and increasing its own production at lower prices. The overall effect was to undercut other producers, especially the poor African countries of Zaire and Zambia.

With the worldwide copper business in a state of persistent oversupply, metal prices as well as stock prices were driven down. Gradually the entire industry underwent a broad change, as the major oil companies moved in, buying up existing copper companies and taking positions for themselves in copper reserves. Beginning in 1963, with the purchase of a copper holding by Cities Service, oil companies bought outright or acquired an interest in six of the thirteen largest domestic copper companies.

The oil companies looked forward to the day when they could cash in on their bargain basement purchases amidst rising prices. And there were other dreamy prospects: extracting uranium for the then-budding nuclear industry and enjoying new markets for copper in what then looked like a flourishing solar industry. As it turned out the nuclear industry went bust after

Three Mile Island in the late 1970s, and alternative energy business has proceeded at a snail's pace.

In 2003, in terms of quantities consumed, copper trails iron and aluminum. The electrical industry uses three-quarters of all copper produced, and a great deal of the metal goes into basic construction. Chile is the largest producer, followed by Indonesia, the United States (where the centers of production are in Arizona, Utah, and New Mexico), Australia, and Peru. China has surpassed the United States as the largest consumer of copper in the world.[2]

TIN ▶ Despite the intrusion of plastic wraps and containers, tin remains a viable material for packaging all sorts of goods. It is still produced under a system that harks back to the colonial empires of Great Britain, Belgium, and the Netherlands. In modern times, the colonial apparatus of these three nations exploited and developed the world tin industry in Malaysia, Indonesia, and Zaire. British capital and technology also played an important role in the Bolivian tin industry.

Tin is seldom used on its own, almost always appearing as an alloy. While it is best known because of the tin can and other containers, it also is employed widely as a solder for joining pipes or electrical conductors and in bearings and other alloys. Pewterware is made largely from tin.[3]

The occurrences of tin in the world are fairly remote. The main deposits are scattered irregularly along a belt that surrounds both sides of the Pacific Ocean. The formations on the Asiatic side are the more valuable. They extend from Siberia, just a few miles across the Bering, through China and Japan on down into Southeast Asia, to Indonesia and Australia. Indonesia has the world's largest reserves. On the American side of the Pacific, there are a few scattered sites extending from Alaska to British Columbia, Colorado, and Mexico. A much more substantial deposit is found in Bolivia. There also is tin along the periphery of the Atlantic Ocean, at Cornwall, United Kingdom, and in Spain, Nigeria, Zaire, and South Africa.

The history of tin goes back to the Bronze Age, when it was mixed with copper to form bronze. The Phoenicians, who had a settlement north of Gibraltar, were probably the first to introduce tin to the Mediterranean world. They may have discovered deposits not far away. But major supplies could not have reached the Mediterranean until after the conquest of Britain by the Romans. Indeed, Cornwall seems to have been the most important source of tin until the thirteenth or fourteenth centuries. The Great Plague slowed output, and, while it later recovered somewhat, Cornwall tin never again was of any great importance. There was also mining in China and in Malaya dating back to the ninth century.

Tin mining is concentrated in Southeast Asia, with Malaysia producing 26 percent of the world's supply, Indonesia 11 percent, and Thailand 9 percent. In South America Bolivia accounts for 13 percent. Other substantial producers are Australia, Zaire, and China.

The United States is far and away the largest consumer of tin, absorbing 30 percent of the world's annual output. U.S. tin consumption includes a sizeable amount of recycled tin. Together, the United States and Great Britain provide 40 percent of the world's tinplate. The two largest producers are U.S. Steel Corporation and Bethlehem Steel.[4]

In Malaysia half the tin output comes from over a thousand small mines. Local ownership predominates in the actual mining, and the operators are mostly Chinese. But in 2003 the one active smelter was owned by a firm jointly held by Singapore and Malaysian interests. Smelters, which process the raw tin, are owned by outside interests. In the case of Malaysia, one of the two smelters is owned by the Patino family interests, now based in the Netherlands but originally associated with the Bolivian industry.

In Bolivia the Patino family historically ran one of the largest tin operations. And, although its mines were nationalized in 1952, the family continued to dominate the Bolivian industry because only its British smelters could refine Bolivian tin, which has unusual properties that make the process both expensive and difficult. The Patino interests long maintained smelters in Australia and Nigeria in addition to those in Great Britain and Malaysia. During the last quarter of the twentieth century, Patino is thought to have controlled as much as 40 percent of all tin smelting.

The demise of lead has been a shot in the arm for tin. The European Union has set tough standards for eliminating all lead by 2006, which means that solders in motor vehicles, electronics, cans, and the like will contain a steadily increasing amount of tin. In nearly every imaginable consumer item, tin plays an ever-increasing role. The army is phasing out lead bullets, replacing lead with a tin matte. There now are tin shotgun shells.

Solder, in which lead and tin are mixed together, constitutes the largest market for tin, and, with lead being phased out, that market will grow larger. While U.S. canning manufacturers employ aluminum in packaging beverages, tin-plated steel accounts for about a quarter of the packaging of other food products. Elsewhere in the world tin cans are the rule. Tin is also used in the manufacture of polyvinyl chloride.

ZINC ▶ Zinc is sometimes referred to as the anonymous metal, since its identity is almost lost in such end products as brass faucets, automobile parts, galvanized gutters, and air-conditioning ducts. To the consuming public it is probably best known as a medicinal ointment, zinc oxide. Nonetheless this bluish-white metal is third after aluminum and copper in trade among the nonferrous metals. And worldwide production of the metal grew by more than a quarter during the 1990s to 8.8 million tons.

There are two principal kinds of what is called slab zinc. The purer type, special high-grade zinc, is mixed with aluminum for use in die casting (the manufacture of molds that form auto parts). The second kind, prime western grade, is predominantly alloyed with lead and aluminum in making galvanized metal widely employed in roofing, siding, and ducting material, and with copper in forming brass and bronze faucets, valves, and pumps.

The automobile industry is the largest single consumer of zinc, from which it manufactures parts, tires, radiators, tubes, and trim. About 40 percent of all zinc is used in galvanizing; die casting and brass manufacture each account for 29 percent. Another use is undercoating. Zinc oxide plays a part in the production of rubber, paints, ceramics, floor coverings, and pharmaceuticals.

Canada, Australia, China, and Peru were the world's leading zinc producers in 2002. Canada and Australia are the biggest exporters and dominate the world market. Together they account for more than half the zinc concentrate in world trade (some 15 percent of the world's output comes from Canada alone). More than three-quarters of all Canadian zinc is exported to the United States. All of the major producing countries have substantial zinc reserves. South Africa in particular has large unexploited reserves.[5]

LEAD ▶ Lead is even more closely tied to the automobile than is zinc. Much of the lead mined or recycled across the world goes into the manufacture of motor-vehicle batteries. Of course historically lead is best known as a poisonous additive to gasoline, now banned in motor vehicles in the United States and elsewhere.

Lead has a wide assortment of other uses: in chemicals, as a pigment, for piping and sheeting, in the electrical industry to make television tubes, for cable sheathing, and in alloys.

By the early 2000s batteries accounted for some 87 percent of the lead used in the United States. Other significant uses included ammunition, oxides in glass and ceramics, casting metals, and sheet lead. The remainder was consumed in solders, metals, brass and bronze billets, covering for cable, caulking lead, and extruded products.

The leading lead-producing countries at the beginning of the twenty-first century were Canada—by far and away the largest and most important—China, the United States, Mexico, and Peru. Recycling plays an important role in the lead market. Recycled lead, especially that recovered from old car batteries, is equivalent to two-thirds of domestic consumption.[6]

Lead has come to be viewed as a serious environmental health hazard. Children are especially vulnerable to lead poisoning, which affects brain functions. Lead is ingested in a variety of ways. Many foods contain lead; it is contained in water that is carried through old lead pipes. Houses or apartments built on land filled with rubble, including lead paint, can be dangerous environments. Dust from soil contaminated with lead, and in the case of small children, the soil itself, are sources of ingestion. Historically, lead-additive gasoline in motor vehicles was a major source of pollution.

In the past, lead has been found in association with other metals, most notably zinc and silver. The Greeks mined lead at silver mines in Laurium, and the Phoenicians recovered lead in the mining of zinc in Spain.

In the United States lead has been removed from gasoline and most paints because of its harmful effects on children's health. But there still is plenty of lead used in solders and certain kinds of steel, and the metal is still employed in certain industrial paints.

With the European Union determined to remove lead altogether from use, and the United States cutting back on its use because of environmental reasons, the industry nonetheless has held steady, in large part because of the extensive use of lead acid-storage batteries in motor vehicles and of industrial battery systems to back up computer and telecommunication networks. A personal computer often employs anywhere from four to eight pounds of lead. The demand for batteries at the opening of the twenty-first century was rising throughout Asia, especially in China. And this growth offset declining demand in the United States.

Five countries account for more than two-thirds of the world's production of lead: Australia, China, the United States, Peru, and Canada, in order of size of output. Australia also has the largest reserves, followed by China and the United States. In the United States lead has been traditionally mined in southwestern Missouri along the Viburnum trend, the shores of historic beaches of an ancient ocean that extended from the eastern slope of the Rocky Mountains to the Ozarks. Lead is still mined in Idaho and Montana, and new deposits are being explored and developed in Alaska.

IRON AND STEEL METALS

IRON AND STEEL ▶ The origins of the steel industry are closely linked to warfare. The introduction of steel in the mid-nineteenth century laid the base for modern armaments, which, over a period of time, have provided a steady and increasing market for the industry.

While man used iron as early as 1000 B.C., the age of steel really began with the discovery in 1856 by Sir Henry Bessemer of a process for combining molten iron with oxygen to produce steel. (Actually, Bessemer was not the first person to hit on this process. An American, William Kelly, in search of a better way to make good iron sugar kettles, had invented the process a full ten years earlier, but Kelly's improved iron was ridiculed because it was not made in the "regular way.")

At the time of his discovery Bessemer had been commissioned by the Emperor Napoleon III to design a new artillery shell. The shell itself was a marked improvement on previous projectiles, but the cannon that shot it was of such a light construction that it could not accommodate the shell. The French were prepared to abandon the project unless some sturdier iron for cannon was found. That led Bessemer into experiments with iron, culminating in his steel discovery.

The Bessemer process helped to quicken the pace of the Industrial Revolution in England. Production of steel led to the manufacture of improved textile machines, which in turn increased the production of cotton for export. In England coal and steel found great markets in the railroads. But these markets were limited, and the British steel industrialists and the financiers who backed them sought expansion abroad. Railroads were built in, and machinery exported to, the continent of Europe, Turkey, and Egypt, and eventually to the United States and Australia. This search for markets contributed to colonialism: The railroads brought food and raw materials from the interior of colonies to ports where they were loaded aboard steel ships for the trip to England. Manufactured goods were returned for sale in the colonies.

The steamship business was a good market for steel after railroad building tapered off. Indeed, in England after the depression of 1893, the steel industry became dependent on the British Navy. In the last quarter of the nineteenth century Britain experienced one shipbuilding binge after another, each one resulting in increased budgets for navy ship programs.

In the United States the British capitalists enthusiastically invested in construction of canals. Then they financed railroads on and across the prairies. Financiers in London encouraged the U.S. Congress to enact the railroad land grants, which ultimately made possible the building of the continental railroad system.

As the Civil War drew to a close and the plans for building the first transcontinental railroad were finalized, the demand for iron to make the rails grew. Until then the business of making iron had been left to many smaller firms.

The prospects for making a fortune in the expanding railroad business aroused the interest of young Andrew Carnegie. After emigrating to America as a thirteen year old, Carnegie had settled with his family in Allegheny (now Pittsburgh), Pennsylvania. His father was a handloom weaver, and his mother mended shoes. Carnegie eventually got a job as a clerk on the Pennsylvania Railroad, becoming a telegraph operator. Soon Carnegie became the private secretary to the line's superintendent. When the superintendent retired, Carnegie took over his job. In these capacities he had access to inside information on which he could make investments. At this time the iron business was blossoming, and Carnegie joined with a boyhood friend, Henry Phipps, in buying an iron forge.[7]

By dint of his work on the railroad, Carnegie was well placed to sell iron for rails. With the knowledge that the railroads were beginning to build steel bridges, he set up a new company to provide steel for that purpose. Next Carnegie combined forces with Henry Frick, another young Pennsylvania businessman who had established himself in the manufacturing of coke, a key ingredient in making iron and steel. As their enterprise grew the three entrepreneurs sought holdings in iron ore, and they bought from John D. Rockefeller a portion of his deposits in the Mesabi Range of Minnesota. (Rockefeller then was busy establishing the Standard Oil Trust.) With control of coal and iron ore in their grip the Carnegie company's influence in steel grew still larger.

Then came the financial panic of 1893. Just as the depression changed the nature of the steel industry in England, making it more heavily dependent on the military, so too in the United States did it have a profound effect.

Fearful of the dangers of ruinous competition steelmen began to argue for a new spirit of cooperation that came to be known as the policy of "friendly competition." J. P. Morgan, the Wall Street banker, led a movement to combine the different American steel companies into one big firm. Carnegie, who desired to retire, wanted no part of this spirit of cooperation and preferred to sell out rather than join the group. He resisted Morgan, and in doing so came to loggerheads with his two partners, Phipps and Frick. Carnegie proceeded to set a trap for Morgan. He waited until the Morgan Bank had become so deeply involved in the steel industry that it could not back out. Then he announced vast new plans for expansion of his own company. If these plans were carried out, the Morgan interests and Carnegie would be plunged into vicious competition.

Panicking at the thought of senseless competition inveighed by the "pirate" Carnegie, lesser steel industrialists pleaded with Morgan to buy out Carnegie at any price. And this he did, paying Carnegie $447 million, far more than he could have hoped to realize in other circumstances. Having got rid of Carnegie, Morgan proceeded to draw together into the United States Steel Corporation the different steel firms along with the Rockefeller ore interests in Minnesota and his fleet of ore boats. At the time of its formation in 1901 U.S. Steel accounted for nearly two-thirds of all American steel production.

The spirit of friendly competition prevailed within the steel industry over the next decade, with the steelmen getting together to set prices at dinner. In 1911, however, the government accused the company of monopoly and sought its dissolution. The case was not decided until after the First World War, when the U.S. Supreme Court in a 4–3 decision held that U.S. Steel need not be broken up. And so it continued as the largest company in the industry, but its share of the business declined. The Great Depression sharply reduced production, and it was only the American entry into the Second World War that reinvigorated the industry.

The decline of U.S. Steel is attributed to different factors. For one thing the spirit of cooperation or friendly competition sought to head off government trustbusting by voluntarily limiting any one company's share of the market to 50 percent. For another, the company was devoted to heavy steel products, while new markets were being opened up for lighter-weight products, in such industries as automobile manufacture. And third, aggressive, independent firms sprang up to challenge the leader.

Still and all, by the end of the Second World War, the steel industry was dominated by a handful of major firms, of which U.S. Steel was still the most important. The grip of this oligopoly was made more secure when the government decided to sell off the plants it had built during the war to the existing companies.

The manufacture of steel has since proliferated. More than seventy-one nations make steel today, compared to thirty-two in 1950. Nonetheless, it remains very much an industry of the developed world.

Within the United States by the end of the twentieth century five big firms, led by U.S. Steel, accounted for over half of the production. As in the days of Carnegie, the American industry is vertically integrated, with major steel companies owning coking plants as well as coal and iron ore deposits and to a lesser extent participating in mining ventures in cobalt, manganese, and other alloy metals employed in steelmaking.

Because of steel's uncertain future many companies sought to diversify into real estate, financing, aluminum, seabed mining, and engineering at the end of the twentieth century. Most of these investments went nowhere, although their holdings in certain natural resources may yet turn out to be a valuable addition to the industry.

Since the beginning of the steel industry in the United States, the main companies have sought control over the basic raw materials—coal and iron ore. As a result the ownership of iron ore reserves has worked to strengthen the concentration within the industry.

Although the United States has been blessed with very large quantities of superb iron ore in the Mesabi (Minnesota) and Marquette (Michigan) ranges, the most valuable deposits have been exhausted, and the companies are left with low-grade taconite ore. To make up the difference they import foreign high-grade, inexpensive ore from Canada, West Africa, and elsewhere. They also have joined with companies from other countries in building steel plants in less-developed countries, where energy and resources are less expensive than in the United States, and where labor is much cheaper.

There is an extraordinary environmental cost to this. Much of the mining is open pit, which has its own destructive potential. Before the end of the twentieth century, it was discovered that the residue of taconite contained asbestos, a confirmed carcinogen. For years these taconite residues, or tailings, had been dumped into Lake Superior, where they contaminated the water supply of Duluth, Minnesota, and eventually drifted throughout the Lake's system into the Mississippi River. The growing pollution set off a long, stormy battle between the steel industry and the environmentalists, who either sought to ban mining operations outright or establish safeguards against dumping the tailings into the water.

The American steel industry has been in real trouble since the 1980s. The Asian financial crisis of 1998 sent it reeling. Thirty-six firms filed for bankruptcy, among them such well-known names as Bethlehem Steel, National Steel, and LTV. Bethlehem and LTV together accounted for about half the steel-making capacity and jobs in the industry. During the Second World War, when there was great demand for steel to build armaments, U.S. Steel, the industry leader, employed 340,000 people; Bethlehem Steel, another 165,000. Over sixty years later those two companies together employ some 34,000 workers.

The U.S. government has sought to keep the industry above water with tariff barriers to stave off lower-cost competitive foreign imports and with bankruptcy laws to keep the business from crashing altogether and to help in reorganization. But these factors were overshadowed by imports at bargain basement prices, along with the decline of the dollar, and, as the companies claimed, with growing costs of pensions and health benefits for their workers.

The United States is not at the top of the list when it comes to producing the raw iron coming out of a blast furnace. It follows the European Union, Japan, and Russia, in that order. When it comes to raw steel production, China heads the list, followed by Japan, the European Union, the United States, Russia, South Korea, and the Ukraine.

By the end of the twentieth century China had emerged as a major player and today is a key middleman in the international steel trade. In part the nation's low labor costs allow it to undercut others in the manufacture of various steel alloys. As a result instead of processing the raw ore themselves, steelmakers around the world, send it to China, where it can be processed and added to various alloys. Much of this steel goes to Japan.

MANGANESE ▶ Manganese is to steel as yeast is to bread. About twelve pounds of the metal are added to every ton of steel as an oxidizing agent to remove sulfur, nitrogen, and oxygen. In addition to removing impurities, manganese also is employed as an alloying element to make steel harder and more wear resistant. Such products as army helmets and railway fastenings contain manganese.

In nature the metal never occurs alone, but always in connection with one or another of 300 minerals. The reserves are vast, extending throughout tropical, subtropical, and warmer temperate zones. Almost half of the world's identified reserves are in South Africa, which provides substantial amounts of manganese to American and western European steel firms. Another 35 percent is in the former Soviet republics of Ukraine, Georgia, and Kazakhstan. To avoid reliance on the Soviet Union during the cold war, U.S. companies allied themselves with the South African industry. The remaining deposits of manganese are scattered around the world. Australia is an important producer. Brazil has manganese, and the world's most productive mine is in southeast Gabon. This Moanda mine annually puts out 2.3 million tons of manganese ore that is processed by a company 38 percent of which is owned by French interests.

Generally the business is dominated by a few large producers that provide the metal to a small group of major steel firms.

The South African Department of Mines reports that the country contains an immense 4 billion metric tons of manganese ore reserves, which amounts to 80 percent of the world's resources. In 2001 that nation produced 1.5 million metric tons of ore, about half of it consumed domestically in the manufacture of stainless steel. The South African industry is dominated by three companies: Samancor, Ltd., which is owned jointly by BHP Billiton and Anglo American Corporation of South Africa; Assmang, Ltd.; and Highveld Steel and Vanadium, Ltd.[8]

CHROME ▶ Without chrome there would be no stainless steel, which is such an important ingredient in modern industry. By definition stainless must contain at least 10.5 percent chrome, and, unlike other alloys employed in the manufacture of steel, there is no substitute for chrome.[9]

Stainless steel is essential in the manufacture of jet engines, and it is a crucial material in the chemical and petrochemical industries. Stainless steel is used in the production of high-temperature materials of all sorts.

Two-thirds of all chrome is employed in the manufacture of stainless steel; it is also used as a refractory material, as a chemical, and for strength in the manufacture of various steels and cast iron. One of the earliest uses of chrome, dating from the 1800s, was in coloring and tanning leather.

Chrome ore is always found in conjunction with other metals as an oxide. The two largest deposits are in South Africa and Russia. The United States, which is the world's foremost consumer of the metal, has no domestic sources itself, and for most of the last century imported supplies from Zimbabwe. In the 1970s the United States sought to force change in South Africa's apartheid policies by placing sanctions on chrome and diversifying its supply by turning to the then Soviet Union. Then a new process by Union Carbide that allowed for the use of lower-quality ores and improved recycling enabled the United States to reduce its trade with Russia. Today America relies on recycled chrome and a big stockpile that can be released for national security reasons. Apartheid as a policy is gone, but the once mighty Zimbabwe source is declining in significance. Early-twenty-first-century producers of chrome ore include the now independent Kazakhstan, along with India and Turkey. But these nations have relatively small reserves, and are far surpassed by enormous reserves in South Africa. It is safe to say that 90 percent of the world's reserves are in South Africa, Kazakhstan, Finland, and Zimbabwe.

In making steel, chrome is added as ferrochrome. This substance is produced by the reduction of chrome ores in electric furnaces. Most of the world's ferrochrome has been supplied by Japan, the United States, and, increasingly, by South Africa, because of the growing tendency to build ferrochrome plants near the mine site. The Scandinavian countries also supply ferrochrome. The manufacture of ferrochrome is dependent on the availability of sufficient inexpensive power, which limits possibilities for production in most parts of the world. South Africa has ample low-cost electricity.

Some two-thirds of the world's chromium reserves are located in South Africa, which produces half the world's chrome every year. The United States obtains 45 percent of its ferrochrome needs from South Africa, which is, indeed, by far and away the leading player in the chrome business, producing one-third of the world's chromite ore and half its ferrochrome.

NICKEL ▶ Nickel, a crucial ingredient in high-strength steels used by the military and aircraft industries, until recent years has come either from eastern Canada or the French southwest Pacific island possession of New Caledonia under which 25 percent of the world's nickel reserves are thought to lie. Two companies have been the major suppliers. The International Nickel Corporation of Canada (INCO) Ltd., the Canadian mining giant, long has provided most of the high-quality nickel from its enormous ore body at Sudbury, Ontario. Le Nickel, the French firm controlled by the Rothschild family, has supplied ores of lower quality from New Caledonia. As the high-quality ore reserves run down, however, the structure of the business is changing.

Nickel is tough and corrosion resistant and melds easily with other elements. It has been called the "war metal" because of its use in heavy guns and for armor plating. But, with the coming of the automobile and the creation of high-strength alloy steels, nickel became an important ingredient in an entirely different range of steels, used widely in aircraft and power plants, in agriculture, and for pipelines. Nickel works well at sub-zero temperatures and thus is employed in making the tanks that hold liquefied natural gas and pipelines in Alaska. In automobile manufacturing nickel provides a base over which shiny chromium can be laid. In 1979 nickel was used as a substitute for cobalt, which was then in short supply.[10]

The metal was first isolated and identified in 1751 by a Swedish chemist, A. F. Cronstedt, but because of impurities such as carbon and sulfur, it was suitable only for alloying. Then in 1867 nickel was discovered in New Caledonia in usable deposits. At the turn of the century workmen building the Canadian Pacific Railroad came upon a massive outcropping of ore at Sudbury. At first, they thought they had discovered copper, but on investigation it turned out to be nickel. This ore body became the basis for INCO, which fifty years ago held 80 percent of the world nickel business. Since nickel is mined in combination with other metals, INCO also was a major producer of copper, platinum, cobalt, and other metals from the rich Sudbury body.

But INCO's hegemony was challenged during the 1970s from several different directions. Within Canada itself ownership of Falconbridge Mining Company changed hands, with Superior Oil taking a stake and coming to play an important role. Falconbridge began to undercut INCO's prices. At the same time steelmakers began more widely to employ lower-quality nickel ores at lower prices. That opened the way for increased competition from other sources, especially New Caledonian nickel, which was mined before the Canadian discovery, but had been eclipsed by Sudbury because of poorer quality and high costs of both mining and refining. To keep ahead of the growing competition, INCO set out to build up its own holdings of lower-grade nickel ore in such places as Guatemala and Indonesia.

At the beginning of the twenty-first century INCO's big Canadian operation supplied most of the nickel to the United States. In addition to its large Sudbury resource, the company wants to develop a new complex in Labrador. The world's largest nickel reserve to date is in Canada, but Russia's arctic mines are the largest single producers of nickel in the world. New finds in Australia promise to make that nation an increasingly important player. A large source of nickel is in Cuba, and, despite the U.S. embargo on trade with the country, Canadian and Australian companies are actively mining the metal there in conjunction with a state-owned firm. The United States has legislation on the books that seeks to punish anyone doing business with

Cuba by banning their executives from entering into or doing business in the United States. But the globalization of the market makes this sort of embargo more and more difficult to uphold.

Nickel could turn out to be more important as time goes on, because it is widely used in the manufacture of batteries for hybrid cars and has uses in cellular phones and computer parts. The metal's use in coinage, however, has declined. Although the Europeans have banned it from their coinage because of fears people will be stricken with nickel Dermatitis, the United States will continue to employ the metal in coins.

COBALT ▶ Cobalt occupies a small, but key, position among the world's metals. Seldom mined on its own, it often is produced along with copper or nickel. It is used in super alloy metals, which must hold up under great pressure and in high-temperature situations. (Cobalt is unscathed at temperatures as high as 2,000° F.)

Until the late 1970s half the world's cobalt production came from Shaba province of Zaire. The United States was especially reliant on this region, drawing three-quarters of its cobalt from its resources. But fighting there made cold war American defense contractors uneasy, and the United States worked on developing new techniques to obtain more cobalt from other metals and sought to diversify the source of supply. About one-third of the cobalt used in this country goes for super alloys, the heat- and corrosion-resistant alloys used chiefly in jet-aircraft engines and chemical-processing equipment. Magnetic alloys (everything from anti-lock brakes to electronic equipment) account for another 10 percent or more. The big growth in cobalt is due to its use as a bonding agent in machined carbide cutting tools. It is also a catalyst used in oil refining (10 percent). Batteries, made in Asia, employ cobalt, and this market is growing dramatically.[11]

Cobalt is scattered everywhere under the earth, but easily mined deposits are hard to come by. The metal is often extracted in conjunction with mining nickel and copper. In Montana the metal is extracted in platinum mining.

At the beginning of the twenty-first century, Zambia played a major role in the cobalt market, providing 22 percent of the world supply. Another 17 percent came from Australia. The U.S. Geological Survey's list of major cobalt producers includes Canada, Congo, Kinshasha (in Zaire), Russia, and Cuba.

As with other steel-alloying metals, there are substitutes for cobalt, and, as a result of the fighting in Zaire in 1978, western industry began to make changes rather than continue to rely on a limited supply at high prices.

Japanese television companies, for example, developed a magnetic material for TV sets that requires greatly reduced amounts of cobalt in their electron-beam guidance magnets. The electronics industry reduced its use of the metal. Nickel was substituted for cobalt as a substrate for integrated circuits. In the aircraft industry the Pratt and Whitney group reduced cobalt consumption by substituting nickel-based alloys for cobalt-based ones and by recycling cobalt from scrap and using technologies that do not require cobalt for engine assemblies. Nickel-based alloys will be used for jet-engine turbine blades on new airliners.

Even without substitution ample supplies of cobalt exist in the world. Manganese nodules—black, potato-like objects found on the ocean floor along the equator in the mid-Pacific—contain cobalt along with other important metals. Any serious shortage of metals would signal the go-ahead for the enormous transnational consortia poised to exploit the seabed.

Over the near term mining conglomerates may well turn to another ready source of cobalt: nickel. Depending on the type of deposit nickel ores can yield cobalt as a co-product. Cuba and New Caledonia both have such nickel ores, and thus they may become potential suppliers of cobalt in the future.

LIGHT METALS

BAUXITE ▶ Bauxite is sometimes called "red gold." Aluminum, its end product, helped win two world wars. And the development of aviation has depended on this metal.[12] For the United States the production of aluminum has involved the creation of a colonial system whereby the economies of a few poor Caribbean nations have been given over to the production of bauxite, all of which is consumed abroad. Today a similar colonial economics is practiced around bauxite in the western African nation of Guinea.

Bauxite ore is a chemical combination of aluminum oxide (alumina), silica, ferric oxide, titania (crystalline titanium dioxide), and water, with the alumina content running up to 60 percent. It generally requires over four long tons of bauxite to produce one short ton of aluminum metal.

There are three basic steps to making aluminum. First the ore is dug out of huge open pits, then crushed and dehydrated in kilns. The alumina is extracted by washing the bauxite in a solution of hot caustic soda. In the final stage aluminum is separated from the oxygen in the alumina by running a powerful electric current through the mixture. This yields molten metal, which is cast into ingots. The smelting facilities that accomplish the last stage account for about two-thirds of the industry's capital cost, and they are located primarily in industrialized countries.

Together the United States and Canada produce 50 percent of the world's aluminum and account for 45 percent of its consumption.

At the outset North American production was based on bauxite produced in Arkansas. Alcoa, which had been founded in Pittsburgh in 1888 and had enjoyed a monopoly for over half a century, began mining in the Caribbean region as early as 1916, when it moved into Guyana and Surinam. At about the same time French and German companies began to exploit the bauxite resources of southern and eastern Europe.

The real growth in aluminum occurred with the Second World War. Between 1939 and the end of the war, smelting capacity had increased seven times over. Washington contracted for 40 new plants. The Reynolds Metals Company, which had entered the business in the 1930s, received a large, low-interest federal loan to expand its capacity. With the war, the companies began an intense search for low-cost, high-quality bauxite ore. Since Alcoa controlled most of the domestic sources, the new companies—Reynolds and Kaiser—turned abroad for sources.

Deposits in Jamaica became especially attractive because of low extraction costs and the very large quantities available. Jamaican ores were cheaper to transport to the United States than those in either Guyana or Surinam because Jamaica is much closer to American ports on the Gulf Coast. The Jamaican ores were also of higher quality, which made them less expensive to refine. Finally Jamaican bauxite, which lay six to twelve inches underground, could be gouged out much more easily than ore in Guyana, which was buried as much as fifty feet below the surface. The political climate in Jamaica, a former British colony with a parliamentary system, was encouraging to the Americans. Labor was plentiful and cheap.

Aluminum companies acquired large tracts of land in Jamaica during the 1940s, and began to develop these reserves a decade later. They also began to construct refineries, in part because of pressure by the Jamaican government, which wanted more of the income generated by the aluminum industry to remain on the island. It also made good economic sense. By refining the bauxite into alumina before shipping, companies could save on the cost of transporting the bulky ore.

During the Korean War, the U.S. government introduced subsidies to the American aluminum companies in the form of tax incentives and a stockpile program that guaranteed a market. Moreover, companies received a direct subsidy from the government in the form of loans. (Reynolds, for example, was granted over $8.5 million to finance its mining and processing facilities—this covered 85 percent of the investment outlay.) At home, the government provided massive subsidies in the form of cheap electricity, so crucial to the smelting stage. One-third of all U.S. smelting capacity is located in the Pacific Northwest and in the past has been dependent on relatively inexpensive electricity from the government-owned Bonneville Power Administration. At one point, toward the end of the last century, the aluminum companies held long-term contracts for one-third of the entire BPA electric power output. In the southeastern states other smelters relied on government-subsidized power from the Tennessee Valley Authority.

The development of bauxite in the Caribbean accompanied a transfer of influence from British to American hegemony of the area. In years past Jamaica had been a standard plantation society, ruled by a handful of families who had risen to preeminence in the sugar trade. Typically there was little heavy industry. Most of the inhabitants, who were descendants of slaves, lived in rural areas. Half of Jamaica's trade was with Britain, based on the export of sugar, bananas, and rum. One-quarter of its trade was with North America.

By the mid-1970s over half of Jamaica's exports went to North America, and 60 percent of its imports—including food—came from the United States and Canada. In contrast to the pre-bauxite period, when nearly half of Jamaica's export earnings came from sugar, in the last quarter of the twentieth century Jamaica relied on bauxite for 46 percent of its foreign-exchange earnings.

From 1915, when the first bauxite concessions were granted in the Caribbean, until 1973, the different bauxite-producing nations sought without much success to make the American and Canadian aluminum companies give them more money and control over the industry. Both Surinam and Guyana, endowed with hydroelectric potential, were anxious to establish alumina plants, which would add value to the bauxite they were mining. The U.S. companies refused, and so did the international banks. In Surinam Alcoa was finally persuaded to build an alumina plant, but because of the company's transfer pricing mechanisms, the nation received little more in revenue than it would have had it continued to yield up the raw bauxite. In Jamaica, which had some leverage because it was the single largest bauxite producer, the government eventually succeeded in increasing taxes.

The OPEC oil boycott of 1973 changed the nature of the business. In the 1960s bauxite producers had explored the possibility of a producer cartel, but they dropped the idea on grounds it was doomed to failure. When OPEC raised oil prices, however, the bauxite-producing nations, dependent on imported energy, were forced to move. Once again they began to pressure the companies for an increased part of the take and for more control over the industry. While Guyana outright expropriated its aluminum works, the pattern of action was set by Jamaica, which increased taxes and based payments on the sale price of aluminum in the United States. The Manley government also negotiated purchase of 51 percent of the bauxite operations, bought back land from the companies, and joined with them in joint ventures for the production of alumina. As a show of confidence, Jamaica's central bank purchased shares in the companies.

In 1974 the major producing nations joined together in an association, the International Bauxite Association (IBA), to confront, OPEC style, the aluminum makers. The members of this new association included Jamaica, Australia, Guyana, Surinam, Guinea, Sierra Leone, and Yugoslavia. Together they accounted for 63 percent of the world's annual production.

The association's principal adversary was the international, vertically integrated aluminum industry, backed up by the U.S. and European governments. Fully 76 percent of aluminum capacity was then controlled by six companies—Alcoa, Alcan Aluminum, Ltd. of Canada, Reynolds, Kaiser, Anaconda (division of Atlantic Richfield), and Revere.

There was a big difference between the IBA and OPEC. Recognizing its weaknesses IBA stayed clear of open confrontation with the companies. It was true enough that the Caribbean nations were the main providers of ore to the United States, and that their economies had become dependent on its sale. But Australia, by far and away the largest producer, was not dependent on aluminum.

The international companies worked through Australia to moderate the IBA. At the same time they set in motion plans to make themselves less reliant on Caribbean producers by setting up operations in other, more-friendly nations, such as Brazil. And finally the American companies began to think more seriously of developing bauxite from clays and sandstone mixtures within the United States. The aluminum industry always has manifested a wistful interest in a stretch of white kaolin clay running through Georgia, which yields alumina but in far smaller amounts than bauxite.

The overall result of the formation of the bauxite association and the negotiations with the companies was to exchange company ownership of bauxite mining and alumina refining stages for long-term supply contracts and local control. But, since the major capital investments are at the smelting stage, the real control of the industry remained well beyond the reach of the producing nations.

Today the emphasis in the bauxite business has shifted somewhat to Australia and Guinea. Australia is the largest producer, accounting for more than one-third of the world's production. Guinea is second largest and sits on 30 percent of the world's bauxite reserves. The economy of Guinea is dominated by bauxite. It accounts for 15 percent of the nation's GDP and 90 percent of its exports. The future world bauxite supply will depend increasingly on Guinea because of that nation's immense resources rather than on Australia.

Total world reserves run from 55 to 75 billion tons, with 33 percent of that located in South America, 33 percent in Africa, and 17 percent in Asia. Guinea alone has 7.4 billion tons. At the beginning of the twenty-first century the main producers were Australia, Brazil, Guinea, and Jamaica.

The U.S. aluminum industry is the world's largest, with an output valued at about $39 billion. The United States produces small amounts of bauxite in mines in Alabama and Georgia, but for the most part imports bauxite and alumina. Australia supplies nearly one-third of America's total demand for alumina. Its major supplies of bauxite ore come from Guinea (40 percent), Jamaica (25 percent), Guyana (20 percent), and Brazil (15 percent).

MAGNESIUM ▶ Magnesium is a light metal which might well compete favorably with aluminum save for the generally lower cost of the former. But, because of the growing movement toward increased fuel efficiency within the United States, magnesium has come to play a growing role. Automakers are experimenting with the metal for door handles and hinges, brake master cylinders, and engine parts.

Since 1941 Dow Chemical was the principal magnesium supplier, but in 1998 it dropped out of the business, opening the way for suppliers from around the world. China is the largest producer of magnesium, followed by

Turkey, North Korea, Russia, and Slovakia. The United States, which consumes almost two-thirds of the world output, now imports magnesium from Russia, China, and the Ukraine.[13] When it shut down its Freeport, Texas, plant, Dow was facing increasingly stiff competition from Norway's Norsk Hydro ASA in Quebec. Magnesium can be produced from various minerals. In Salt Lake City Magnesium Corporation of America is perched on the edge of the Great Salt Lake and uses salt from the lake. Noranda wants to produce magnesium from asbestos tailings in an abandoned Quebec mine.[14] The industry is becoming more and more tied to the auto manufacturers, with vw having set up a Dead Sea magnesium plant in Israel. Ford has explored interests in Queensland, Australia.[15]

About 40 percent of all magnesium goes into aluminum, which, in fact, is an alloy containing 1 percent magnesium. Magnesium is an essential metal in easy-open soda and beer cans. But it has many other uses: as an alloy with aluminum, zinc, and manganese; and in jet engines, rockets, missiles, luggage, frames, power tools, cameras, and optical instruments. The metal can also be employed in incendiary bombs, flares, and fuses. It prevents corrosion and is used in pipelines and for ship hulls.

TITANIUM ▶ One of the oddest gatherings during the cold war occurred in the late 1970s when executives from the United States, the Soviet Union, Japan, and Britain gathered in Moscow for what appeared on the surface to be a rather academic meeting on the future uses of the Cinderella metal—titanium. Pleasure-boat hulls, heat-exchanger tubing, and other such uses were the ostensible topic of conversation. But everyone knew the real business at hand was armaments. In particular it was the development of the B-1 bomber. If its production went ahead, the then-enemy, the Soviet Union, stood to make millions of dollars through the increased sale of titanium. Moreover, the Kremlin would respond to the new American bomber by building one of its own, thereby further boosting titanium sales.

Those days are gone, but the future of the titanium business still looks to the development of airplanes, which provides three-quarters of the market in building engines and air frames. In addition to new fighters, which will use more titanium than ever before, the big manufacturers look forward to marked expansion of the passenger-airline fleet, which is expected to quadruple during the early part of the twenty-first century. Currently, actually relatively little of all titanium produced goes into the manufacture of planes. Most is used in the making of titanium dioxide for paper, inks, plastics, textiles, and ceramics. Golf clubs have provided a big market for titanium. DuPont is the largest producer of titanium dioxide.[16]

Titanium is made from two metals that are found in conjunction with other metals. These consist of ilmenite, which currently is produced in large quantities in Australia, and of which there are deposits in Russia, Ukraine, and Kazakhstan, and rutile, a material found almost exclusively on the East Coast of Australia on beach properties mostly owned by British and American companies. Although the various minerals used to make titanium are among the most common in the earth's crust, rutile is most easily transformed into a metallic form. The other minerals all have elements that are very difficult to remove and that, if not removed, cause fracture of the metal under even a light strain.[17]

Titanium metals are mainly found in Australia, which is the largest producer, and in South Africa and Canada.[18]

PRECIOUS METALS AND STONES

SILVER ▶ Together with gold and copper, silver was among the earliest metals used by man. Unlike the other two, however, silver was not immediately recognizable, since it was hidden away in a sulfide form within different ores. One of these ores, galena, was fairly common in Europe and Asia Minor. When fires would ravage the forests covering outcroppings of galena, the ore would become molten, and the silver would run out. The historian Diodorus Siculus, writing in the last century before Christ, described the occurrence: "These places being covered with woods, it is said that in ancient times these mountains (the Pyrenees) were set on fire by shepherds and continued burning for many days and parched the earth so that an abundance of silver ore was melted and the metal flowed in streams of pure silver like a river."[19]

From ancient times there were evidences of silver ornaments, indicating that the metal was a token of wealth, and exchangeable for goods and services. The earliest actual mining seems to have occurred sometime in the fourth millennium B.C. by the predecessors of the Hittites. They inhabited Cappadocia, an area almost in the middle of modern Turkey. By 2000 B.C. silver jewelry and metalwork were common. Open-pit and then shaft mining of silver had begun. Mining moved east, with deposits in Armenia being explored. In 500 B.C. the Laurium silver-lead mines in Greece were opened. They are believed to have been the mainstay of Greece for three centuries and to have financed the Persian wars. They were shut down in the first century A.D.

By this time silver—more than gold—was in great demand because of its high economic value, and the metal was exploited under the cruelest conditions, with natives and criminals made to serve as slaves in the silver-lead mines of the Iberian peninsula, first opened by Carthage and continued by the Romans after their victory in the Punic wars.

The spice trade created a keen new demand for silver. The trade routes ran from Sri Lanka and the Malabar Coast of India to the Red Sea, across the deserts of Egypt to the Nile, thence down to Alexandria, where first Phoenicians, then Carthaginians, and ultimately the Romans, took possession of the spices, silks, fine cottons, ivories, and jade. Silver from the Iberian mines paid for it.

In the eighth century the Moorish invasion of the Iberian peninsula put an end to mining there, and from then until the fifteenth century silver was obtained largely as a result of redistribution of war plunder. Then, just as a period of great expansionism was beginning in the sixteenth and seventeenth centuries, the Spanish Empire discovered new large deposits of silver in Mexico, Bolivia, and Peru. Not only were these deposits much larger than any previous ones, but this silver could be much more simply refined since it was not mixed with lead. (Mercury became a key ingredient in the refining process.)

Spanish America provided the world with silver until 1820, when Spain's colonies successfully began to revolt. A severe crisis was averted partly because Europe went back to using large existing stocks of silver and partly because of the development of banking systems. The shortage of silver was relieved with discoveries in the Sierra Nevada of the United States; in fact, the United States soon became the world's largest producer of silver, a position it retained until 1900. From that point on, there was never again a shortage of silver. Indeed, silver began to appear as a byproduct in mining such other metals as copper, lead, and zinc.

Silver originally was traded in ingots or lumps called pieces of silver. The value was fixed by weight. Early units of money included the Phoenician talent and the Hebrew shekel; then, in due course, there were the English pound, Indian tola, and Chinese teal. Generally coins were of three distinct classes: gold for governments and the wealthy; silver for merchants and their trade; and copper, brass, or bronze for the day-to-day needs of ordinary people. The Spanish dollar was the normal currency in the Americas and came to be the basis of currency for the United States.

The discovery of silver in the Americas led to transfer of the spice trade from the Mediterranean to Mexico, with galleons passing from Acapulco to Manila. About 1850 the Mexican dollar became the principal currency all along the Yangtze valley and in the ports of China.

Silver vied with gold as a form of money until the eighteenth century, when a series of circumstances began to turn Europe from silver to gold. As the Portuguese began to receive increasing amounts of gold from their Brazilian territory, they set up a gold standard and demonetized silver. Britain went to gold in 1816, and by 1916 few countries were left on the silver standard except China. The process of demonetizations was helped along with each succeeding discovery of silver, making the metal more and more available.

In the early 1930s scientists began to consider silver in an entirely new light—as an industrial metal. Over time industrial uses made silver far more valuable than it was as money. About one-third of all current production goes into chemicals. The largest single user of silver has been the photographic industry, which was based almost entirely on silver-containing light-sensitive halides, derived from silver nitrates and other related compounds. Image definition is unsurpassed with silver salts, and, while there are photographic processes that do not require silver, these processes are not adaptable to color films.[20]

Another major part of silver production, some 15 percent, is used in the manufacturer of silverware. A further 5 percent goes into the making of jewelry. A great deal of silver also is employed in the manufacture of batteries and electronic components.

Silver is often found in conjunction with lead and zinc, and copper and gold—not on its own. It is often not even the primary purpose of mining, but an unintended consequence. The main producers (in order of production) are Mexico, where two companies—Industrias Penoles, SA de CV, and Grupo Mexico—predominate; Peru, where the largest producer is Cia de Minas Buenaventura; and Australia, with BHP Billiton as its the largest player.

GOLD ▶ The oldest man-made objects of gold discovered so far, dating from the late Stone Age, have been found in excavations at Ur. It is believed that the gold used in these objects may have been mined in Arabia, then transported along the Euphrates River to the Ur communities. Later, Crete, which had no gold of its own, accumulated the metal, probably from the Balkan highlands and possibly from within Egypt. There is even speculation that Cretan sailors may have brought back gold from the Iberian Peninsula. Until 2000 B.C. Egypt produced most of the world's gold. After that gold began to appear in the Mediterranean area from Spain.

In the earliest times the sources of gold were a carefully guarded royal prerogative, but as the supplies of the metal grew, gold jewelry filtered down to ordinary people. Gold became a type of portable wealth, first in the form of gold rings and later as all sorts of other jewelry.

The modern history of gold effectively begins in Russia in 1744, when the metal was discovered on the eastern slopes of the Urals. Over the next hundred years the gold fields spread; the mining was either directly for the czar or for a few landlords. By 1847 Russia had become the leading producer of gold, mining three-fifths of the world's supply.

The gold discoveries in California, beginning at Sutter's Mill and quickly running up and down the creek beds of the Sierras, changed the entire picture. Western mining was the province of the lone prospector, not of any concerted organization. The supply of gold from the United States was immense. Most of it stayed within the country, but some also flowed into the banks of England and France. The U.S. discovery was followed by a gold rush in Australia. Most of that gold was handled by London. From then on gold finds were few and far between.

In 1867 the great diamond fields at Kimberley along the banks of the Vaal River were discovered, and everywhere men who had successfully prospected for gold turned to diamonds and sped to South Africa. Their fortunes in gold allowed them to participate in the hunt for diamonds. All along there had been small traces of gold in evidence in South Africa, but they had not enticed most prospectors, who were by then used to scooping up nuggets from the California or Australian streambeds.

The gold in South Africa was of an altogether different sort. It consisted of specks or dust embedded in a pebble conglomerate, almost as if in a sandwich of stones. This conglomerate, or reef, extends for mile upon mile and varies in thickness from a few inches to several feet. The reefs extend down into the earth for miles and are covered at the surface with thousands of feet of hard rock. Tracking the reefs below ground is an intricate geological detective game. The actual mining of South African gold requires immense amounts of capital and engineering skill.[21]

Because this new type of gold mining costs so much, the diamond men quickly established themselves as gold kings, and the descendents of those original miners remain in charge today. The gold was hard to separate out until the invention of a process using cyanide to filter out the gold. This was an important step in developing the industry.

By 1898 South Africa was providing one-quarter of the world's gold. Since 1910 the nation has produced one-third of all new gold. London was key to the South African industry, for not only did capital come from London, but London bankers also played an important role in selling the gold.

Before the California gold rush gold was in short supply. Some estimates are that up to 1850 only about 10,000 tons had been mined since the beginning of time. It was only the swelling supply, first from Russia, then California and Australia, and ultimately South Africa, that provided gold in sufficient quantities that enabled the metal to become the accepted standard of value, while forcing silver to be demonetized.

Britain went on a gold standard in 1816 but dropped it by the twentieth century. The United States clung to a bimetal standard until 1900, when it briefly adopted gold. Today most gold is used in the manufacturer of jewelry. But because it has represented a standard of value, people continue to purchase gold as a hedge against currencies of declining value.

Instead of petering out gold mining at the beginning of the twenty-first century once again became of industrial importance, this time because of the demand for gold in the products of modern technology. Because of its superior electrical conductivity, resistance to corrosion, and other desirable combinations of physical and chemical properties, gold has become a valuable industrial metal. It performs critical functions in computers, communications equipment, spacecraft, jet aircraft engines, and a host of other products.[22]

All told, three-quarters of all the gold mined in the world will one way or another end up as jewelry, and much of that jewelry is absorbed in India, where women, who often have no wealth on their own, are effectively valued on the basis of the amount of gold in their dowries.[23]

Advances in mining have allowed the big international mining companies to return to mines long ago exhausted to find slivers of gold that in the nineteenth century were too small to process. Using a method developed by the U.S. Bureau of Mines in the 1960s, miners use cyanide to leach out gold from tailings—leftover piles of residue from previous mining. Low-grade ore with minute gold residue is crushed, put on the ground, and sprayed with a cyanamide solution. Inevitably some of the cyanide leaks into the water, causing serious pollution. In one instance at a Summitville, Colorado, mine, the government spent $100 million to contain the cyanamide leachate from just one mine.[24]

South Africa produces more gold than any other country, followed by the United States. Well over three-quarters of all the gold mined in the United States comes from California and Nevada. World resources are estimated at 100,000 tons; of that perhaps 20 percent results as a byproduct. South Africa has one-half the total world resources; the United States and Brazil are tied at 9 percent each.

According to the U.S. Geological Survey, "Of an estimated 140,000 tons of all gold ever mined, about 15 percent is thought to have been lost, used in dissipative industrial uses, or otherwise unrecoverable or unaccounted for. Of the remaining 120,000 tons, an estimated 33,000 tons are official stocks held by central banks and about 87,000 tons are privately held as coin, bullion, and jewelry."[25]

Modern mining in the United States is mostly carried out in enormous open pits, ringed with barriers and appearing like small islands or redoubts set in the middle of the hill and valley geography of Nevada. Most of the mining is in Nevada, where hard-rock mining uses more water than all the people in the state put together (one mine every day sucking up as much water as the entire city of Austin, Texas). To get one ton of gold the mine goes through 3 million tons of waste rock.[26]

Gold mining in the United States is attractive, in part, because of federal government subsidies of $5 an acre. If the mine is located on an Indian reservation, then the mine owners are in luck, since the pollution standards for Indian reservations are less stringent than those for most other land. The subsidies sometimes appear to be extraordinary; by May 1994, when U.S. Interior Secretary Bruce Babbitt signed the Barrick Gold Company's mineral patents, it was estimated that Barrick was getting $10 billion worth of gold for less than $10,000. Babbitt was quoted as saying that "it's the biggest gold heist since the days of Butch Cassidy. But these folks stole it fair and square. The West has long been settled but the giveaway continues unabated."[27]

Anglo American PLC is among the largest gold-mining companies. It is a sprawling combine of mining companies founded by Sir Cecil Rhodes in 1917. J. P. Morgan originally put up some of the capital. In modern times this company has been most closely connected with the Oppenheimer family.

Anglo American, De Beers Consolidated Mines, Ltd., and Minerals and

Resources Corporation (Minorco) are all part of the same mining group. Anglo and De Beers are joined together like Siamese twins, with Anglo owning 34 percent of De Beers and De Beers owning 34 percent of Anglo. The Oppenheimer firm owns 8 percent of Anglo American. Through a 51.5 percent share interest in AngloGold the group has gold mining interests located in South Africa, Australia, Mali, Tanzania, the United States, Namibia, Argentina, and Brazil.[28]

Another player in gold is Barrick, an upstart which merged with Homestake in 2001 to become a major player. It has operations in Argentina, Australia, Canada, Chile, Peru, and Tanzania, as well as the United States, where its flagship Goldstrike property is located on the Carlin Trend in Nevada. Also worth mentioning are Echo Bay, a Canadian firm with holdings on public lands in the United States, as well as Canadian operations; Freeport-McMoRan, with gold and copper mines in Indonesia; Newmont Mining Corporation, the biggest U.S. producer, also with holdings in Nevada; Noranda, which is controlled by the Bronfman family, owners of Seagram's, and has extensive holdings in the Carlin Trend in Nevada; Pegasus Gold, in Montana; and Rio Tinto Zinc, the world's largest mining conglomerate.[29]

PLATINUM ▶ The platinum group consists of six related metals that commonly occur together in nature: platinum, palladium, rhodium, iridium, ruthenium, and osmium. They are among the scarcest metallic elements, and their price is correspondingly high. Together with gold and silver, the metals of the platinum group are referred to as the "precious metals." The group is generally found in association with nickel and copper.[30]

Nearly all of the world's supply of platinum-group metals is extracted from lode deposits in three countries—South Africa, Russia, and Canada. Actually, 92 percent of the world supply comes from Russia and South Africa. South Africa produces two-thirds of the total platinum; Russia provides two-thirds of all palladium. Half of the world's reserves of platinum-group metals are in South Africa.

At one time platinum was used mainly in jewelry. Indeed, Japan, which consumes more of the metal than anyone else (50 percent of the world production annually), still employs most of it as a base for jewels.

But over the last quarter century the platinum group has become important to industry because of its extraordinary physical and chemical properties. A sizable proportion of the metal is consumed in the manufacture of catalytic converters used for auto-exhaust emission systems. Platinum also is employed in oil refineries as a catalyst for upgrading octane in gasoline. Other metals of the group are employed as corrosion-resistant materials in the chemical, electrical, glass, and dental industries. Palladium is in keen demand by the telephone companies, which use it in exchange relays.

Outside of Russia three companies account for most of the platinum produced. In South Africa Rustenburg Platinum Mines, Ltd., puts out two-thirds of that nation's platinum. Impala Platinum, Ltd., is a second major producer. Much of the platinum is mined in the western Transvaal.

INCO, Ltd., is the third-largest producer. It operates nickel mines in Ontario and Manitoba, where platinum is produced as a byproduct. The U.S. Geological Survey has stated that almost all Russian output is a byproduct of nickel-copper mining at Sorilsk, in northwestern Siberia.

There is some platinum to be found in Colombia, too, where it is recovered by gold-platinum placer mines. In the United States small amounts are recovered from copper sludge at refineries owned by AMAX Mining, Asarco, and Kennecott Minerals Company. There are small amounts (less than 0.5 percent of world production) recovered from nickel-copper refining in Japan and Finland.

Even in cases where platinum may be produced as a byproduct of metals mined elsewhere, the refining is often done in South Africa.

Because the platinum business is so tightly held by a mere handful of companies, the market in the metal can be easily manipulated and is subject to large swings. Before the Soviet Union broke apart Moscow and Johannesburg vied with one another. The Soviets on occasion dumped platinum on the world market to raise foreign exchange to purchase wheat during a poor harvest year. Platinum prices would drop accordingly. After the Soviet Union pulled out of the market, the South African merchants could reap greater profits in economic downturns, when investors turn to precious metals, including platinum, as a hedge, thereby driving prices up. And the market is influenced in other ways: since platinum is produced along with nickel, its supply can rise or fall in pace with nickel mining. As a result price swings in platinum can be wild. In early 1998 worries about Russian supplies sent the price of palladium soaring from $198 per troy ounce at the beginning of that year to $417 by mid-May, the highest price ever recorded for it.[31]

DIAMONDS ▶ Diamonds represent the most concentrated form of wealth in existence anywhere in the world. They are tiny in size, lightweight, and highly portable. Over the long history of their exploitation in Africa by

British colonial corporations, diamonds have been marketed through an intricate private cartel which keeps surplus from flooding the market and maintains control of the business in a few South African and European hands.

During the late stages of the cold war and continuing into the twenty-first century, open warfare swept through the major diamond producing areas of Africa. In Sierra Leone rebel armies financed arms purchases through the sale of diamonds taken from areas under their control. Diamonds were used to pay for entire private armies imported to fight for control in the name of the nominal government.[32]

A UN report states, "The wars in Angola, Sierra Leone and the Democratic Republic of the Congo are currently the most notable examples of where rebels have used diamonds in this way. However diamonds and the wealth they generate are not sensitive to borders and the profits have been used to finance conflict abroad as in the case of Liberia."[33]

According to the Diamond Registry, an industry group, diamond production in 2002 amounted to 120 million carats—with considerably more gem than industrial diamonds. A very rough estimate of their worth is $7.6 billion. About half came from nations with a small number of mines that are regulated by the government, in Africa as well as in Canada and Australia. They represent the traditional diamond-mining business, historically controlled by De Beers of South Africa, and hence the once long arm of British colonial capital. Today's main producers include South Africa, Namibia, Botswana, Canada, and Australia. These nations produce about half of the world's annual output. The other half comes from Russia. Angola and the Democratic Republic of the Congo also produce diamonds. In fact all in all diamonds are produced, often in small quantities, in twenty-six different countries. Thirty nations are involved in the processing of diamonds.

A small amount of diamonds (some 20 percent of total production) are sent from the mines to be polished for jewelry. Diamonds for jewelry in the United States, which account for somewhat less than half the total market, have a value of $56 billion at the retail level. Rings constitute most of the end product, with pendants a fast-growing second. In the United States the sale of jewelry (including diamonds along with other stones and metals) represents almost one-quarter of the value of all consumer goods sold. As readily seen from these statistics, the diamond is a most compressed form of wealth.

Most diamonds are used for industrial purposes. The industrial diamonds are those that, because of color, structural defects, size, or shape, do not meet the requirements for gemstones. Diamonds are much harder than any other natural or artificial abrasive material. Diamond grinding wheels and diamond tools are used extensively in sharpening carbide-cutting tools. Diamond bits are used in drilling for oil, and diamond cutting implements are routinely employed in cutting and shaping concrete highways and other concrete structures. Some of the demand for industrial diamonds has been taken up by synthetic diamonds produced by General Electric, De Beers, and others, but the technology of synthetics has not yet yielded sizable stones, which are so important in cutting and drilling. Therefore the industrial demand for natural diamonds is keen and continues to grow. Zaire is the largest producer of industrial diamonds, followed by Russia.

Diamonds play a big role in the economies of South Africa, Botswana, Namibia, and Guinea.

Most diamonds—rough and polished—go through a trading center at Antwerp. (Other trading points are in Tel Aviv, New York City, and Bombay.) De Beers still controls the business through its cartel called the Central Selling Organization, based in London.

An arm of the Anglo American Corporation, the South African mining conglomerate De Beers remains king of the business and mines half of all the world's diamonds. In postcolonial Africa De Beers shares the business with governments through jointly owned companies. Debswana is equally jointly owned by De Beers and the government of Botswana, and Namdeb is also equally jointly owned by De Beers and the government of Namibia. Half of the $300 million spent by the industry in exploration comes from De Beers, and, quite unlike other mining ventures, a diamond mine can recover its costs in just two years.

Alrosa accounts for all official Russian production of diamonds, with its Udachny mine alone producing approximately 75 percent of the company's total diamonds by value and 68 percent by output in 1998, although this is due to change soon as another mine increases output. Argyle of Australia includes a 60 percent holding by Rio Tinto and 40 percent by Ashton Mining. BHP Diamonds, Incorporated (a wholly owned subsidiary of Broken Hill Proprietary Company Ltd.), in a joint venture with Dia Met Minerals Ltd. and two geologists, is mining all the production from Canada's Northwest Territories under the Ekati name. Its chief mine produces about three million carats a year, about 5 percent of world diamond production. MIBA (80 percent of which is owned by the government of the Democratic Republic of the Congo and 20 percent by the Belgian firm Sibeka) controls the productive mines at Mbuji Mayi in the Democratic Republic of the Congo. A significant number of medium-sized companies also contribute to world diamond production.

Nine out of ten diamonds used in jewelry are cut and polished in India, where the business has an enormous workforce of some 700,000 jobs. Israel exports half its diamonds to the United States, accounting for about half the American business. Thailand, the United States, and Mauritius are other cutting centers. New York, the biggest diamond market, with about 1,800 dealers, gets most of its diamonds from De Beers.

Some of the so-called "conflict diamonds" from Angola and Sierra Leone reportedly have been sent to the United Arab Emirates which apparently has set up factories for polishing. This country has been hiring Indian cutters to do the job.

Overall the business is in flux, with a squeeze on the middlemen as producers link up with retailers. And the industry is worried about the impact of synthetic diamonds and what effect laser and heat treatments— that can seem to perfect a stone—will have on the market. That has led to toying with a scheme of "diamond passports" to reassure consumers.[34]

Angola provides an example of how American- and Chinese-backed guerilla insurgents used diamonds to finance their war against the government there. For years UNITA, a joint creation of the United States and China, and in its day partly financed by the CIA, sold diamonds to finance the war. Diamonds helped the rebel army amass more than $3.7 billion over a 6-year period. An army financed by diamond sales prevented peace in Angola for many years.

While UNITA could never control Angola outright, it controlled the diamond-producing areas there. It sold the diamonds it acquired, through several different countries, to raise money, or bartered them directly in exchange for arms. A boycott extended by the United Nations proved porous, and UNITA traded diamonds easily through Namibia, Liberia, and Rwanda.

UNITA placed a tax on diamonds from diggers working within the territory it controlled, usually in the form of rough diamonds and sometimes in cash. It also granted various diamond buyers to operate in its territories in exchange for a commission. A buyer from the Congo operated in such a manner.

A United Nations report described the operations: "To protect and to monitor its diamond mining operations UNITA is said to have organized a special diamond protection force, which operates under the command of General Antonio Dembo, the Vice-President of UNITA."[35]

It continued:

The Panel learned that generally when cash is required by UNITA, the required quantity of diamonds are packaged and either sold for cash or exchanged for the required commodities. In a typical arms transaction, UNITA prepares parcels of diamonds (allegedly valued between US$4 million and US$5 million each), and diamond experts provided by the arms broker and by UNITA agree on the value of each parcel based on the number and quality of the stones presented. UNITA specifically seeks out arms dealers willing to accept diamonds as payment. In a typical non-arms related deal where cash is needed to purchase commodities, support operations, or assist family members, for example, the diamonds are usually carried to a safe destination outside Angola, and a meeting is arranged with interested buyers. The diamonds are then exchanged for cash.[36]

The report also noted:

Sometimes the diamonds were taken directly to Antwerp and evaluated or sold there. Sometimes the diamond traders and UNITA traveled to a third country to make the deal. In the latter case, the favored locations were Burkina Faso, Zaire (during the Mobutu era) and Rwanda (after 1998)—because of the protection given to UNITA personnel by the authorities in those countries. The Panel also learned that protected diamond deals had in the past taken place in a number of other countries, particularly Côte d'Ivoire.

Burkina Faso is a safe haven for UNITA diamond transactions. The Panel learned that Ouagadougou was a particularly favored safe haven for transactions between UNITA and diamond dealers based in Antwerp. Typically, Savimbi would call President Compaoré in order to alert him that a delegation would be arriving. General Bandua recalled a conversation in which Savimbi told Compaoré that "all those who are coming to sell or buy, they are all my friends."[37]

The panel also received credible evidence of similar types of transactions and similar facilities being provided by Rwandan authorities, and by the former Zairian authorities prior to the fall of Mobutu. Diamonds were smuggled through Namibia, and on occasion taken to South Africa and roughly polished to disguise their origin before being mixed with other diamonds in the legitimate trade, and reportedly marketed through a South African jewelry concern. Eventually the diamonds worked their way into regular commerce, and often would end up in the Antwerp market, which handles 80 percent of the world's diamonds. The UN panel found controls at Antwerp were lax. The diamonds were also handled in London, another major market.

UNITA used diamonds to cement friendship with Zaire, which helped Savimbi on various occasions. "The Panel heard testimony from a source close to Savimbi that with the exception of the President of Burkina Faso the UNITA leader regarded his political friendships with African leaders as being essentially business relationships," the UN report noted. "Certain services were provided and in return certain payments were made. In the case of Togo, the source recalled an incident in October 1998 when Savimbi had refused to pay what had been asked of him by President Eyadema, and Eyadema had as a result refused to allow the release to UNITA of a missile system that had been delivered to the airport at Kara for UNITA, and that was to be sent to Andulo. The matter was a source of considerable tension between the two."[38]

During the 1970s a Liberian named Charles Taylor worked his way up the ladder in Liberia, helping to overthrow its president Samuel Doe and ultimately capturing most of the country before winning the presidency in 1997. Under his rule, Liberia was even more anarchic and violent. In 2003 Taylor was driven from power but he remained—at least temporarily—as an active political figure behind the scenes.

An exhaustive UN probe, which in 2000 produced its *Panel of Experts Report on Diamonds and Arms in Sierra Leone*, spells out how Taylor became a player in the violent civil war in Liberia's neighbor. He arranged financing and military training for the Revolutionary United Front (RUF), the rebel movement in Sierra Leone, thereby making himself a key cog in the world diamond business.

Packets of Sierra Leone diamonds passed directly to Taylor, according to the UN report, and Liberia became the brokerage where millions of dollars' worth of what became known as "blood diamonds" were traded for military hardware, mostly light weapons, to supply the RUF.

IN ALL OF THIS the role of De Beers was crucial. As the main player in the diamond business it could squash or support the diamonds coming from

Angola. The company's position has always been obscure. Whilst in Russia in October 1997 Gary Ralfe, De Beers' CEO, said,

> You are absolutely right to say that in fact it is UNITA that has over the recent few years been responsible for most of the production in Angola. One of the essential jobs that we De Beers carry out worldwide is to ensure that diamonds coming onto the markets do not threaten the overall price structure and therefore although we have no direct relationship with UNITA, there is no doubt that we buy many of those diamonds that emanate from the UNITA-held areas in Angola, second-hand on the markets of Antwerp and Tel Aviv. And as the diamond markets have weakened recently (inaudible) . . . in buying up this Angolan production which otherwise will be threatening the overall price structure has increased.[39]

But in a June 1999 letter to the London *Observer*, Tim Capon, a director of De Beers, wrote "We have never purchased diamonds from UNITA." He repeated this position on August 22, 1999: "Contrary to your assertion, we have never purchased diamonds from UNITA . . ." Another article, in the *South African Mail and Guardian*, points out that "UNITA gems went to De Beers." Before the UN diamond sanction of 1998, "the situation was murkier—the company said it did not knowingly buy UNITA diamonds with the qualifier that it could not identify where the diamonds came from."[40]

Whatever the case by the time the UN report came out, De Beers was getting out of the business (if it ever had been in the business). The UN report stated: "De Beers in London, which is the main buyer of rough diamonds in the world, in 1999 decided to cease buying any Angolan diamonds (except for the production of one particular mine, which De Beers is contractually obligated to purchase)." It concluded: "The Panel came across substantial anecdotal evidence that the measures taken by De Beers to ensure that it does not purchase UNITA diamonds directly or from third parties, and De Beers' subsequent withdrawal from the diamond market in Angola have made it more difficult for UNITA to sell its diamonds thereby raising the costs to UNITA and effectively lowering the price that UNITA would be able to get."[41]

BY THE END of the twentieth century the diamond business was in considerable flux. The turmoil in southern Africa has begun to have an effect on De Beers, and some nations have abandoned the syndicate to sell direct to dealers. Ghana, for instance, has dropped De Beers as a selling agent. Guinea, where production is small but where there is a trove of untouched diamonds, operates independently of De Beers. The fighting in the Shaba province in Zaire in 1978 forced out De Beers. The Central African Empire has cut out De Beers, instead opting for a consortium led by a former Israeli general. (Israel has become a center for cutting diamonds.) Angola, which has just begun producing diamonds after its long war of liberation with Portugal, is still offering diamonds through De Beers.

The De Beers position is potentially more tenuous than it might seem at first, since most of the company mines are leased from governments other than South Africa. The company itself mines about a third of the almost 40 million carats of diamonds produced in the world, and buys most of its supply on fixed quotas from other producers.

De Beers has begun to lessen its dependence on southern Africa by shifting its investments away from diamonds and, through the vehicle of Anglo American, to other parts of the world. The company also is moving into the cutting and polishing end of the diamond business, where, in effect, it can compete with the dealers to whom it has been selling all these years. Joint ventures in this area have been formed, including one with the government of India. The company also is involved in joint mining ventures abroad, as in Australia, where there has been a diamond rush.

At one level, the former colonies of the European powers either had been formally cut into the De Beers network, i.e., Namibia and Bechuanaland, or found themselves, either unintentionally or on purpose, working through a separate network which conceivably would operate beyond De Beers control, and hence beyond the control of the traditional market. The emergence of the United Arab Emirates as a polishing center meant that potentially this network could run all the way from production through wholesale completely independent of De Beers. At first De Beers tried to handle these rogue players with free-market play. But the quantity of diamonds from Africa alone made this next to impossible. The result has been that De Beers has come out for UN sanctions, and in 2001 was backing legislation in the U.S. Congress to throw American clout behind a passport system for outlaw diamonds, that is to say, diamonds entering the market out of the company's control.

In an effort to stimulate sales De Beers formed a joint venture, LVMH Moët Hennessy–Louis Vuitton, which sells luxury goods for retail outlet with high-class stores in London and New York. The United States is an important diamond market since it consumes half of the world output of cut and polished diamonds. De Beers sought to maintain an arm's-length distance from the new retail chain because of possible American antitrust violations. Officials at the retail outlet said they were buying diamonds in competition with Tiffany and Cartier from independent dealers or from "sight holders"—the dealers who have been authorized to buy diamonds for cutting and polishing from De Beers itself.[42]

In sum diamonds did indeed in the case of Angola and in Sierra Leone finance the armed insurgencies. Getting control of the market, not through any free trade but through Western governments' sanction, proved crucial for the organized traditional diamond business, i.e., De Beers, to maintain its faltering presence. This is an ongoing and fragile cartel.

GEMSTONES ▸ There are no consistent estimates of gemstone occurrences in the world. Following are some of the existing sources of different stones:

— Afghanistan: Emerald
— Australia: Opal (95 percent of the world's supply), sapphire
— Brazil: Agate, beryl, ruby, sapphire, topaz
— Colombia: Emerald
— Former Soviet Union: Garnet
— Kampuchea: Sapphire
— Kenya: Tsavorite, rhodolite, ruby, sapphire
— Madagascar: Beryl, rose quartz, sapphire, tourmaline
— Mexico: Agate, opal, topaz
— Myanmar: Ruby (although Mogok Valley mines, which yield high-quality rubies, are nearly exhausted), jade (much of it smuggled out), beryl, sapphire, topaz
— South Africa: Emerald
— Sri Lanka: Beryl, ruby, sapphire, topaz
— Taiwan: Jade
— Tanzania: Beryl, emerald, garnet, rhodolite, gem zoisite, amethyst, aquamarine, chrysoprase, opal, gem, corundum, sapphire, ruby, tourmaline, zircon
— United States: Emerald (North Carolina), opal and sapphire (western states), turquoise (southwestern states)
— Zambia: Emerald (Israelis have a mining venture here)
— Zimbabwe: Emerald

Forests

TIMBER ▶ The timber business is among the oldest international industries on the planet. In the United States—long at the center of the industry as producer and exporter—this industry played a central role in colonial history, and is intricately linked to westward expansion. In more recent times the industry—which is controlled by a handful of corporations—has been involved in some of the most heated and high-profile controversies over environmental regulation and control of the public domain. The story of timber speaks to core questions regarding the use of land and resources.

When the English first settled on American shores in 1607, most of the forests in England were gone, and those on the European continent had been conserved. As settlement of its new colonies developed, Britain considered American forestlands as "naval stores," with New England, and eastern Canada after 1763, providing a reserve of timber for the masts and planks needed by the celebrated British Navy, while the southern pines provided tar, pitch, and turpentine. As time wore on the colonists wanted the forests for their own shipbuilding, and the struggle over their ownership was one cause of the American Revolution commonly overlooked by later historians.[1]

The development of the U.S. timber industry followed cycles of industrialization and expansion. During the nineteenth century the lumber business was among the top industries in America, providing fuel and the raw materials for the growing cities of the East and for the settlement of the West. By mid-century the progress of the timber industry became intertwined with that of the railroads. Abraham Lincoln had represented railroad interests in Illinois, and, as president, he signed into law the railroad land grant act, which gave continental railroad builders land to lay tracks on across the continent, along with adjacent land for stations, warehouse buildings, and other railroad structures. Then, in order to provide the railroads capital for their venture, the companies used the land as collateral against mortgages from banks in the Northeast and Britain.

In this way the railroad companies obtained large tracts of forest and mineral-bearing lands in the West. For example, in 1864, in the midst of the Civil War, Congress created the Northern Pacific Railroad Company to build a line from Lake Superior to Puget Sound. To help finance the railroad Congress gave the company 40 million acres, consisting of every other square mile stretching out from the tracks on either side in a 40 mile band—in total, an area equal to 2 percent of the contiguous United States and larger than the nine smallest states put together. Investors in the Northern Pacific included such individuals as the future presidents Rutherford B. Hayes and Ulysses S. Grant. The company eventually went bankrupt, and recovered by merging with another railroad, to become the Burlington Northern, owned by the infamous financiers J. P. Morgan and James J. Hill. The lands adjacent to 25,000 miles of track in 23 states held vast amounts of coal, gold, natural gas deposits, and other resources of commercial and industrial potential. It also included 10.5 billion feet of old growth timber on 1.5 million acres.[2]

The railroad land grant spawned a handful of timber companies, including three—Weyerhaeuser, Potlatch, and Boise Cascade—that long remained interconnected through directorates and stock ownership. These firms came to dominate the American timber business. Typical of timber companies they were responsible for widespread overcutting and other environmentally damaging practices—a phenomenon made additionally controversial because it—and the companies' considerable private profits—was made possible by free grants of the public domain.[3]

From the seventeenth century through the early twentieth, wood was the most valuable raw material in America. In addition to railroad ties and fuel for steam engines, it provided the timber for houses and buildings, firewood to warm the houses, and the charcoal that was key to making iron. The high demand for timber, accompanied by continuing population growth and settlement, transformed the American landscape. When the Europeans arrived, some 850 million acres of America was covered by forests. By 1920 this had been nearly cut in half. Since then forests have been growing once again, and nearly one-third of the nation is covered with trees.[4]

By the end of the nineteenth century the rapid deforestation, along with the outcry against it, was in large part responsible for Theodore Roosevelt's conservation movement. Congress set aside some 200 million acres as protected national forests. Even so, under the Civil War–era Homestead Acts, it continued to offer up great hunks of the unprotected public domain for $1.25 an acre. The Homestead Acts in theory were intended to give ordinary settler families the chance to have their own small holdings, but in effect they often led to a land grab for large corporations. (This was, in fact, not antithetical to Roosevelt's conservation scheme, which called for the efficient exploitation of resources and thus in practice usually favored big business.) The national forests themselves were, however, left untouched until the housing boom after the Second World War created demands for more wood and resulted in a drive to open these set-aside lands for cutting as well.[5]

By the beginning of the twentieth century the industry was responding to shifts in the demand for timber. Coal surpassed wood as a source of fuel. By 1920 oil and gas were also coming into their own; thirty-five years later they supplied two-thirds of the nation's energy needs. At the same time charcoal gave way to coke in iron making. Most important of all, more and more trees were cut down to make paper and paper products, everything from newsprint to Kleenex. Increasingly, the U.S. timber industry reached toward a global market—a trend that has continued to this day.

The global supply of timber is concentrated on a number of continents, with South American and Russian forests combined containing almost half of the world's total (24 and 23 percent, respectively). Africa accounts for 17 percent of the world's timber supply. Well over half of the earth's natural forests are tropical, and most of those are found in South America. In 1995 a UN study found that Russia, Canada, and Brazil accounted for half the world's remaining old-growth or virgin forests.[6]

The United States and Russia are the world's greatest exporters of logs, with New Zealand a distant third. All three sell most of their logs to Asia, notably Japan and Korea. There is active trade in timber between the United States and Canada, another large producer. While some kinds of American timber are exported to Canada, Canada also exports much lumber to the

United States, which in turn ships it abroad to Asia. Other key trading patterns include the export of Russian timber to Finland, Swedish timber to Norway, and German timber to Austria.

With so much of the Northern Hemisphere's forests already cut down to provide the material and fuel for the Industrial Revolution over the last 150 years, today's big timber companies are closing in on what remains of the planet's great timber stands along the equator and in remote regions of Russia.

At the same time the resilient industry is continually reinventing itself, finding new ways to chop up cheap, fast-growing softwood like pine into small pieces and then glue them back together into fiberboard, which is steadily replacing lumber as a building material. Pulp and paper, which also use "junk" wood, is the fastest growing segment of the business worldwide. By some estimates, however, half of the world's timber is still used to produce charcoal, much of it in the poorer countries, which lack supplies for their basic fuel needs.

THE U.S. FOREST-PRODUCTS industry is the largest producer of wood and paper products in the world. In 2000 American timber production stood at 17.6 billion cubic feet. About 30 percent of this output went into pulp and paper production. The United States produces nearly one-third of all the pulp and paper products in the world, half of which is for writing paper and printed pages. Timber is still a huge business in America—the sixth-largest by one reckoning—and accounts for 8 percent of America's manufacturing output.[7]

American companies have grown into major multinationals that dominate the world timber industry. They are engaged in its every facet, from logging and manufacturing different types of fabricated board to the making of pulp for paper. Much of the world's lumber trade is dominated by three multinational corporations: Weyerhaeuser, International Paper, and Georgia Pacific. Weyerhaeuser prospers from exports to Japan. International Paper is one of the world's leading paper producers. Georgia Pacific concentrates on construction materials, especially plywood from North American forests, to supply U.S. demand.[8]

In the United States Weyerhaeuser owns outright 6.5 million acres of woodland and leases another 800,000, making it the largest private landowner in the world. Historically Weyerhaeuser's land came from late-nineteenth-century Northern Pacific railroad grants that Frederick Weyerhaeuser bought from the railroad, along with other land purchases in the Midwest. In the early twentieth century the company acquired more lands in the South and Northwest. "By its own estimate, Weyerhaeuser has clear-cut four million acres in the U.S. since 1900, including 98,000 acres in 1998," according to George Draffan of Public Information Network. "In the 1930s, Weyerhaeuser had thousands of acres of cutover land in Oregon, Washington, Idaho, and Minnesota. . . . In addition, Weyerhaeuser subsidiaries and affiliates cut—and left behind—several million acres in the Philippines, Malaysia, and Indonesia in the 1960s, 1970s, and 1980s."[9]

In 2000 Weyerhaeuser bought SR of Australia, one of the world's biggest building and construction firms, which included sawmills and related assets, as well as a 70 percent stake in Australia's biggest softwood timber distributor, Pine Solutions. In Canada Weyerhaeuser holds long-term licenses to 34.7 million acres. The company operates through wholly owned subsidiaries in Uruguay, New Zealand, Australia, Ireland, and France. In Uruguay it owns a venture that is turning 239,000 acres of grazing lands into plantation forests. In New Zealand the company participates in ventures on over 200,000 acres. In February 2002 Weyerhaeuser acquired Willamette Industries, expanding the paper, packaging, and timberlands segments of its business.[10]

International Paper Corporation, headquartered at Purchase, New York, has operations sprawled across the world. In the United States it owns or manages 9 million acres of land, making it one of the largest landowners in the world. It runs operations in some 40 countries, in North America, Europe, Latin America, and the Asia-Pacific region. It is a 50 to 51 percent shareholder in Carter Holt Harvey, operating in New Zealand (810,000 acres) and Australia. Through a 1999 merger with Union Camp, International Paper acquired 1.6 million acres of timberland, along with Union Camp's operations in countries throughout the world. It has future harvesting rights on timberlands in Canada and Russia.[11]

Georgia Pacific, headquartered in Atlanta, grew to prominence in the 1930s and '40s, becoming the largest supplier of wood to the U.S. military in the Second World War, and expanded to the Pacific Northwest. By the 1970s it owned 4.5 million acres of land in the United States, Canada, and Brazil, with cutting rights to another 1.5 million acres. The company had become so large that a federal judge ordered it to sell off 20 percent of its assets to meet with federal antitrust laws. Even so Georgia Pacific kept on growing, buying and selling huge swaths of timberlands, including many acres in the state of Maine. Its overseas holdings in 2002 included building-materials facilities in Canada, a 50 percent interest in South Africa's leading formaldehyde supplier, and subsidiaries in Brazil, Panama, Bermuda, China, Turkey, the United Kingdom, and continental Europe.[12]

Corporations have come to own outright some 80 million acres of timberland in the United States and have access to huge chunks of forests in the public domain, which still covers about one-third of the nation.

By the end of the twentieth century there was an ongoing intense battle for control and ownership of the last of the world's best timber stands. In the United States that meant gaining access to previously protected parts of older forests. President Clinton reflected these policies by endorsing an act that purported to save timber, while it actually widened a loophole giving companies access to old-growth timber. Under this salvage rider, companies could cut trees otherwise thought to be doomed.

Still the public domain more or less remained an off-limit trove of America's natural resources, including timber. Industry sought access to one of the largest stands of timber in the Tongass forests of Alaska.

But the big environmental organizations with their thousands of members fought hard to block more logging. At the edges of the environmental movement, such individuals as Judy Bari, a California activist, were at the center of protest demonstrations that saw people chaining themselves to trees, sitting down in the road to stop trucks, and even climbing trees and refusing to come down to draw attention to logging practices.

Timber workers were caught off balance as companies, trying to cut costs, sent raw timber up and down the West Coast to locations in Mexico, where it could be cheaply milled and then sent back north. Whole communities on the West Coast plunged into near poverty as jobs were eliminated and installations shut down in favor of the cheaper works south of the border. All this was enhanced by the NAFTA free-trade acts that opened much of Canada, the United States, and Mexico into one huge trading zone.

At the same time some timber from Mexico worked its way into the United States, where it was finished. Riding the timber loads north were destructive native Mexican bugs that threatened to spread new diseases in American forests. The World Wide Fund for Nature issued a report in March 2001 arguing that just ten companies could put an end to logging what remains of the old-growth forests. Among the ten are the five largest wood-processing firms: International Paper, Georgia Pacific, Weyerhauser, Stora-Enso, and Smurfit Stone Container. These five companies process about 20 percent of the world's industrial wood. The five largest wood buyers are Home Depot, Lowes, IKEA, Kimberly-Clark, and Proctor and Gamble.

RUBBER ▶ The Second World War dramatically changed the rubber business. At the beginning of the twentieth century almost all rubber came from trees that grew wild along the equator, mostly in Brazil and Africa. The Anglo-Belgian India Rubber Company of Belgium's King Leopold II produced much of the world's rubber. Using mercenaries the company expropriated hundreds of thousands of acres of rubber trees in the Belgian Congo.[13]

The demand for rubber increased with the invention of the pneumatic tire in the latter part of the nineteenth century and the growth of the automobile industry in the early twentieth century. Rubber prices doubled between 1900 and 1910. Because of the profitability the British and Dutch established rubber plantations in their colonies in Southeast Asia. By the 1920s the British controlled three-quarters of the world's production. Most of the world's rubber at that time was consumed in the United States. The predominant areas of production, then as now, were Malaysia and Indonesia.

Until the Second World War virtually all rubber in use was natural, although in the 1920s and 1930s German, Russian, and American scientists had experimented with synthetic rubber. In the 1920s Standard Oil, then the world's leading petroleum corporation, and I. G. Farben, the German chemical concern, formed a cartel. The two companies agreed to share developments in chemistry, while at the same time promising to respect each other's markets. Farben chemists had developed a process for turning coal into synthetic gasoline, which Standard Oil feared would seriously disrupt its oil markets. At the same time chemists for both companies were well along with another development—synthetic rubber.[14]

Under the Third Reich, Farben became even more closely involved with Hitler and assisted Nazi war preparations. While the German army command showed little interest in synthetic rubber, believing sufficient quantities of natural rubber existed at depressed prices, Hitler insisted on constructing plants to make synthetics. One of these factories was established within the concentration camp complex at Auschwitz.

As the United States entered the war, and the Japanese invaded the rubber areas of Southeast Asia, the American government moved to break Standard Oil's hold on synthetic rubber patents. Because of the Farben cartel the United States had looked the other way rather than prosecute for violating the law. Washington encouraged pooling of patents and then built plants to manufacture synthetic rubber. After the war the plants were sold off to the rubber companies.

Since the 1950s natural rubber has provided only 30 to 40 percent of all elastomers (natural and synthetic rubbers). It is stronger than synthetic rubber but more susceptible to weathering. Most of it is grown by small farmers in Thailand, Indonesia, and Malaysia. The great bulk of world rubber production is synthetic, a direct result of the war effort. Synthetic rubber is produced from chemicals that are byproducts of petroleum production—butadiene and styrene. Asia is the center of production, accounting for 95 per cent of world output.[15]

About three-quarters of all rubber is used in the transport industry, with most going into tire production. Goodyear, with headquarters in Akron, Ohio, is the world's largest tire company. It has 90 plants in 153 countries and produces 220 million tires annually.[16]

Ranked behind Goodyear are Michelin of France and America's Bridgestone-Firestone, Cooper Tire and Rubber, and Continental.[17] Shanghai has emerged as a leading tire-manufacturing center, not only for mainland China, but for the entire Asia-Pacific region. Michelin has a joint venture with Shanghai Tire and Rubber.[17]

Fibers

COTTON ▶ The manufacture of cotton textiles was one of the very first factory industries for many of the world's industrialized countries. Until the eighteenth century, the production of cotton goods was a cottage industry, done on handlooms in various parts of the world. But the invention of the water-powered spinning frame in England brought the industry out of homes and into mills located on rivers and streams. As soon as cotton cloth could be manufactured cheaply, world demand soared, and England began industrializing the countries of Asia that have come to dominate the world trade in cotton goods.[1]

Cotton has been seen as the world's most valuable nonfood crop. All parts of the plant are useful, but it is valued primarily for its fiber, which can be made into lightweight, absorbent, inexpensive cloth. The idea of making clothing from cotton originated in the subtropics, where the plant grows. Varieties of cotton are indigenous to parts of South America, East Africa, and the Indian subcontinent; large-scale cotton cultivation is thought to have first been practiced in the Indus Valley of India, 4,000 or 5,000 years ago. Indians were wearing hand-spun, locally woven, and dyed cotton clothing as early as 500 B.C., although it was originally considered a rare and precious item. Cotton textiles have been found in ancient Peruvian tombs, and when the Spanish explorer Cortés arrived in Mexico in the sixteenth century, he received cotton clothing as a gift from the natives.

Extensive handloom industries developed in India, China, and sub-Saharan Africa. India was the first country in the world to produce cotton goods for export. The Greeks and Romans imported Indian hand weavers, as did England in the seventeenth century. China's production was extensive but for home consumption only. In precolonial Africa many different societies enjoyed a flourishing textile industry, and woven cloth was so important to the internal trade that it was used as money in some areas. In the seventeenth and eighteenth centuries, European traders sought out African hand-woven cloth, especially the printed cottons of the western African coast and the machira cloth of southern Africa.

Hand-woven cotton goods were imported into Europe long before they were produced there. The processes of spinning and weaving, the most labor-intensive and time-consuming steps in the manufacture of cotton textiles, may have come to southern Europe by way of the Mediterranean states, which imported textiles from India. Spinning and weaving spread slowly from southern to northern Europe, and were brought from the Netherlands to England by Protestant refugees around the end of the sixteenth century. The English wove some cotton textiles during the 1600s, using raw cotton from the colonies in the West Indies, but the inefficient process of hand-spinning and -weaving limited cotton's importance until the Industrial Revolution.

In the mid-eighteenth century the Arkwright spinning frame was invented in England, making mass production possible, and in the decades that followed, the cotton textile industry expanded very rapidly in Britain. By 1820 cotton goods accounted for 45 percent of England's overseas exports.

The West Indies and Guyana remained England's main source of raw cotton through the eighteenth century and the early nineteenth. Since the end of the American Revolution, the American South had been expanding its plantation system rapidly; then the invention of the cotton gin in the early 1790s made it practical to use in textile manufacturing the type of cotton grown in the United States. By 1830 America was supplying three-quarters of the cotton used by Britain's textile industry.

Great Britain dominated the world cotton trade for most of the nineteenth century. As early as the Napoleonic wars cotton goods were in such great demand that its cotton monopoly helped Britain to survive the conflict. One of Napoleon's strategies was to weaken Britain economically by preventing European countries from importing British goods. But demand on the Continent for tropical colonial produce—especially sugar, coffee, and cotton—was so strong that merchants in northern Europe and Russia persisted in trading secretly with England. After 1814 the largest and fastest-growing market for British cottons was India, where the domestic handloom industry was temporarily undermined by the flood of cheap British goods. During the same period, however, a number of other countries were beginning to develop their own cotton-textile industries, which they protected with tariff barriers. The manufacture of cotton textiles is a perfect "threshold" industry for countries just beginning to industrialize. It requires little capital investment beyond a few pieces of basic equipment; it is labor intensive and uses mostly unskilled or semiskilled workers; and economics of scale are limited, meaning that the first factories do not have to be large. Transportation costs are low, and cotton goods find an internal market everywhere. In the United States, Italy, France, Germany, and Brazil, cotton-textile manufacture was either the first or one of the first industries to be established on a factory basis. Cheap mass production of cotton goods depends above all on a supply of cheap labor. As a country industrializes, competition from other industries drives the price of labor up—as happened in Britain in the nineteenth century.

Between 1880 and the First World War serious competition for British cotton exports emerged from the United States, Japan, and Italy. The first two moved into the Chinese market, while Italy competed in Latin America and the Middle East. At the same time India and China were mechanizing their own handloom industries. Between the two world wars Japan emerged as the world's leading exporter of cotton textiles, and British exports began a steep decline. In the early days Britain had tried, through stringent laws prohibiting the export of mill technology and the emigration of skilled textile workers, to keep other countries from developing competitive textile industries. The United States was the first country to circumvent these restrictions. In 1789 an English textile worker named Samuel Slater managed to immigrate to America and re-create a British water-powered spinning frame. The Rhode Island mercantile house of Almy and Brown had a mill built according to Slater's design, an innovation that marked the beginning of the factory system in America. Unlike the hand-operated spinning jennies that had preceded it, the water frame used unskilled labor, required minimal initial capital investment, and manufactured thread in quantity.

Two more cotton-related innovations in the next few decades had far-reaching consequences for the United States. These were the cotton gin and the power loom. Invented by Eli Whitney in 1793 the cotton gin removed the seeds from cotton fiber 50 times faster than was possible by hand. This gave a tremendous impetus to the development of cotton plantations in the South and, consequently, to slavery and the African slave trade. The steam-powered loom was copied from textile mills in England by Francis Cabot Lowell, who managed to re-create the design from memory after a trip to Britain in 1811. This and other refinements in mill technology turned cotton-textile manufacture into a large-scale, profitable operation. Entire towns—like Lowell, Massachusetts—were built around the mills to house mill workers. The textile industry attracted capital investment from a number of Boston-based mercantile firms. Using profits from the mills these merchants began to diversify, expanding their investments into real estate, railroads, shipping lines, banks, and insurance companies. Their interests became so extensive that they found it convenient to delegate actual management to agents, use a high degree of planning in their investment ventures, and arrange for as little direct competition as possible among themselves. This marked the emergence of the corporate structure of organization in America.

New England remained the center of the American textile industry until the close of the twentieth century, when most of the mill investment began to move to the South. After Reconstruction the South needed to diversify its economy. The slave system was gone, replaced by sharecropping, and in many places cotton cultivation had exhausted and eroded the land. Southerners began to start up textile mills, encouraged by the availability of cheap labor. Until about 1910 the southern mills were mostly owned by small investors, but from then on, mill capital became concentrated in fewer and fewer hands. Mill owners operated "mill villages" according to a paternalistic system not unlike that of the plantation. They benefited from a close relationship with the local churches, which helped to mold public opinion in favor of the textile industry and to discourage any expression of discontent among workers. In the period between the two world wars, New England textile firms began to relocate their mills to the South, taking advantage of the region's low taxes, inexpensive electric power, and cheap, nonorganized labor.

Unions and labor laws had raised the price of labor in New England, and textile manufacture shifted to the South in the same way that it later shifted to Asia. The northern firms' owners generally operated as absentee land-lords in relation to their southern mills, and workers enjoyed even fewer benefits than they had under the old paternalistic southern system. But the South's strong tradition of antiunionism and its persistent surplus of labor discouraged any serious organization of workers. Although sporadic labor revolts occurred in 1929, they were unsuccessful, and the involvement of communists in one strike linked unionism with anti-Americanism in the eyes of southerners. As late as 1976 only 10 percent of some 600,000 southern textile workers were unionized.

Today the American mills are still concentrated in the Southeast, but most of the cotton farming has shifted to the West and Southwest. The soil of the former slave states has been so depleted by decades of cotton and tobacco growing that only two areas—the Mississippi Valley Delta and the Black Belt of Alabama—are still able to produce cotton in quantity. In fact Texas is now the leading cotton-growing state, followed by California and competition from less-industrialized Asian countries.

In the American textile industry of today mills buy raw cotton from growers; card, comb, weave, and dye it; and sell the finished fabric to apparel markets. There apparel makers may have the garments made in this country, or they may ship the fabric to contract firms in countries with low wages (primarily Mexico and Brazil), where the cutting and sewing are done. Burlington Industries is the largest textile company in the United States, and J. P. Stevens is second. Over half of all textile workers are employed in three states—Georgia, South Carolina, and North Carolina. The last mentioned has the lowest industrial wage in the nation. Although mill villages are a thing of the past, many mills are still located in small rural communities, and the textile company is frequently the only show in town. However, much of the business is now based abroad in Pakistan, India, China, Southeast Asia, Mexico, and the Caribbean nations because of inexpensive labor costs.

Polyester fibers have become major competitors to cotton, and in 2001 their world production ranked above cotton, with 93.1 million bales com-pared to cotton's 91.8 million bales. All in all man-made fiber use stands well above cotton at 139.7 million bales worldwide in 2001. The United States remains the largest producer of cotton in the world, and cotton is grown in 17 states from Virginia to California, covering more than 19,000 square miles. Each year farmers harvest 7.2 billion pounds of raw cotton, with over half the crop destined for apparel, while a quarter goes to home furnishings of one sort or another. A side product in the growing of cotton is cottonseed, which is used as feed for livestock, and appears as well in human foods, such as margarine and salad dressings.

The business is vertically organized, with American companies participating in every part of the industry—growing the cotton, spinning it into yarn, making it into fabric, and finally cutting and sewing the cloth into garments or using it for industrial purposes, such as the interior fabric of automobiles. American firms sometimes send fabric to the Caribbean, where cheap laborers sew it into clothing that is reimported. The United States also imports products at every point in the chain—yarn, fabric, apparel.

Cotton consumption and production in the United States were at a low ebb in the first decade of the twenty-first century. During the 1990s the industry lost 700,000 jobs. Four hundred plants shut down. Total output dropped by some 20 percent. Companies that had moved South from New England in search of cheap labor began moving to Mexico.

As it departed America the cotton industry changed. Cotton grown in the United States is now shipped to Mexico, Turkey, Indonesia, and India as yarn and fabric. The state-run enterprise in China has become the largest manufacturer of cotton textiles and apparel. Central Asia emerged as a big cotton-producing region, with Uzbekistan becoming the world's fifth largest producer and third largest exporter. Originally state run, its business in recent years was opened to private investment. Egypt, which produces one-third of the world's long-staple cotton, is another major producer. It is notorious for forcing children between the ages of 7 and 12 to work long hours in the cotton fields. They are paid 81 cents a day. Millions of farmers in western Africa compete to grow cotton but cannot make inroads in the U.S.-dominated international market.

The key to American hegemony in raw cotton is government subsidies—some $3 billion in 2003 spread amidst 25,000 growers. These subsidies, which allow the United States to dump cotton on the world market at prices below the cost of production, effectively exclude much of the rest of the world from obtaining anything like equal status in the business.

SILK ▶ Silk has always been the world's preeminent luxury fabric. Elegant clothing has traditionally been made of silk, which is prized for its luster and brilliant color when dyed. Until the invention of nylon in the twentieth century, silk was in great demand in the United States for the manufacture of women's stockings.

The secrets of silk were closely held by the Chinese. Its production originated in 3000 B.C. and became an industry around 1,600 years later. Silk reached Persia around 100 B.C. The Persians, in turn, tried to keep the secret to themselves. At about this time the fabled Silk Road, stretching from Japan in the East to Genoa in the West, had opened. It was devoted largely to the trade in silk, but along its path traveled other luxuries such as gold and jade. The Silk Road was also the transmission route for culture and ideas. While other secrets of silk slowly filtered westward, the Chinese successfully kept its actual methods of production a secret and thereby remained at the center of the business for centuries.

In the sixth century the Roman emperor Justinian contracted with two Persian monks to smuggle the secrets of silk production into Byzantium. The monks transported silkworm eggs and the seeds of the mulberry tree to Constantinople in the hollow segments of their bamboo canes. Silk made Byzantium wealthy for centuries afterward. From there sericulture (silkworm raising) spread to Italy, France, and Spain, where it became a profitable industry during the Middle Ages.

By the sixteenth century the knowledge of silk production had spread to Tuscany and along the Rhone Valley throughout Europe. By the early seventeenth century silk was being made in England. By the beginning of the twenty-first century, most silk was being produced in its Chinese homeland or Japan and Korea.[2]

Making silk is an intricate and time-consuming process. Silkworm eggs are hatched and closely scrutinized for any sign of disease. Then the larvae are fed cut-up mulberry leaves, and they climb twigs set near them where they spin their cocoons. After various steps silk filaments are pulled out from the cocoons into bowls of water and are combined and turned into yarn, which then is dried and wound upon reels before marketing.

Since the maturing silkworms eat only fresh mulberry leaves, sericulture involves the large-scale cultivation of mulberry trees. The silkworm eggs must be incubated, except in tropical climates, and their hatching timed to occur when the mulberry tree is in leaf. During their period of growth, caterpillars hatched from one ounce of seed eggs consume about one ton of ripe leaves.

The cocoon is spun from glandular secretions present in the mature worm. Two separate fluids are excreted together and solidify on contact with air, forming a single thread. The worm spins this thread into an oval cocoon about one and a half inches long. When unwound an average cocoon yields a filament about 1,000 yards long.

In the last quarter century of the twentieth century silk production doubled, with China and Japan accounting for more than 50 percent of all the silk manufactured in the world. China emerged as the single largest supplier of silk.[3]

While silk comprises less than 1 percent of the textile trade, it is highly valuable. China is thought to make anywhere from $1 to $1.5 billion in the silk trade every year. Italy is at the hub of the trade, importing more raw silk than any other country, then exporting finished products. France is second. The U.S. market is among the largest, importing as much as $2 billion in silk products annually from China. The United States is also a big market for knitted silk products from China, such as thermal underwear and T-shirts. Germany is the largest European market. With Japanese investment Brazil has emerged as a player in the silk business, although declines in the Japanese economy have hurt it. In addition Vietnam and India have been developing their silk industries.[4]

The popularity and value of silk made it a natural target for chemical companies seeking to make man-made fibers. Rayon, the earliest synthetic, was smooth and shiny but lacked silk's elasticity, and failed to replace silk in the nineteen-teens, as it did not make satisfactory stockings. In 1939 DuPont introduced nylon, the first completely man-made fiber. Nylon had the elasticity of silk as well as its sheen, and it proved to be a successful, inexpensive replacement for silk in hosiery. Since then the substitution of nylon for silk has been so complete that today only a few small items like scarves and ties are commonly made of silk. Silk now accounts for no more than 1 percent of the world's fiber consumption.

Fertilizers

Modern industrial agriculture depletes the soil of various nutrients, which then are replaced in the form of chemical fertilizers. The most important ingredients in these fertilizers are nitrogen, which is "fixed" from the atmosphere in the form of ammonia; phosphorus, which promotes root growth and is obtained from phosphate rock; and potassium, an important factor in growth and in photosynthesis. Potassium comes from potash.

NITROGEN ▶ Throughout most of the nineteenth century nitrogen for fertilizers came from deposits of nitrates concentrated in Chile. These nitrates also were used in the manufacture of gunpowder. By the end of the century scientists became increasingly concerned that the world population would outrun its food supply. Malthusian arguments were resurrected, and one promising solution seemed be raising farm yields by using fertilizers. But the limited nitrate supply in Chile was unreliable and subject to monopoly prices.

In anticipation of an expanding market in agriculture, German scientists at BASF, part of the I. G. Farben chemical complex, rushed to synthesize nitrates. Among those working under BASF grants was Fritz Haber, a technical-school instructor. Using great pressure and very high temperature,

Haber succeeded in combining the nitrogen in the atmosphere with hydrogen in water to form ammonia. The "fixing" of nitrogen in the Haber process soon became the basic method for production of nitrogenous fertilizers. It represented a great advance over undependable and limited natural resources, such as the Chilean nitrate deposits.[1]

Although nitrogen is freely available in the atmosphere, the process for fixing it in the form of ammonia requires large amounts of expensive natural gas. It is a big business, essentially dominated by major chemical corporations and farmer cooperatives. Because of increasing prices for natural gas, prices for ammonia, and hence fertilizers, have skyrocketed.

PHOSPHATE ▶ Phosphorus is the second most common element in chemical fertilizers. It promotes root development, aids in seed formation, stimulates blooming, and is often regarded as critical for plant growth.

Phosphorus in fertilizers derive from raw rock phosphate. The rock is mined, then washed, ground up, and treated with sulfuric acid to produce the concentrate.

Phosphorus occurs in almost all the rocks in the world, often in small amounts. Most known reserves are concentrated in a few major deposits, although phosphorus also is found on the ocean floors. By far and away the largest world reserves are located in Morocco and the western Sahara. China has become a major producer as well. Historically the South Pacific island of Nauru had major deposits, but by the twenty-first century these had seriously diminished.[2]

Within the United States Florida is a large source of phosphate. Most of it occurs in two great geologic formations, the Bone and Hawthorn formations. Bone is far and away the world's best deposit. The Hawthorn formation, which extends into Georgia and has offshoots in the Carolinas, is a prime site for future mines. All in all the phosphate resources of Florida have been variously estimated at 25 to 200 billion tons. Not only was phosphate Florida's third-largest industry, but at the beginning of the twenty-first century one-third of the world's phosphate supply came from Florida, with about one-half of that total representing the output of one company—IMC Phosphates MP, Incorporated. Because its phosphate was easy to get at and cheap to mine, Florida became the world's biggest supplier. But things began to change as labor costs rose and growing pollution from mining threatened drinking water supplies along the Peace River.[3]

There is considerable world trade in phosphate rock. As the world's largest phosphate producer, the United States exports two-thirds of its annual output. The biggest buyers are China and Morocco. Perhaps the most prominent symbol of change is the South Pacific island of Nauru.

Nauru, a tiny—21-square-mile—island, once was a center of a highly profitable phosphate mining industry. Because of the scarcity of easily mined phosphate elsewhere and the prodigious quantities on the island, Nauru grew rich, and even possessed an airline equipped with the latest planes, which crisscrossed the southern and central Pacific. The country of 12,000 inhabitants boasted of having the second highest per capita income in the world. But its phosphate resources ran down, and Nauru turned to offshore banking. By the end of the twentieth century its government had issued licenses to 400 international banks. After international banking authorities cracked down on these dubious operations, Nauru enjoyed a new, unexpected windfall. It turned itself into what amounted to an Australian prison camp, housing refugees from Indonesia and elsewhere in Asia as well as a growing stream from central Asia and the Middle East, all of whom Australia did not want to accept as immigrants.[4]

POTASH ▶ Potash is the third major element of chemical fertilizers. It includes naturally occurring potassium salts and the commercial products derived from them. Potassium contributes to healthy plant growth, aids in photosynthesis, and helps the plant withstand adverse climate and soil conditions and resist disease.

There are immense amounts of potash in the world, and the largest deposits—enough to last for perhaps 2,000 to 3,000 years—are in Saskatchewan. Russia and Belarus account for another 30 percent of world reserves, and substantial reserves of potash are also known to exist in Thailand.

In terms of current production Canada and Russia equally produce about half the world's potash. Another quarter comes from the industry in western Europe.

During the 1970s Saskatchewan's then-socialist provincial government moved to obtain ownership and hence control of the potash. By 1979 it controlled 4 of 10 operating mines, owning three of them outright and having a controlling 60 percent interest in the fourth. That gave the Saskatchewan government 41 percent of the total production. By the beginning of the twenty-first century political tides had turned against state-run industries all over the world, not the least of all in Saskatchewan, where the province's valuable holdings were put on the auction block and privatized.

Foods

Since before the earliest European settlements, farming has been at the center of American life, and for much of the nation's history it has been America's largest industry.

The myth of the sturdy, determined, independent farmer, transforming the wilderness into tame countryside, dominates popular histories of the Westward expansion. And the settlement of the American Midwest and West was indeed largely an agricultural endeavor. The railroads were financed and built to carry settlers west, often with government assistance in the form of tools, seed, and cheap land to farm. The food they raised went to feed the populace of growing cities in the United States, as well as in Europe. Almost from the beginning American farmers produced more food than was consumed at home, and time has only increased that discrepancy. The United States, in large part, produced the food to support two world wars, and selling our immense farm surplus has become an important factor in U.S. foreign policy.

Despite the enduring myth of the American family farmer, the steady trend in American agriculture has been away from the independent small holder and toward large-scale corporate agribusiness. Under this theory, by imposing a corporate-style regimen, the farm could be transformed into an efficient business operation, which would hum along like a steel mill or an automobile assembly line. Efficiency, in turn, would lead to steady profitability, at long last ending the boom or bust cycles of agriculture that had plagued the farmer throughout history.

This project, to industrialize agriculture, has proceeded in fits and starts. Industrialization of the farm has been nudged along by economic recessions and depressions that have forced farmers out of business and led to the consolidation of once small independent holdings into larger and larger spreads. Governmental farm subsidies, including cheap loans, have helped to push forward this massive consolidation, despite the fact that they are most often justified by sentimental homages to the struggling family farmer.

In today's industrialized agriculture, farmers are squeezed on one side by the banks and insurance companies that finance their operations, and on the other side by the large food processors that buy their goods. The terms of their work are set by these big institutions, often times reducing the independent farmer to little more than a renter of his own land. Consider the process: Before the growing season begins the farmer draws up a schedule and goes to the bank for financing. If the bank determines that the farmer can meet the schedule, it provides enough money to produce the projected yields. The yields themselves are often largely determined by other interested businesses, such as the petroleum, chemical, and biotech industries that manufacture the fertilizers, pesticides, and genetically altered seeds. Once harvested, the food goes to a few big companies for processing and eventual sale. These companies also play a role in farming, through their decisions of the type and quantity of crops to buy, which influences what crops farmers plant.

As for the worthy family farmer, he tries to adhere to the harvesting schedule set for him by the finance industry. If he meets the yields, but finds the price has dropped, his financiers may carry him for a year or two. If the downtrend continues, they may require a refinancing at a higher interest rate, or the banks will foreclose directly on their tenant. Farm spreads that are steadily losing money are ripe for purchase by corporations, banks, or syndicates of investors. The purchasers can combine their holdings bought at bargain-basement prices into large agribusiness ventures. Often the decline of small holders coincides with rapacious urban sprawl. A study by the American Farmland Trust showed that the greatest loss of prime farmland occurred in areas of rapid growth, such as on Long Island, New York, where potato farming has been replaced by expensive suburban vacation homes, or the steady march of suburbs into California's central coastal valley, or on the Snake River plains in Idaho.

The national agricultural system is based on a regional pattern of production, with the Midwest growing grain; California, vegetables and fruits; and the western plains, cattle. By the end of the twentieth century this regional system had expanded to become a global system. A company that sells canned tomatoes, for example, can now obtain its tomatoes in season in California, then in Mexico, and then farther south, wherever the cheapest and most plentiful supplies are found.

It is the hope of some ambitious agribusiness planners that the system of the future will be controlled by satellites, whose steady gaze from space can harmonize growing cycles on earth, determining what crops can be grown where, turning on and off the sprinklers in fields of strawberries in Mexico or dousing an African orchard with pesticides as needed. This project is not without pitfalls, however. For one thing it has been confounded time and again by the uncontrollable weather, be it drought, a severe hurricane, or floods.

While factory farming is promoted as an efficient part of the farm-to-market food chain, it can result in unexpected, costly problems. A report by the Institute of Medicine, a division of the National Academy of Sciences, in 1989 identified the creation of antibiotic-resistant bacteria as a cause of serious human diseases. It singled out as a primary cause the factory farm:

> New agricultural procedures can also have unanticipated microbiological effects. For example, the introduction of feedlots and large-scale poultry rearing and processing facilities has been implicated in the increasing incidence of human pathogens, such as salmonella, in domestic animals over the past 30 years. The use of antibiotics to enhance the growth of and prevent illness in domestic animals has been questioned because of its potential role in the development and dissemination of antibiotic resistance. Approximately half the tonnage of antibiotics produced in the U.S. is used in the raising of animals for human consumption. Thus, concerns about the selection of antibiotic-resistant strains of bacteria and their passage into the human population as a result of this excessive use of antibiotics are realistic.[1]

Around the world twenty-first-century agriculture is built upon what is left of nineteenth-century mercantile foundations, where the European powers organized their colonies to produce farm goods—not to feed the local population but to supply the needs of the mother country. In the French colonies in the Sahel region of West Africa, that meant reorganizing the subsistence economy so as to produce peanuts for oil and cotton for textiles. India, which once had a diverse agriculture, was reorganized to produce cotton and grain for Britain. Gambia switched from rice farming to peanuts. Ghana focused on cocoa, while Dahomey and southeast Nigeria produced palm oil. The American colonies sent timber for the British Navy, along with tobacco, rice, and grain. In some cases the colonizers took over the best land and reorganized the workforce, as in Puerto Rico, where peasant farmers were turned into laborers on American-owned sugar plantations. In other places, like Java, for example, the Dutch turned small holders into laborers through the use of tax policies.

These colonial structures carried over into the last quarter of the twentieth century, when, according to the Institute for Food and Development Policy, "Most of the commodities that provide export income to the underdeveloped countries—bananas, cocoa, palm oil, coffee, and so forth—are controlled by a handful of corporations based in the United States and Europe. The corporations produce the crops themselves, contract with local estate owners for the production, or buy it through marketing boards controlled by a domestic elite. They then market the commodity. The lion's share of the return goes to the foreign corporation, not to the domestic economy."[2]

The systems built by colonialism contained the makings of today's international food industry, an intricate worldwide operation in which farm products are grown, harvested, processed, and sold through a small network of large international corporations.[3]

LIVESTOCK

In the industrialized West, livestock is at the center of agribusiness. And the agricultural engineers have nearly succeeded in transforming the raising of sheep, pigs, cows, and chickens into factory products by removing them from nature, penning them up in feedlots, or organizing their short lives from birth to death in a continual assembly line. And to create a market for these assembly-line products, the engineers have changed what and how we eat. As one author succinctly stated the situation: "A third of North America is currently devoted to the grazing of cattle; over one half of the nation's cropland grows livestock feed, and more than half of all potable water consumed in the U.S. is used to water them."[4]

Today cattle raising and meatpacking are together the biggest part of the food industry, which at the end of the twentieth century stood as the fourth largest manufacturing industry in the nation. Just over 10 percent of all food Americans buy is beef and pork. People eat more beef than any other type of meat—64 pounds every year. Hamburgers are by far and away the single biggest item, with 8.2 billion hamburgers and cheeseburgers being served in commercial restaurants at the beginning of this century.[5] And at the same time the United States had become the world's top beef exporter, sending 1.24 million tons of beef mostly to Japan, Mexico, Canada, and South Korea. Australia was the world's second largest beef-exporting nation.[6]

While beef consumption has been fairly steady, people are eating more chicken than ever. The average American consumes 53 pounds of chicken a year, making that the fastest-growing meat product in the store. Chicken outpaces pork, another rapidly expanding meat.

Chickens provide two food products—eggs and meat. In modern agriculture these living creatures are transformed into an assortment of industrial products. Their manufacture begins with the farmer obtaining as many as 50,000 chicks, which he places in a warehouse without any windows. In *Animal Liberation* Peter Singer, a philosopher and animal rights advocate, describes the poultry-production process as follows: The atmosphere in the warehouse is controlled hour by hour, with chicks automatically receiving set amounts of food and water at timed intervals. As they grow in size, the crowded chickens are apt to cannibalize one another. Sometimes the conditions drive them mad, and the animals race into corners, where the dead and dying pile on top of each other. Because such behaviors cut the rate of production and reduce projected sales, warehouse supervisors and farmers cut off beaks to stop the chickens from eating one another and put them in cages to stop the piling on. When its time for the short-lived chickens to be killed, a main concern is to make sure they do not die with undigested food left in their stomachs, which also would reduce revenue. To keep labor costs down the chickens are literally sucked through a big pipe from one place to another or dropped through the floor of a cage onto a conveyor belt. The end comes while they are hanging by their feet on a conveyor belt and a knife cuts off their heads.[7]

The rearing of chickens is about the best agribusiness can do in the way of turning the farm into an assembly-line industry. Pigs get much the same treatment—crammed into tight quarters, where they thrash about eating one another's tails. Some pigs still live outdoors. In the life of a sow the only real freedom is when she is mated with a boar, as it is still cheaper to have her mated than artificially inseminated. Then the dreary cycle begins: confined in pregnancy, having the babies immediately removed at birth, and once again, mating and pregnancy.

Calves that are bred for veal undergo a short, horrendous life in which they are placed in tightly confining stalls, where they are tethered by the neck and fed a liquid protein-rich concoction until they are judged heavy enough to be slaughtered. The regimen is intolerable to many calves, and they die in their stalls. Farmers are willing to absorb such high losses because restaurants pay so much for veal.

Chickens, pigs, and veal calves have been transformed from farmyard animals into animal products. By comparison, cattle have a relatively care-free life: They are penned up in feedlots but are still free to move about. The last free farm animal is the lamb, but there have already been experiments in raising lambs like pigs.

Profitability in the cattle business is obtained through the workforce of humans who try to keep up with an ever-faster production line in the slaughterhouse. Once decent-paying work, packinghouse jobs are now the most dangerous industrial jobs in the nation. One journalist reported in *Mother Jones* that "In 1999 more than one-quarter of America's nearly 150,000 meatpacking workers suffered a job-related injury or illness."[8] And they are among the lowest-paid industrial workers. The entire workforce is hired fresh every year and consists mainly of Latino workers who jump at the chance of making $9.50 an hour.

The results of the modern agriculture system were readily apparent during the foot-and-mouth disease epidemic that swept through Great Britain in early 2001, resulting in the killing of millions of sheep and cattle. There were few proven cases of foot-and-mouth, but fear of what might happen caused the British government to call up the military to supervise the wholesale slaughter of animals peaceably grazing on small farms, destroying the farms in the process. The spread of foot-and-mouth was due in part to the growing system of free trade and agribusiness. Free trade with the rest of Europe dictates British animals must meet standards of the European community so that they can be freely traded across the continent. Agribusiness in Britain has led to the closing of numerous local slaughterhouses, concentrating the killing of animals in a few large installations. This requires that livestock be transported by truck over long distances from farm to slaughterhouse, in the process, providing an opportunity for diseased animals to spread their infection across the country.

Foot-and-mouth is not a fatal disease. It does not kill the animals, nor does it affect human beings in any way. But it has economic portent in that farmers fear infected animals will weigh less and hence reduce their profitability. More to the point, cattle growers fear the image in the press of infected British livestock being sold as meat abroad, turning people away and ruining the British campaign to sell beef and lamb abroad.

One possible preventative measure would be to vaccinate livestock against foot-and-mouth, but farmers argue against doing so because it only adds to the cost of raising the animals. In the long run it is cheaper to kill them and begin anew. This strategy is certainly better from the standpoint of the companies that sell livestock for breeding purposes.

Turning the farm into a modern factory is turning out to present unexpected problems. For example, to increase the output of milk from dairy cows, the agribusiness industry, led by Monsanto, devised a drug to increase the amount of milk a cow can give at a milking. It is called the recombinant bovine growth hormone. And while this new "input," as the agribusiness experts might call BGH, does appear to increase milk, one of its side effects is to place the cow under considerable stress, making her sick and turning her milk into sour-smelling, pus-filled liquid that no one in their right mind would want to drink. To counter this side effect farmers regularly give the cows antibiotics. This causes more problems, since the repeated use of antibiotics makes the cows more resistant to its curative effects.

And not just the cows. Humans who drink the milk also are imbibing the antibiotics, thus lessening the efficacy of antibiotic medicines in their own systems. Some experts believe BGH also can lead to cancer in humans. And there is no doubt that BGH has an economic impact that works against the farmer. If any number of farmers ply their cows with BGH, they will undoubtedly end up producing more and more milk. The milk will saturate the market, pushing prices down, not up. Marginal farmers who narrowly make money off milk cows can go out of business or sell out to big combines.

The bovine growth hormone is not the only troubling development in the cattle farm factory. Because individuals in herds are grown cheek by jowl in their feedlots or pens, when they get sick they pass disease back and forth among one another. Bovine spongiform encephalopathy (BSE), or mad cow disease reveals the very real fears inherent in this system. During the spring of 2003 Canada reported one case of mad cow disease, and Canadian officials quickly isolated the suspect herds and banned shipment of beef into the United States. With that, Canada announced the disease was contained.

But such claims are risky, since Canadian beef is widely imported into the United States, both on the hoof and as meat and meat products. With NAFTA it is difficult if not impossible to trace the origins of a particular cow, as its point of origin cannot always be fixed. Consumers cannot tell whether or not their meat comes from Canada.

The Canadian Cattle Identification Agency, conscious of this problem, has looked into ear tags containing electronic chips that would allow diseases like BSE to be quickly targeted and contained. But this technology may be years away from adoption, mostly because of the costs.[9]

A General Accounting Office report issued in 2002 stated that "the United States has imported about 1,000 cattle; about 23 million pounds of meat by-products; about 100 million pounds of beef; and about 24 million pounds of prepared beef products during the past 20 years from countries where BSE was later found." Furthermore, the report said that if the disease did enter the country, current safeguards might not be enough to detect it and keep it from spreading to other cattle or to the human food supply.[10]

In Europe the spread of mad cow disease has been tied to feeding cattle the waste products of other slaughtered animals. Supposedly this practice has been banned, but in reality there are loopholes in the law, allowing, for example, blood captured at slaughter to be used as feed for cattle herds. It can also be used as food for chicken and pigs. The blood is important because calves are quickly separated from their mothers after birth, and given other foods. Cow's blood is a common replacement food.

Dr. Michael Greger of the Organic Consumers Association observed, "the Canadian and U.S. feed bans also allows the feeding of pigs and horses to cows. Cattle remains can be fed to pigs, for example, and then the pig remains can be fed back to cattle. Or cattle remains can be fed to chickens and then the chicken litter, or manure, can be legally fed back to the cows. And the cow diagnosed with mad cow disease in Canada may have indeed been rendered into chicken and pig feed."[11]

In a situation like this, where the concept of free trade makes it difficult to pin down the origins of disease, we must rely on our agricultural inspection service.

In a report on mad cow the General Accounting Office report concludes: "BSE may be silently incubating somewhere in the United States. If that is the case, then FDA's [Food and Drug Administration's] failure to enforce the feed ban may already have placed U.S. herds and, in turn, the human food supply at risk. FDA has no clear enforcement strategy for dealing with firms that do not obey the feed ban. . . . Moreover, FDA has been using inaccurate, incomplete, and unreliable data to track and oversee feed ban compliance."[12] When the first case of mad cow disease was discovered in Washington state in 2004, the lax procedures of the Agriculture Department were exposed to view, specifically nonexistent inspection at U.S. borders and the use of so-called "downers"—or sick cattle—in the manufacture of all sorts of processed meats, the most prominent being hamburgers and hot dogs.

Following an E. coli outbreak in the 1990s that killed some children, Bill Lehman, a meat inspector at a Montana port where Canadian beef crosses into the United States, described his work: "I merely walk to the back of the truck." According to his account published in the *Village Voice*, "That's all I'm allowed to do. Whether there's boxed meat or carcasses in the truck, I can't touch the boxes. I can't open the boxes. I can't use a flashlight. I can't walk into the truck. I can only look at what is visible in the back of the trailer." He told one interviewer how he did his inspections: "I've just inspected over 80,000 pounds of meat . . . on two trucks. I wasn't running or hurrying either. . . . I just stamped on their paperwork 'USDA Inspected and Passed' in 45 seconds."[13]

The Institute of Medicine outlined the human costs of antibiotic-resistant germs: "Treating resistant infections requires the use of more expensive or more toxic alternative drugs and longer hospital stays; in addition, it recently means a higher risk of death for the patient harboring a resistant pathogen. Estimates of the cost of antibiotic resistance in the United States annually range as high as $30 billion. Even with the continuing development of new drugs, resistance to antibiotics is an increasingly important problem with certain bacterial pathogens."[14]

With these gaps in the preventative controls, we rely increasingly on government inspectors to spot and stop bad meat. But government meat inspection, as seen above, is minimal and often relies extensively on self-regulation by the big companies. When the government does issue a meat recall, it is usual for less than half of the diseased meat to be recovered. The rest of the bad meat gets through to the consumers. As a result, for example, some 2 million people a year are affected by salmonella-tainted chicken. Congress has historically opposed giving the government the right to impose recalls on the meatpackers. Why? Because the meatpackers are such large financial contributors to the political campaigns of congressional incumbents that Congress shies clear of offending them.

GRAINS

The United States, which often is viewed as the largest consumer of the world's raw materials, is itself a large provider of the world's food, in the form of grain.

Grains make up more than a quarter of the $43 billion annual agricultural exports that account for 21 percent of all U.S. exports. This makes grains the largest single category of exports. Large portions of the American grain harvest are exported, including as much as half the total production of rice and wheat.[15]

Grains have been traded from the time of their earliest cultivation in the Middle East, around 7000 B.C. They subsequently found their way to China and India, and traders introduced grains to Europe via the Danube River. Other traders carried them to Spain and Italy. Neither Greece nor Rome was self-sufficient in grain, and their needs occasioned a brisk trade in the eastern Mediterranean. By and large, however, trade in grains was irregular throughout the world until the eighteenth century. Then new milling techniques made possible wide-scale production of bread, thereby creating a regular market for grain.

Bread soon became the food of the Industrial Revolution. British bakers obtained some flour from the eastern seaboard of the United States and received shipments of wheat and oats from Sweden and Poland; the surpluses that made up for periodic shortages came from an area around Odessa, an early grain port on the Black Sea.

From the mid-eighteenth century on, Britain's farms made an effort to stay abreast of the nation's increasing need for food, but despite improved farm machinery, production could not continue to meet demand. In 1846 the protectionist Corn Laws were abandoned, which threw open the British market to world trade. From then until late in the century Russia was the principal source of England's grain. With the opening of prairie agriculture after the Civil War and the building of the transcontinental railroad, however, the United States began shipping grain to England from the Midwest and California. With the opening of the Suez Canal in 1873, wheat began to arrive in England from India, and then from Argentina and Australia.

As the American surplus developed, so did the search for markets. This search, together with an ever-expanding surplus, has been a major concern of American foreign policy since the beginning of the twentieth century. For many years, agriculture was the biggest industry in the United States, and the production of grain was the single largest part of that industry.

From the New Deal onward the government supported the search for markets through such activities as price supports, set-asides, and purchases by the Commodity Credit Corporation. But during the Nixon administration these federal supports attracted less attention, and the government sought to encourage agribusiness to become more active in shaping farm policy.

American schoolchildren are still taught about the extraordinary grain-producing potential of the American Midwest. But few people realize that the Midwest is two distinct regions—the Corn Belt (Iowa, southern Minnesota, Illinois, northern Missouri, northeastern Kansas, and the western portions of South Dakota and Nebraska) and the Great Plains (northern South Dakota, North Dakota, northern Minnesota, western Kansas, eastern Colorado, Wyoming, and Montana). The major differences between the two areas are in rainfall and soil type. Oats, wheat, and barley need less-fertile soil and less rain than do corn and soybeans, which require at least 40 inches of rain per year. Thus, as demand for wheat rises and new acreage is planted, production of crops like oats and barley has declined and shifted to more-marginal areas. In the Corn Belt, the more-marketable soybeans and corn have replaced oats.

These market-based decisions have been brought about by short-term financial demands on farmers—what Earl Butz, Richard Nixon's Secretary of Agriculture, called the workings of the "free market." In fact this free market in grain is ruled by a handful of big companies which handle much of the grain abroad and substantial amounts of what is sold within the United States.

A quick survey of the top three or four companies in various segments of the U.S.-based grain business shows the extent to which the same company names keep cropping up.

Three American-based companies—Cargill, Continental Grain, and

Archer Daniels Midland (ADM)—and Zen Noh, a Japanese firm, account for 81 percent of American corn exports and 65 percent of its soybean exports. Cargill and ADM again, along with Cenex Harvest States and General Mills, control 60 percent of terminal grain-handling facilities. ADM Milling, Con-Agra, Cargill, Bunge, and AUP control 80 percent of soybean crushing.

Some of these companies also have affiliates dominant in meatpacking industries: ConAgra and Cargill, along with two other competitors, control 81 percent of beef packing and 59 percent of pork packing.[16] Cargill alone is especially powerful. Long America's largest grain exporter, in 1999 it acquired its closest rival, Continental Grain, further consolidating its stronghold. The new merged company in 1999 accounted for about 35 percent of corn, soybeans, and wheat volume.[17] One of the world's largest private companies, Cargill takes in $50 billion in annual sales. It is double the size of the current second largest exporter, ADM.[18]

The keys to controlling grain markets are storage capacity and transportation networks. The large grain firms own elevators throughout the Midwest and at important ports, such as points along the Texas and Louisiana coasts and on the Great Lakes. They also own railroad cars and have interlocking directorates with grain-carrying railroads. They own fleets of trucks, port facilities, steamship lines, feed-manufacturing facilities, milling operations, baking companies, seed companies, fertilizer outfits, corn-refining mills, research laboratories, farmlands, banks, and insurance companies. These facilities are to be found both in the United States and abroad.

For the most part American grain farmers are generally at the mercy of the traders, who not only set prices, but as indicated above, control access to markets. Thus, while the value of U.S. grain exports has gone up in recent years, prices to farmers have lagged behind.

COARSE GRAINS ▶ Coarse, or feed, grains include crops like oats, flaxseed, barley, rye, and grain sorghum as well as corn. An important part of American export programs, coarse grains are used almost completely as feed for livestock, although there is some milling of rye into flour and some use of oats and barley for human consumption.

Production of coarse grains is now centered in areas that, as previously explained, cannot grow more profitable crops like wheat, corn, and soybeans. Two-thirds of the nation's barley crop was grown in five states: North Dakota (20 percent of the U.S. total), Montana, California, Idaho, and Minnesota. Farmers in areas that can produce wheat are gradually turning their land over to that crop, replacing traditional feed crops like barley. Oat production has dropped substantially during the last quarter of the twentieth century because farmers in Corn Belt states have switched to potentially more profitable corn and soybean production. The use of chemical fertilizers has replaced crop rotation, of which oats were an important part. This too helps explain declining oat production. Oats are grown primarily in the Midwest; about 50 percent of the crop comes from Minnesota, South Dakota, Iowa, and Wisconsin.

Sorghum is produced almost entirely in Texas (50 percent of the U.S. total), Nebraska, and Kansas. North Dakota produced about 50 percent of the nation's flaxseed, with the rest coming from Minnesota and South Dakota. Flaxseed is also known as linseed, and its component parts, oil and meal, have traditionally been used in the paint industry and as livestock feed. But, as water-based paints take over the paint market, linseed oil grows less and less important to industry.

Major importers of feed grains include the European Union, the former Soviet Union countries, and Japan. Farm cooperatives, on the whole, no longer produce these feed grains in large amounts, however (sorghum is the exception in selected states). This reflects the reduced profitability of coarse grains and the increasing emphasis on wheat, soybeans, and corn as the staples of American grain exports.

WHEAT ▶ The United States is one of the world's biggest wheat producers, along with China, the European Union, and India. It accounts for 25 to 30 percent of global exports. More than three-quarters of the wheat grown in the United States is winter wheat (mainly hard red wheat), and ideal for baking. Winter wheat crops are grown mostly in the Great Plains, along the Mississippi River, and in certain eastern states. Kansas tops the list of wheat-growing and wheat-products-exporting states. Spring wheat, two-thirds of which is grown in Minnesota, the Dakotas, and Montana, accounts for more than 25 percent of total U.S. wheat production. Hard red spring wheat is used for baking and milling, although lower-quality spring wheat, which has a low gluten content, is used for feed.

In addition to the United States, other important wheat-exporting nations are Canada, Australia, the European Union, and Argentina. Important U.S. grain customers include the countries of Southeast Asia, North Africa, and the Middle East.

CORN ▶ In 2000 nearly 80 million acres of American cropland were devoted to corn—nearly one-third of the total. The United States is the world's largest corn producer and exporter, contributing about 60 percent of the corn sold on the international market. Iowa, Illinois, South Dakota, Nebraska, Indiana, western Kentucky, and Ohio dominate production, with one-third of all the corn coming from Iowa and Illinois. Other important corn-exporting countries include Argentina, China, South Africa, and Russia. Individually they produce only a fraction of U.S. export volumes. The thick, fertile soil of the American Corn Belt offers the unique conditions necessary to have supported intensive cultivation of corn for over the past century.

Most corn is used as animal feed and is sold to the European Union, Japan, Russia, and Mexico. In the United States about one-quarter of the corn crop is used for food and seed and much is refined for starch, sweeteners, and corn oil. The market for corn processed into cereal and other food products is expanding.

The increase in corn production and export in this country has been accomplished primarily through a huge increase in crop yields rather than the introduction of new corn acreage. The use of fertilizers, improved seed-drilling equipment, and new plant hybrids has contributed to the increase but has also jacked up the costs of production. Like wheat, corn is dominated by the big companies. All of these firms have feed-manufacturing subsidiaries that produce high-protein livestock feed. Corn sweeteners provide another market.

RICE ▶ Rice and wheat are the two most important food grains in the world. Rice is the staple food of the East, Southeast, and South Asia, with the region as a whole accounting for more than 90 percent of global production and more than 88 percent of consumption.

Most rice is consumed in the country where it is grown. In fact, trade accounts for only a small share—some 6 percent a year—of global rice production. The major rice exporters are Thailand, Vietnam, India, China, Pakistan, and Burma. Thailand, the world's largest rice-exporting country, accounts for about 25 percent of the global rice trade, and Vietnam is typically number two, with about 17 percent of the trade. Outside of Asia, Brazil is the largest rice producer and consumer. With the largest population in Latin America, it cannot satisfy its own demand for rice and relies on imports from Argentina and Uruguay to make up the difference. In addition, in years when these imports prove insufficient, Brazil turns to the United States for further rice imports.

Although the United States accounts for only 1.5 to 2.0 percent of global rice production, it is an important player in the world rice trade, annually accounting for about 12 percent of exports. It is surpassed only by Thailand and Vietnam, and in some years by India and China. In the Western Hemisphere, Canada and the Caribbean islands do take some Asian rice, but Mexico and Central and South America prefer imports of rough (unmilled) rice from the United States—the only country to ship rough rice—as this keeps their milling industries going. Import regulations and regional trading blocs in Latin America also repel Asian rice exporters from this region.

Outside these areas, Northeast Asia—primarily Japan, and to a lesser degree Taiwan and South Korea—is the largest market for American rice. The United States also ships substantial amounts of rice to the European Union, Sub-Saharan Africa, and parts of the Middle East. However, excluding food aid, the United States typically ships little rice to Southeast Asia—one of the world's top import markets—or South Asia. American rice is typically of too high a quality for these markets to afford.[19]

American rice farming began in the eighteenth century, when English colonists first grew rice along the South Carolina coast. Rice production declined with the Civil War, however, as irrigation systems fell into disrepair. In recent years, the United States was importing rice from China, Japan, and the Philippines.

As cotton culture faded in the South, farmers in Louisiana, Arkansas, Mississippi, and Texas began growing more rice. During the Second World War the government offered high price supports to stimulate production. After the war the need to help feed people in Asia helped to spread rice growing into California. Production expanded rapidly in the Sacramento Valley.

Until 1976 the federal government controlled who could plant rice, how much they could grow, and what price they received. Crop yields increased substantially after 1950, but the price supports held steady at from $4 to $5 per 100-pound bag. By the mid-1950s there was a growing surplus of rice, which the government was buying to sustain prices. The rice-support program was expensive, but it had the backing of powerful men in Congress: leaders such as William Fulbright, who headed the Senate Foreign Relations Committee; Wilbur Mills, who headed the House Ways and Means; and William R. Poage, head of the House Agriculture Committee.

Of the approximately six million tons of rice annually grown in the United States, customers must be found for the three million tons that cannot be sold at home. For California producers, who account for a million tons, the hunt for foreign consumers is especially important. The medium- and long-grain varieties of rice that are produced in the South are favored by domestic packagers, breweries, and markets in Europe and Canada. But the short- and medium-grain varieties grown in California become gummy when cooked and have a much more specialized clientele—in Asia, among ethnic populations in such places as New York City, and in Puerto Rican communities.

During the 1950s Japan produced a surplus of rice, which placed the California growers, who had come to depend on the Asian market, under heavy pressure. The California delegation to Congress labored in Washington to maintain and shore up the Asian rice business. For a short time they succeeded in keeping the Japanese out of Okinawa and maintaining that market for the California producers. But when control of Okinawa reverted to Japan, California lost the rice business there.

The rice glut was partially alleviated by the Vietnam War. In the final phases of the war, in 1973 and 1974, nearly three-quarters of the Food for Peace program was directed at Cambodia and Vietnam. Over one million tons of rice, paid for by the U.S. government, were shipped to those two countries in two years. The fall of Vietnam was a savage blow to the rice growers, but by then South Korea had replaced Vietnam as a market.

South Korea during the last half of the twentieth century had been unable to produce enough rice for its own population. During the 1960s, when the government embarked on a program of rapid industrialization, thousands of people were taken from rural farms and put into the cities. The need for food became intense, and the American rice growers began to fill the need. By 1970 Korea was importing one million tons of rice, about half of it from the United States.

Rice dealing in South Korea became a complex skein of diplomatic maneuvers, secret deals, and corruption. President Nixon undertook to arrange a secret deal to provide Korea with rice aid. In exchange the Koreans agreed to withhold textile exports to the United States. U.S. textile manufacturers in the South had become furious at the influx of cheap Korean goods, robbing them of their home markets. These industrialists were important backers of Nixon, and it was understandable that he sought to help them. At the same time the Pentagon and State Department both pressed for rice shipments to Korea as a form of payment for the Korean troops in the Vietnam War. All during this time, the South Korean diplomats and secret police intrigued among U.S. congressmen, giving them free trips, favors, and outright bribes to maintain support of the Korean rice shipments.

SOYBEANS ▶ Although soybeans have been touted as a wonder-protein food that could rescue the human race from starvation, very little of the world's soybean crop is used as anything but animal feed. A relatively small share of total U.S. production is used to manufacture textured vegetable protein (the substance that makes bacon bits or hamburger extender), soymilk, and other soyfoods like tofu. Soybean meal accounts for the bulk of the commercial value of a soybean, supplying 65 percent of world protein feed for livestock. Soybean oil, a byproduct of the conversion of beans into meal, is used for making margarine and cooking oils and is occasionally used as an animal feed.

The United States produces about two-thirds of the world's soybeans and about one-half of the soybeans sold on the international market. Four states—Ohio, Iowa, Illinois, and Indiana—produce about 40 percent of the American crop. The only other major exporter of soybeans is Brazil, which contributes some 4 million tons annually to the world market.

OILS, FATS, AND WAXES

Tables 1–4 on the following pages provide a convenient summary of the different kinds of vegetable oils and fats, and animal and marine oils and fats, that must at least be mentioned in any discussion of the world's food products. They are produced by countries all around the globe and are valued for numerous uses beyond that of human consumption.

SUGAR

No agricultural crop has brought such misery to the world as sugar. Sugar has ruined land from one end of the earth to the other. It was the prime vehicle for the spread of slavery. And sugar now is widely cited as a major cause of disease. Still, the world craves sugar. Until the sixteenth century Europeans obtained their sweets from honey and fruits. Over the next three centuries sugar was obtained from sugar cane. Then, in the nineteenth century, sugar beets entered the scene. Today, corn syrups and artificial sweeteners compete with sugar.

TABLE 1 ▶ Vegetable Oils

	EXPORTERS	USES
Drying oils		
Perilla	China, Korea, Japan, India	Paint, varnish
Linseed	U.S., Argentina, India, Canada, former Soviet Union	Paint, varnish, linoleum, printing ink
Tung	China, Japan, U.S.	Paint, varnish
Oiticica	Brazil	Paint, varnish
Semidrying oils		
Poppyseed	Levant, India	Salad oil, artists' oil, soft soap
Safflower	U.S., India	Salad oil, paints, resins
Soybean	U.S., China, Manchuria	Food, paint, resins, chemicals
Corn (maize)	U.S., Argentina, Europe	Food
Sunflower	former Soviet Union, South America, Eastern Europe	Food, soap
Cottonseed	U.S., India, Egypt, Mexico, former Soviet Union	Food, lubricants
Sesame	India, Egypt, Levant	Perfume, pharmaceuticals, food
Rape (colza)	India, Europe, Canada, Pakistan	Food, soap, lubricants, chemicals
Nondrying oils		
Almond	Southern Europe, North Africa	Perfume, pharmaceuticals, food
Arachis (peanut, groundnut)	India, West Africa, China, U.S.	Food
Olive	Mediterranean countries, U.S.	Food, soap, lubricants, chemicals, pharmaceuticals

The origins of sugar cane trace back to New Guinea thousands of years ago. Then it was planted in gardens and people chewed it. Around 8000 B.C. sugar cane moved south and east to the New Hebrides and eventually wound up on the Asian mainland. According to G. B. Hagelberg, an expert on the sugar industry, the first definite mention of sugar was in 325 B.C. in Punjab. There is evidence of sugar processing in Persia in A.D. 600. The Arabs carried it westward, into Egypt and Cyprus, and it reached Sicily in the eleventh century. Prince Henry the Navigator brought Sicilian sugar to the Madeira islands, the first "sugar land" of the Atlantic. Sugar continued to show

TABLE 2 ▸ Animal and Marine Oils

	EXPORTERS	USES
Marine oils		
Anchovy	Peru	Resins, leather currying, paints, food
Sardine	West Coast of North America, Japan	Resins, leather currying, paints, food
Menhaden	East Coast of North America	Resins, leather currying, paints, food
Herring	North Sea, Japan	Leather currying, paints, food
Cod Liver	North Sea, East Coast of North America	Vitamins, leather currying
Shark liver	North American coasts	Vitamins, leather currying
Seal	Arctic and Antarctic	Food, leather currying, soap
Whale	Arctic and Antarctic	Food, soap, fiber dressing, leather currying, greases
Sperm whale	West Coast of South America	Lubrication for delicate machinery
Terrestrial animal oils		
Neat's-foot	U.S., South America, Europe	Lubrication, high-grade leather

up on a westward course to the Azores, the Canaries, the Cape Verde Islands, and then to America. But while it moved west, its movement north was much slower. In Europe it was viewed as a delicacy well into the Middle Ages. Sugar reached England in 1319.[20]

The islands of the eastern Atlantic bear testimony to the terrible destructiveness of sugar. Madeira, originally a timber island, was stripped of trees so sugar could be grown for the European market.

The sugar industry gradually became the basis of a triangular trade in which merchants brought goods from England to Africa. There ship captains bartered the goods for slaves, who were hauled to the West Indies and exchanged for rum and sugar, which were sped back to England. Ships from New England carried rum to the Slave Coast of Africa, slaves to the West Indies, and molasses from the West Indies to New England to make more rum. From the colonial era sugar and its byproducts—rum and molasses—were closely linked. Adam Smith quoted as a common saying of his time, "A

TABLE 3 ▸ Vegetable Fats and Oils

	EXPORTERS	USES
Mahua (illipe)	India, Malaysia	Food, soap, candles
Shea butter	West Africa, Sudan	Food, soap, candles
Palm oil	West Africa, Indonesia, Malaysia, Brazil	Soap, candles, tinplate industry
Cacao (cocoa) butter	Indonesia, Malaysia	Chocolate, pharmaceuticals, perfume
Babassu oil	West Africa	Food, soap
Coconut oil	Philippines, Indonesia, India, Sri Lanka, South American coasts	Food, soap, chemicals
Japan wax	China, India, Japan	Polishes

TABLE 4 ▸ Animal Fats

	EXPORTERS	USES
Lard	U.S., central Europe	Food, soap, pharmaceuticals, chemicals
Bone	U.S., India, Europe, Argentina	Soap, candles
Tallow (beef)	Argentina, U.S.	Food, soap, candles, chemicals
Tallow (mutton)	Australia	Food, soap
Butter	U.S., Europe, Australia, Canada, former Soviet Union	Food

sugar planter expects that the rum and the molasses should defray the whole expense of his cultivation, and that his sugar should be all clear profit."[21]

As the sugar trade grew, so did the slave trade, which provided the industry with more workers. While growing sugar cane required considerable agricultural labor, manufacturing sugar from cane also necessitated expensive machinery. Thus, there grew up an association of European overseas capital, sugar cane, and slavery in the plantation system.

The stories of sugar and slavery diverged in the nineteenth century. The slave trade was outlawed by Britain in 1807 and, with the passage of the Abolition Act in 1833, gradually gave way to indentured or contract laborers from India. That is why today there are large populations of East Indians in the sugar-producing countries of Guyana, Trinidad, and Fiji. The British colonies that employed slaves to produce most of the world's sugar in the early part of the century lost their prominence.

Napoleon sought to break the British hold over world trade by banning the importation of sugar from the British colonies into the countries of Europe under his control. In its place he substituted sugar made from beets, a process he had observed in Silesia. For a time France became the center of a sugar beet industry. The Russians also built up a large-scale beet industry.[22]

Sugar beets are biennials, which are rotated with other crops to maintain soil conditions and are viewed as a beneficial part of farm diversification. In addition, beets can be used for animal feed.[23] Sugar cane is a perennial grass plant that takes from ten months to two years to grow. It is seldom grown in rotation, but is a monoculture crop that tends to dominate the economy of a region, and is destructive of its soil. Cane sugar, however, is the commodity traded in international commerce.

While the sugar beet and sugar cane are two different crops, their final product is basically the same, and the manufacturing process is the same for both plants: The sugary juices are separated from the solid material by crushing and shredding. Impurities are removed. The water is boiled off in a vacuum, and sugar crystals are separated from the final liquid by centrifugal action. This leaves uncrystallizable sugar and residual impurities in the molasses.

A byproduct of sugar cane, molasses has been used as a fuel in sugar-cane factories or has been returned to the land as fertilizer. As noted above it played an important part in the early sugar trade as an ingredient in rum, and still is employed in the West Indies for that purpose. Molasses also has been used in the distilling industry in the production of ethyl alcohol, although this use is meeting competition from oil-based products. While sugar is generally grown on plantations, a considerable amount comes from small holders.

Historically, most of the sugar-exporting nations have had a common agency or association to help market the sugar sold abroad. Amidst the pressure to privatize, however, many of these state-run agencies became for-profit concerns, either in whole or in part. In certain cases sugar is supplied according to long-term bilateral trade agreements, the most famous of which tied Cuba to the Soviet Union during the cold war. Over the last quarter-century there have been other examples: Australia's links with Japan, for one; and the British Commonwealth's ties to the European Union, another.

The output of the sugar industry and the number of producers grew markedly during the twentieth century. However, as the number of producers swells, the processing end of the business has become ever more concentrated. And it is in processing and sales that control of the business lies.

At the beginning of the twenty-first century, there were some 90 million tons of sugar in world trade. The Caribbean nations contributed about one-third; the European Union and the Philippines also had substantial outputs. The United States, Great Britain, Russia, and Japan were major importers. Sugar is mostly used in beverages, bakery goods and cereals, confectioneries and candy, ice cream, dairy products, and general foods.[24]

While millions of people have died toiling in the sugar fields over the centuries, the fortunes created by their labor have been enjoyed by the relatively few. The situation is little changed today. A few families and a few corporations enjoy the wealth from sugar.

Today's sugar cane is grown in some 80 tropical and semitropical countries; sugar beets, across an even wider ambit.

Three Florida counties (645 square miles) west of Palm Beach produce more than half the sugar cane grown in the United States. Cane also is grown in Louisiana, Texas, and Hawaii. Sugar beets are raised in Minnesota, Michigan, Ohio and elsewhere in the Midwest.[25] As America's top cane producer, Florida produces some 3 billion pounds a year and employs 4,000 full-time and 3,000 part-time workers. The *Miami Herald* reported in 1990 that the Florida Sugar Cane league estimated the industry adds $1.5 billion to the state's economy. The big users are soft drink and candy manufacturers.[26]

In the United States the origins of the sugar business can be traced back to settlers and Indians who grew cane on their small farms across the South. By the 1920s both Louisiana and Hawaii had become the centers of a small, but growing, industry. At the same time sugar beets gradually were being grown in the Middle West. It was just before the Great Depression that investors started to explore the agricultural potential of Florida. The precipitous economic situation brought that to a temporary halt. Under the New Deal Congress sought to assist sugar by stabilizing prices, controlling production, and placing a limit on imports, and Florida sugar took off as a result. One of the most important investors was Charles Stewart Mott, the General Motors magnate turned philanthropist. He put together the United States Sugar Corporation, which became the largest sugar refinery in the nation.[27]

Meanwhile farmers found they could boost sugar-cane yields through the use of fertilizers laced with nitrogen and phosphorous. Even so after the

Second World War the United States imported substantial amounts of sugar from Cuba. When Castro took over in 1959, he seized the sugar mills, and their owners fled. The United States responded by placing an embargo on Cuban sugar. This was an immediate shot in the arm for American farmers, and Mott's U.S. Sugar Corporation grew in size and political clout.

Among those fleeing the Cuban revolution was Alfonso Fanjul, the heir to a Cuban sugar fortune that included 10 mills and owned 150,000 acres before Castro. Fanjul set up shop in the posh winter vacation capital of Palm Beach. He proceeded to acquire large parcels of sugar lands. By the time he died in 1980, Fanjul's sons, Alfie and Pepe, were managing a $30-million-a-year business. The Fanjuls continued to buy land, and enlarged their operations through control of sugar plantations in the Dominican Republic. The family eventually came to account for one-half of all Dominican sugar production. Its enterprise, called the Flo-Sun group, surged ahead of U.S. Sugar to become the largest cane grower in the United States. Along the way it became a major political force, doling out money to both Democratic and Republican parties.[28]

By the beginning of the twenty-first century the American sugar industry had become a thoroughly anachronistic business, with the general citizenry propping up a highly concentrated business that seemingly was surrounded on all sides by various enemies and hostile forces. On the one hand there were congressionally mandated price supports. On the other hand, because sugar was protected by quotas, the price was kept considerably higher than the market would naturally bear. In addition, government programs kept the costs of labor cheap by mandating a system bordering on indentured servitude, in which all kinds of civil and economic rights were abandoned. The workers would arrive at a work camp straight from Jamaica or else-where in the Caribbean. There the company would provide for their basic needs, housing, and food, at a cost. Soon the workers found themselves paying off the usurious company loans with their small earnings. (The wage system itself was scarcely believable: instead of setting a wage based on time worked or even by the piece, sugar wages were determined by a supervisor who would eye a swath of sugar cane and then, off the top of his head, set a price for harvesting the whole acreage.)[29]

And there was another subsidy. In Florida, where more than half the cane sugar in the United States is harvested, the growers save money because of cheap water, subsidized mostly by urban dwellers and taxpayers. In addition the land on which sugar cane is grown was a former swamp, drained at no cost to the growers by the U.S. Army Corps of Engineers. In the 1990s the Fanjuls and President Clinton negotiated a deal aimed at reducing pollution pouring out from the sugar lands down into the Everglades. The final arrangement appeared to have the industry put up anywhere from $230 to $330 million over 20 years, while American taxpayers through the federal government would fork over anywhere from $400 to $700 million. Soon after this arrangement was completed, critics on both sides—industry and the environment—said it would not work, and it was too late to save the Everglades.[30]

This system, sometimes referred to as Big Sugar, has produced its share of enemies: conservatives who do not like farm subsidies, environmentalists worried about pollution, and unions and civil rights advocates who stormed over the treatment of workers. But none of them have made any difference. Grassroots support, which sometimes makes a difference in American politics, is stymied in the case of sugar because of its financial resources. The companies assiduously lobbied in Tallahassee where they have long held enormous influence over state government, and on Capitol Hill in Washington, where sugar is also a big player. In 1995 the Center for Responsive Politics, which tracks election expenditures, reported $11.9 million in total sugar contributions to all federal political candidates from 1979 to 1990, with most of the money going to Democrats.[31]

Different studies have estimated that the government price-support programs added to the cost to consumers anywhere from $1.4 to $3.7 billion a year. Viewed from another perspective, in 1993–94 the Fanjuls received $64.6 million in federal benefit payments while making $1.2 million in campaign donations to various federal candidates.[32]

The support programs were rationalized, as all agricultural programs are, as measures designed to help the family farmer. In fact the support system, if anything, worked to make the industry more concentrated than before. Thirty-three farms in Florida and Hawaii each receive more than $1 million in annual benefits. Four Florida companies get more than $20 million each. Seventeen of the estimated 1,705 cane farms—1 percent—received 58 percent of all cane-grower benefits in 1991.[33]

Cutting sugar cane is one of the worst jobs faced by any American laborer. The work was so draining that the sugar companies bused in workers from Mississippi and Alabama and treated them almost as indentured servants, keeping tight control of them in migrant camps and locking them up if they tried running away. The federal government eventually sued to free the workers from their onerous conditions, which amounted to "slavery," as the government put it. The industry beat down the government suit, but it changed its ways. After the Second World War it started recruiting workers from the Caribbean, about 10,000 a year, many from Jamaica. They were treated harshly in a Byzantine wage system through which a company could pay workers less than they had rightfully earned.[34] These wages and working conditions in the sugar fields benefited the owners of the Big Sugar firms, including, by the end of the century, the Mott Foundation, a charity supported by one of the most ferociously antilabor sugar companies in the business.

This entire system depended on a narrow base of Big Sugar money (mostly from Florida) to influence members of the House and Senate Agriculture Committees along with continuous manipulation of the U.S. Department of Agriculture. There never has been any broad political base to the sugar industry in the United States. And by the beginning of the twenty-first century, the big industries that use sweeteners were in open rebellion. The candy manufacturers such as Kraft (part of the tobacco giant Philip Morris) and soft-drink firms (Coca-Cola and Pepsi) began closing down plants in the United States and moving their sweetener operations abroad, where they could take advantage of various tax advantages and, most of all, cheap labor cutting cane in original colonies.

That meant added importance to such large international sugar refineries as Tate and Lyle, the British conglomerate. With 150 subsidiaries in over 30 nations, Tate and Lyle dominates the sugar business in Great Britain and operates refineries in Canada (where it also dominates the market), the United States, and southern Africa; it also has a 14 percent interest in a major French refiner. Booker McConnell and Lonrho are two other major British-based sugar refineries with interests abroad.

SPICES

The United States is the world's largest importer and consumer of spices. Of the over 40 different kinds of spices, just 7 (vanilla beans, black and white pepper, capsicums, sesame seed, cinnamon, mustard, and oregano) account for more than 75 percent of the total annual value of American spice imports. Over half the imports come from a handful of countries: Indonesia, Mexico, India, Canada, and China.

VANILLA ▶ The major spice discovery by early explorers of the New World was vanilla. During the sixteenth and seventeenth centuries, vanilla was popular in Europe as a food flavoring, a poison antidote, and an aphrodisiac.[35]

Made from the bean pod of a perennial orchid vine native to Central America, natural vanilla ranges in quality from the strong Tahitian variety, which is better suited for perfumes than foods, to the delicate Mexican variety, considered the best in the world.[36]

Vanilla is widely used in ice cream, soft drinks, chocolates, candy, tobacco, baked goods, desserts, liqueurs, and perfumes. It is also administered to ease stomachaches. This is one reason for the supposed effectiveness of Coca-Cola, which contains vanilla, against that complaint. Madagascar and Indonesia produce 90 percent of the vanilla crop each year. Other major producers are Mexico, where the vanilla orchid was first found, and the island of Tahiti.[37]

Vanilla is a highly labor-intensive crop. Only in Mexico do native insects and birds pollinate the flowers; in Asia and Africa, hand pollination is required. Vanilla plants also needs intensive cultivation, and the beans undergo a complicated five- to six-month curing process before they become marketable.

CINNAMON ▶ One of the first spices used by man, cinnamon has been valued in foods, medicines, perfumes, and incense. The Egyptians were importing it 4,000 years ago; wealthy Romans luxuriated in cinnamon-scented baths; and every medieval magician kept cinnamon on hand as an ingredient for love potions. Used today primarily in bakery products, beverages, and candy, cinnamon is also used in perfumes and soaps and to disguise the flavor of some imbibed medications such as cold remedies and antibiotics. In India cinnamon is used as a cure for colic and diarrhea.[38]

Many Americans have never tasted actual cinnamon. Almost all of what is called cinnamon in the United States is really cassia, a less-expensive substitute that is considered slightly inferior in flavor. Cassia is reddish brown, while cinnamon is tan in color. Both spices are made from the bark of tropical evergreen trees, most of which are harvested in small orchards and on plantations in Sri Lanka, India, Brazil, and Indonesia. China, Laos, Cambodia, and Vietnam are also producers. Twice a year shoots are cut from the trees, and their bark is peeled off, scraped, and dried in the sun.

MUSTARD ▶ Native to Europe and southeastern Asia, mustard has been used since prehistoric times, first as a medicine and later in food. Pythagoras put mustard on scorpion stings, and Hippocrates also made medicines from it.

The green leaves of the mustard plant are a popular vegetable dish in many cultures. Dry mustard powder, the ground and sifted seeds of the plant, has no flavor. It must be moistened with an acid such as vinegar or wine to begin the enzyme activity that creates its pungency. The flavor disappears after about an hour, unless the powder is remoistened.[39]

Mustard powder is also used as a preservative in mayonnaise, curries, and salad dressing, and in drugs as a stimulant, diuretic, and emetic, as well as a plaster remedy for rheumatism, arthritis, and chest colds. The Chinese used mustard as an aphrodisiac. The Danes thought it could cure a woman's frigidity.

A hardy annual, mustard grows in most temperature climates. World production is widespread and totals some 200,000 tons a year. Over 20 percent of this crop is imported by the United States, largely from Canada.

CLOVES ▶ Since the eighth century, cloves have been one of the principal oriental spices in European commerce. Bitter wars were fought within Europe and with Indonesian natives to secure exclusive rights to the profitable clove trade, which was eventually monopolized in the seventeenth century by the Dutch East India Company, which brutally protected its monopoly by reorganizing clove production.[40] All clove trees except those in a carefully patrolled area were ordered destroyed—a harsh cultural shock for Indonesia's natives, who planted a clove tree on the birth of each child and believed that the child would die when its clove tree died.[41]

After the French managed to smuggle some clove seeds into their colonies, profitability declined, and the Dutch lost interest in the clove trade early in the twentieth century. Today, Tanzania's Pemba island in the Indian Ocean, 30 miles off the east coast of Africa, is the world's leading clove producer.[42]

Indonesia, which uses up to 50 percent of total world production, is the largest consumer of cloves. In fact, after petroleum and timber, cloves are its key source of foreign exchange.[43]

PEPPER ▶ One of the earliest articles of commerce between the Orient and Europe, pepper was first brought West by Arab traders from India's Malabar Coast some 4,000 years ago. Because it can be stored for many years without losing its flavor, pepper long ago became the dominant spice in world trade. Today it accounts for one-quarter of the entire world spice trade.[44]

Over the years many fortunes were founded on pepper, including those of the first American millionaires, Elihu Yale and Elias Derby. During the 1800s Salem, Massachusetts, was at the center of the trade.[45]

But these riches never reached pepper farmers, most of whom still cultivate the perennial pepper vines on small plots that require constant weeding, mulching, tying, nourishing, and protection against disease and pests. India is the world's leading pepper producer, followed by Indonesia and Vietnam.

Black and white pepper are made from berries of the same vine. Black pepper is picked unripe and dried in the sun. White pepper, more expensive than black, is the ripened berry that is trampled on or otherwise macerated to remove the hull before drying. Pepper drying is done by the grower: Large, deep piles of peppercorns are spread on the ground and walked through every day to bring the bottom berries to the top for sun drying. Grinding is done by the processor.[46]

Pepper is used generally as a food flavoring in almost every nation on earth. The United States is the world's largest pepper consumer.

SALT ▶ Because salt is now so plentiful and cheap, there is little international trade in the substance. But empty salt mines are prized as storage places for all sorts of things, from old movie films to oil to atomic wastes.[47]

Because so much salt is used to de-ice roads (not on food, as one might think), the auto companies have coated the bottoms of cars with anticorrosive zinc, thereby giving a boost to that industry. Indeed, if salt were not used on roads, the bottom would fall out of the zinc industry.

Salt has long been important to the human diet because it slows down the decomposition process of meats, and then can easily be removed by boiling. After gaining early commercial value as a food preservative, salt became an expensive and prized commodity. It is still highly valued in some parts of the world; in northern Africa, for example, it is used as money.

Salt has been used throughout history as an economic tool by those in power to apply political pressure on their subjects. In England during Queen Anne's reign the salt tax so enraged the populace that it was finally removed by Parliament. But the British government continued to prohibit the salt trade in some American colonies, to maintain control over the colonial American fish trade (as salt was essential to preserve fish). The French Revolution was sparked in part by a salt tax. As the industrial age emerged, salt became less important as a preservative (with the advent of refrigeration) and more important as a raw material in industry.

The United States is the world's biggest salt producer, followed by Germany and India. Nearly half of the American supply comes from brine wells owned by chemical companies in Texas, Michigan, and West Virginia. The main markets are in North America and Europe, but the business is slowly shifting to eastern and southeastern Asia.

About 60 percent of this production is used by industry, mostly in the manufacture of chlorine and caustic sodas. About 20 percent of salt production is used for road deicing.

Salt and its components are also used in the production of soap, rocket fuel, water softeners, and agricultural chemicals. Home use constitutes only about 1 to 3 percent of total consumption. There are three basic methods of salt production: deep mining, solution mining, and solar evaporation. In deep mining, "rooms" are dug out of salt deposits, leaving big salt pillars for support. The rooms' size varies from 40 to 70 feet in the smaller bedded deposits to as much as 100-foot lengths in a large dome deposit. Solution mining involves forcing water into salt deposits and processing the brine.

Approximately 45 percent of the world's salt is produced by solar evaporation. In many areas this method has remained unchanged for centuries. The process involves about nine major concentrating ponds and a series of smaller ponds. The brine is moved in succession from one pond to another, depending on the salt concentration. In the final stage there is a six-inch crust of crystallized salt, which is harvested. The entire process can take anywhere from 18 months to 5 years, depending on the climate.

Salt deposits are valued for their geological properties. The domed caverns left by salt mining have valuable storage capabilities. Films are often stored in salt mines because the constant temperature and humidity preserves the celluloid better than aboveground storage. In recent years it has been suggested and acted upon that the United States build up a year's reserve of oil stores in underground cavities created by solution salt mining. And because of their geological stability, salt deposits deep in the earth have been proposed as storage sites for radioactive wastes.

The company that is today the best-known name in salt was started in 1848 and turned a profit the first year. In 1879 Joy Morton invested $10,000 in a one-fifth ownership of the company. By 1885 he had become the sole head of the business. Today, Morton Salt is a division of Morton-Norwich Products, Incorporated, a multinational corporation with 65 subsidiaries.

COFFEE ▶ Coffee is one of the most valuable commodities in world trade. And after oil it is the second most important source of income for the developing nations that sell it. Some 20 million people are engaged in growing and selling coffee. Sales in the industrial world have steadily grown, even in the face of high prices ($3 for a cup of latte in the United States in 2003). But while the consumer pays more and more for specialty coffees, the price to the grower is steadily falling, so much so that millions of people involved in the coffee business face dire poverty.

The business is highly concentrated and is incongruously dominated by a big cigarette manufacturer and a baked goods outfit: Philip Morris (Maxwell House) and Sara Lee (Chock full O'Nuts and Chase & Sanborn). The United States and Europe consume half of the world's coffee output.[48]

Most coffee is still grown in Brazil and Colombia. They are the biggest producers, accounting for about 40 percent of the world output. In addition, there are substantial amounts of coffee produced in Central America and Africa.[49]

The amount of income received for coffee in the third world depends on how the conglomerates view coffee in their overall product mix and whether they devote sufficient funds for advertising. And all of this for a crop that has little nutritional value.

It takes three to four years for a newly planted coffee tree to produce fruit, and then, depending on how well it is cared for, the tree can produce beans for up to 50 years. In general, yields begin to decline after 15 years, and most trees peter out after 20 or 30 years.[50]

There are two main types of coffee: Arabicas, grown mostly in Latin America, and Robustas, produced in Africa and Asia. Consumers usually prefer the Arabica coffees because they are milder and contain less caffeine than the Robustas. But the Robusta yield is greater, and the price is lower. Thus, Robustas gradually have gained in use, now accounting for perhaps one-third of all coffees consumed worldwide.

Among Latin American countries Brazil still provides most of the supply. Colombia, is the second largest. African nations producing Robustas include Uganda, Angola, and the Ivory Coast. Kenya grows both Arabicas and Robustas, as does Tanzania.

The distinction between Robustas and Arabicas has somewhat eroded over time because the major coffee manufacturers sell not by type but by brand name. Using sophisticated blending techniques they can change the mix depending on the price of the different coffees and still maintain the basic blend. In addition Robustas are widely used in making instant coffees, which since 1951 have steadily increased in popularity until they now account for some 20 percent of the market.

Coffee is boom one day, bust the next. Weather can be an unpredictable and important factor. There was a manageable surplus until 1970s, when a severe frost in 1975 destroyed half of Brazil's coffee trees. An earthquake in Guatemala and floods in Colombia cut into coffee production in both those countries. Coffee-growing areas were the centers of guerilla warfare during much of the 1980s. Central American wars involving El Salvador and Nicaragua are examples, as are Angola and Ethiopia.

In general, coffee remains an archetypal colonial crop. It is grown in poor countries—former colonies of European nations—and exported for consumers in the United States and western Europe. Worldwide, the crop is thought to provide employment for 20 million people on three to four million farms in some 70 nations. About half of the world's crop is grown on fairly small farms (from 20 to 30 hectares, or about 50 to 75 acres); a third on huge estates; and the remainder on peasant holdings of less than 2 hectares (5 acres) each.[51]

There is no question that coffee is an important source of income for these poor nations. In her 1975 book *The Commodity Trade of the Third World*, Cheryl Payer wrote:

> [E]leven countries received 25 percent or more of their foreign currency earnings from it in 1972. In that year coffee earned 27 percent of Brazil's foreign exchange (although this proportion has steadily declined in recent decades); the figure is 52 percent for Colombia; 50 percent for Haiti; 50 percent for Ethiopia and 61 percent for Uganda. Many of these countries also depend on internal coffee taxes for a substantial proportion of their government revenue: In El Salvador, for example, the coffee tax produced 20 percent of the total fiscal revenue in 1973; in Haiti, Guatemala and a few other Latin American countries it has contributed 10–15 percent. In Colombia, the coffee tax in 1973 represented about 20 percent of the total central government revenue.[52]

At the beginning of the twenty-first century three nations remained overly dependent on coffee sales: In Uganda coffee accounted for 95 percent of all exports; in Burundi, over 85 percent; and in Rwanda, 75 percent.[53]

In the early twentieth century Brazil was king of the coffee trade, providing three-quarters of the world's supply. It maintained its monopoly by stockpiling coffee in years when harvests were large, thereby avoiding the dreaded glut. Then, however, in an effort to undercut Brazil's hegemony, Britain and France began to encourage the cultivation of coffee in their African colonies.

Concerned about possible Axis intervention in Brazil during the Second World War, the United States signed an agreement with coffee-producing nations to keep them in the Allied camp. Under this arrangement the Office of Price Administration set quotas and guaranteed prices—most of them higher than the prevailing market—to the producing countries.

After the war and during the Eisenhower years the United States tried another approach. The State Department argued that a sharp break in coffee prices would be a threat to national security, for it claimed to fear communist intrigues among the Latin coffee producers. From then on both government and industry sought firm coffee supports for producers. The International Coffee Agreement of 1962 was aimed at keeping up prices by restricting the amount of coffee sold through a quota system. By the 1990s the agreement was discarded.

Forty years earlier coffee ran head on into the soft drink battle for the youth market. It simply could not keep up with the withering advertising campaign put on by Pepsi and Coke. As the business became more difficult, coffee companies merged, until by 1965 eight firms accounted for three-quarters of the world's business. Innovations helped the business, such things as the Mr. Coffee brewing system and GI coffee shops during the Vietnam War. Most important, of course, was the rapid rise of Starbucks in the specialty or gourmet brands where coffee was turned into several different drink concoctions.

Today the business is even more concentrated in the hands of a few suppliers. Philip Morris, best known for cigarettes, controls 14 percent of the world coffee market and 20 percent of the instant coffee business. Next comes Sara Lee, with 11 percent; Proctor and Gamble, 8 percent; and Lavazza (Italian), 2 percent. In recent years attention has focused on specialty coffees. However, in terms of sales, the biggest increase in the business came through fast-food bakery outlets such as Tim Hortons in Canada and Dairy Queen and Dunkin' Donuts in the United States.[54]

By far the largest and most profitable coffee company is Nestlé, selling over half of all the instant coffee in the world as well as owning certain other firms that make regular coffee. Instant coffee accounts for 20 percent of coffee sales by volume and 40 percent by value. Nestlé is well situated to market instant coffees in Eastern Europe and Asia, which have a taste for them.

TEA ▶ In some countries with a high degree of malnutrition and hunger, millions of agricultural acres are devoted to producing a crop that is of dubious nutritional value, requires considerable hand labor, and uses large amounts of the best arable land—tea. (Tea's main contribution to public health is an indirect one: to make it, water must be boiled, which sterilizes it and presents a safer alternative to untreated water in many poor countries.) India and China are the two largest producers of tea, the largest exporters, and the largest consumers. Most tea is grown in Asia, and almost half of all tea is imported by Great Britain. On a per-capita basis, the British drink more tea than anyone else—3 to 4 cups a day. In recent years tea prices have been going down, not up, which translates into more and more land given over to production of tea in the very poor parts of the world.[55]

Over 70 percent of world tea is sold at auction, primarily in London; Colombo, Sri Lanka; Calcutta and Cochin, India; and Nairobi, Kenya. A tea agent handles these sales, supposedly acting for the producer to get the highest bids possible. From the successful bidder, the tea then goes to a blender for processing, a shipper for exporting, a packager, and finally a retailer.

Tea first appeared on the European continent in the early seventeenth century. It was brought from China by English, Dutch, and Portuguese traders, but it took another century for the tea trade to hit its stride, with the beginning of direct commerce between Europe and China.[56] By the eighteenth century tea fleets were plying the oceans, and one merchant estimated that every inhabitant of England and its American colonies consumed one pound of tea a year. The English placed a high tax on tea, which led to a considerable black-market trade, and was one factor in sparking the American Revolution. Tea never caught on on the European continent the way it did in England. By the mid-seventeenth century the British East India Company had entered the picture and came to monopolize the business. The structure of the business has generally changed, but this early colonial pattern persists in many places today. The function of the British East India Company is now carried out by the food and drink giants Unilever and Nestlé.

Unilever, the international holding company celebrated as the largest consumer-goods company in the world, is the most important player in the tea business. It owns the former independent companies Lever Brothers, Monarch Foods, Lipton, and Shopsy Foods, and has 500 companies doing business in 72 nations, including huge plantations in Cameroon, Colombia, Ghana, Malaysia, Nigeria, the Solomon Islands, Thailand, and Zaire.[57]

Unilever rules tea through its ownership of Brooke Bond Liebig (BBL), itself a holding company that provides close to one-half of all the tea sold in Britain. BBL's tea operations comprise subsidiaries in every phase of the market—plantations, agents, blenders, shippers, packagers, wholesalers, and retail distributors. While tea is the firm's biggest source of revenue, the company also has interests in coffee, cattle ranching, meatpacking, and other food products. Its brand names include Red Rose, Blue Ribbon, and Oxo.

Through its ownership of Lipton, Nestlé is another major player in the international tea business. Best known for its Nestlé Crunch chocolate bar, it is also a major player in coffee through ownership of instant coffee giant, Nescafe, and in bottled water. The company owns Perrier, Poland Spring, and San Pellegrino. Its brand names include Buitoni pasta, Stouffer's frozen meals, Kit Kat candy bars, and Alpo dog food.[58]

Third-place contender is Tata Tea, a multinational company headquartered in India, which, through ownership of Tetley Tea, is the world's second-largest producer of tea bags. Tata is the largest producer of tea in India.[59]

Tea plantations, by displacing traditional subsistence agriculture such as rice growing, have made tea economies dependent on tea exports for enough foreign exchange to import food. It is little wonder, then, that virtually every major tea-producing country has severe problems of starvation, hunger, and malnutrition.

By the end of the twentieth century tea drinking got a shot in the arm with several new twists in marketing. Once tea was sold on the coffee aisle of supermarkets. But now tea drinks compete with other soft drinks. In addition the established firms are offering herbal blends. Green tea has achieved a sudden popularity because of its alleged beneficial effect on certain cancers. Tea is also sold through vending machines and at drug stores and gas stations. Tea has become competitive with coffee in coffeehouses, especially with the popular chai—a mixture of tea, milk, and spices. In the United States, where tea-industry sales are around $4.6 billion, more than half of the total is provided by nontraditional markets. By the twenty-first century

China trailed India and was the second-largest tea producer in the world. There is more land under cultivation or growing tea in China than anywhere else in the world—1.1 million hectares (2.7 million acres). Eighty percent of China's tea is green tea, which is generally of lower quality than many other teas, but is also much cheaper (80 percent cheaper in Japan, for example). For that reason alone China has built export markets in such places as Morocco and Japan, won niches in the central Asian countries of Uzbekistan and Turkmenistan, and penetrated the markets of other tea-exporting nations. In 2002 China provided 60 percent of the world's growing green tea market. It also produces large quantities of black tea for the Russian market. Because its costs—especially labor costs—are low, China has begun to attract foreign investment, with big international companies staking out acreage and beginning to produce their tea there. But China is by no means close to taking over the tea market, because its teas are laced with poisonous pesticides, which already has led to a fall in the German quality-tea market, and it faces major obstacles in the European Union countries, which have stiff pesticide-residue regulations.[60]

COCOA ▶ Chocolate is by far the most popular sweet in the United States and much of the world. The chocolate habit in Europe dates to the sixteenth century, when the Spanish and Portuguese explorers brought cocoa beans back from the New World. In 1519 Cortés observed Montezuma's court in Mexico drinking thousands of cups a day of a bitter drink made of wine or sour mash mixed with cocoa beans and called chocolate. What impressed Cortés was the value the Aztecs placed on cocoa. Ten beans would fetch a rabbit; one hundred, a slave. Cocoa was imbued with other properties. Montezuma is supposed to have imbibed chocolate before visiting his harem of 100 wives so as "to be in good form." Indeed so valuable were cocoa beans that counterfeiters stuffed dirt into old bean shells and traded them as the real thing.

Distraught Catholic bishops excommunicated parishioners "who sought to give themselves a foretaste of paradise" by drinking "this wicked beverage" in church.

Cortés planted cocoa beans on his way back to Europe—in Trinidad and Haiti, and on Fernando Po, the island off Africa from which centuries later cocoa was taken to the west coast of Africa. Arriving in Spain and France from Mexico, cocoa beans slowly worked their way into the Continent, but no one knows exactly how. As the author Susan Terrio explains, "The most popular theories feature the arrival of chocolate at the seventeenth-century French court on the occasion of royal nuptials uniting Spanish princesses with French kings: either the Infanta's marriage to Louis XIII in 1615, or Maria Teresa's marriage to Louis XIV in 1659. Another theory posits the diffusion of chocolate among clerics and monastic orders and still another the royal grant of refuge in southwest France to Iberian Jewish chocolatiers escaping religious persecution in the late sixteenth or early seventeenth centuries."[61]

The cocoa tree grows best along the equator. It is an evergreen, with brilliant leaves that start out pale green, pink, or red and change to a glossy, dark green as they mature. The tree produces flowers and fruit all year long. The fruit of the cocoa tree is a pod with seeds in it. These pods appear after the fifth year, sprouting up directly from the tree truck or on the branches. They look like long melons. At harvest the pods are cut from the tree and split open, revealing the cocoa beans inside, enmeshed in a white pulp. At first, they are allowed to ferment, being dumped into a hole in the ground and covered with leaves. This fermentation cuts the beans' acid taste. Then they are dried, roasted, and opened so that the dark brown particles, or nibs, can be removed. The nibs, which are the basis for all cocoa and chocolate, are ground up to create chocolate paste. (The shells can be used as fertilizer or as cattle feed.)

The chocolate paste is processed in two basic ways. If it is put through a press, all the cocoa butter is squeezed out, and a powder remains. This is pulverized into cocoa. The other process is to take the chocolate paste and add more cocoa butter until chocolate is obtained. Cocoa butter on its own is used in cosmetics, skin oils, suntan lotions, soaps, and creams. Chocolate bars are made by pouring the chocolate into a machine that squirts it into molds.

Until the end of the nineteenth century, most of the world's cocoa was grown on giant estates in Latin America and consumed in Europe. Spanish merchants dominated the business. By the twentieth century, however, Africans began to grow cocoa, partly under the persuasion of the British, who saw its important potential as a commodity in colonial trade. Africa gradually won the cocoa trade away from Latin America.

Cocoa is an especially tricky crop. Both tree and fruit are sensitive to disease, which can destroy them. The cost of combating disease is expensive, and if the price of cocoa is not high enough, growers are likely simply to let their trees perish. Since it takes five years to bring a tree to fruit, that means that the supply may fluctuate wildly.

This fact helps to explain the decline of Latin American cocoa farming: Because of high costs, large plantations fell into ruin or abandoned cocoa for such other crops as coffee or bananas. But there were other reasons. Latin American plantations produced especially fine cocoa varieties, as compared to the hardier, higher-yielding varieties introduced into Africa. The Africans could thus out-produce Latin America, and as the chocolate business burgeoned into a mass market, the need for the finer-quality Latin beans diminished. Finally the big Latin American cocoa estates were more susceptible to the wildly fluctuating cocoa markets than were the small African farms, where a peasant could grow a few trees and harvest the crop without hired labor.

During the 1990s 8 developing countries produced 80 percent of the world's cocoa and accounted for 85 percent of the exports.[62]

In the Ivory Coast the leading producers are small family businesses. Buyers come from nearby villages to purchase cocoa, which they then sell to exporters. The exporters tend to be rich Africans, French, or Lebanese. They send the product to the West, where companies like Nestlé and Hershey make it into chocolate. One journalist for the *New York Times* who visited the Ivory Coast to explore cocoa production there reported that numerous children as young as seven are imported as slaves to harvest cocoa. Ivory Coast officials deny the charge, insisting that only a few youngsters meet this fate.[63]

The Ivory Coast produces more than twice as much cocoa as the next-largest producer, Ghana. In addition to Africa, plantations in Asia and the South Pacific are producing substantial amounts of cocoa. When the bottom dropped out of the cocoa market in the 1980s, Ghana, where cocoa provides 46 percent of all export earnings, was hard hit, as was the Ivory Coast, where cocoa accounted for nearly one-third of its export income.[64]

The United States imports 22 percent of the world's cocoa production, followed by Germany, with 13 percent. But in terms of sales the best market is Great Britain, where per-capita expenditures stand at $90. Overall more chocolate is eaten in western Europe than anywhere else. Almost all cocoa is used to manufacture chocolate, a highly concentrated business dominated by large companies in western Europe and the United States. The big international grain traders—ADM and Cargill—are major players in grinding up the raw beans, which then go to the major chocolate and candy makers—Mars, Nestlé, Unilever, and Philip Morris.

Mars is a reclusive but important company which has grown from sales of

$300 million in 1970 to $14 billion today. It sells food products, drinks, pet-care products, vending equipment, and electronics. Through its Master-foods, Mars produces Snickers, the top chocolate bar in the U.S. market—with sales of $235 million—as well as M&Ms, Milky Way, and Twix. Mars is the third-largest privately held company in the United States.[65] An overall decrease in candy eating (nutritionists have successfully attacked candy as junk food) has brought about a decline in the industry and caused the major companies to diversify. (Mars, for example, owns Uncle Ben's Foods, which makes rice, and Kal Kan, a pet food concern.)[66]

In 2001 the candy business in the United States had sales of $23 billion, with growth in breath fresheners and snack and granola bars. Otherwise, sales remained generally flat. That year the Chocolate Manufacturers Association, the trade association, worked hard to protect the industry from charges that American chocolate candy came from cocoa trees in West Africa harvested by slave children. This revelation threatened to engulf chocolate in a buyers' boycott. But the industry headed off the attack, at least temporarily, with a protocol that tied companies to eliminating child labor by 2004.[67]

The major manufacturers have persisted in efforts to develop a substitute for chocolate, but this will not suffice for connoisseurs. Susan Terrio interviewed Sonya Rykiel, the fashion designer, on her "chocolatism": "I am pursued by chocolate. I can't remember having ever lived without it. It's part of me. When I read a book I eat chocolate, when I go to the movies, I eat chocolate, when I travel I eat chocolate. I keep chocolate hidden in a special place at home and it happens that sometimes I share it, but only with my sisters. Chocolate is a drug and a mystery you shouldn't try too hard to solve."[68]

FISH

Fishing is an enormous industry that sprawls across the globe. Over time it has devoured the original riches of the sea. As a result many wild fish are simply disappearing and being replaced by domestic varieties grown in fish farms. The image of the tough, independent fisherman eking out a living on his own boat (most recently memorialized in *The Perfect Storm*) still persists. But in truth the fish business is almost all international, dominated by large enterprise. And the fish in the oceans and streams are being hunted down faster than their numbers can be replenished. Fisheries are the most globalized food industry that exists. Over 75 percent of the world marine-fisheries catch—over 80 million tons per year—is sold on international markets.[69]

The ocean's vast international waters, and the commodities they contain, are beyond national sovereignty and resistant to regulation. For the most part, the modern fishery industry has been a case of survival of the fittest—and the biggest. Through the mid 1970s American fishermen watched helplessly as the factory ships owned by the Soviet Union and Japan lay off the Atlantic and Pacific coasts of the United States waiting to pounce on the once-plentiful, but now fast-disappearing, schools of fish. They had become the world's top fishermen.

During the 1970s the Soviets steadily increased their catch as a result of large government investments. While most fishermen are among the lowest-paid workers in the world, in the Soviet Union fishing was then the fourth-highest-paid industry. Throughout the 1970s the Soviets invested more than any other country in fishery expansion. Their huge factory-boats—capable of processing some 50,000 tons of fish in a single voyage—traveled in tandem with trawlers thousands of miles away from Russian shores. These "floating factories" stayed at sea for as long as six months. The small independent fishermen who must return to shore each evening so their catch does not spoil cannot begin to compete with the production volumes of such vessels—even though the small fishermen's methods may be more efficient.

If fishery expansion was a sound decision for Soviet industry, it has been a vital necessity for the Japanese. About 55 percent of the animal protein consumed in Japan is fish and seafood. With limited land area and a mountainous terrain largely unsuitable for livestock grazing, Japan is dependent on fish, and this is unlikely to diminish. And even with its active fishing industry and substantial annual catch Japan is a net importer of fish.

And the Japanese are not alone. Over half of the world's people—especially in Asia—depend on fish for most of their animal protein. But the rest of the world consumes so much beef and other meat that fish overall represents only 10 to 13 percent of animal protein in the human diet.

In part the humiliation of the American fisherman—watching helplessly as the Japanese and Soviets took huge hauls of fish from American coastal waters—led to the passage of the Magnuson Fishery Conservation and Management Act (MFCMA), with the aim of putting a halt to over-fishing. The government got behind a capital construction program with such measures as price guarantees and deferring taxes. Fishermen were encouraged to spend more and more. By the 1980s the Farm Credit system (which also finances fishing-related enterprise) was pumping money into the industry while foreign countries denied their poaching rights, such as Norway, bought into American operations.[70]

American fishing revived. The number of fishing vessels jumped by 40 percent, and the number of commercial fishermen went up by 60 percent. In part the resurrection of the industry can be attributed to such things as technological innovation and government subsidies, but rising consumer demand played an important part. The expanding frontier was not without limits, however. To get around the U.S. restrictions on foreign fishing boats gouging out dwindling schools of fish—especially off Alaska—the Norwegian interests, backed by their government, bought hulks of old naval vessels or discarded oil tankers, then stripped them to the keel and rebuilt them in Norwegian shipyards into sleek 250-foot factory ships that can catch and process fish into such products as Alaska Pollock fillets and surimi. These ships flourished in Alaska in the 1990s. With their crews of up to 100 workers, they can stay at sea for months, traveling from one fishing ground to another. They can process, then freeze, up to 550 pounds of fish every day.

The lure of fishing profits brought big international corporations into the picture, with Tyson Foods, the U.S. chicken giant, getting into the business in Alaska, along with Canada's Fishery Products International and the Pescanova Group S.A. from Spain. Pescanova, partly subsidized by the Spanish government, operated joint ventures with South African companies in Namibian waters and worked off Argentina and through ownership of France's largest industrial fishing company—Jego-Quere. The European Union, an important underwriter for expanded fishing activity, "increased fishing support from $80 million in 1983 to $580 million in 1990," according to the *Economist*. A fifth of that went to build new boats or to improve old ones. Instead of protecting scarce resources, government subsidized their destruction.[71]

As more and more money was pumped into expansion, the overall stock of fish began to fall. By 1993 65 of a total 231 U.S. marine fish stocks were classified as over-fished. There were too many fishermen trying to catch too few fish.

The most dramatic situation took place in the western Atlantic, where commercially viable schools of cod vanished. It became so bad that 30,000 people in the fishing business in eastern Canada lost their jobs, and the Canadians took it upon themselves to start policing not just their own territorial waters but applied the law in international waters as well. The fast-growing fishing industry pushed aside ineffective laws, and over-fished, but such species as cod suffered from more than just being over-fished. Their reproduction was decimated in the so-called by catch, the process of dragging the ocean bottom like a road scraper, hauling up not just the fish, but everything else on the bottom. This ruined the spawning grounds of the cod. Sports fishermen got into the act as they poached fish. And the commercial operators refused to put in place basic safeguards to protect the future catch, such as banning by catch. Southeastern shrimpers in the Atlantic get three to four pounds of by catch with every pound of shrimp. In the Gulf of Mexico they get seven to nine pounds of by catch for every pound of shrimp. The overall shrimp by catch adds up to one billion pounds of fish a year.

These practices resulted in the demise in the 1990s of haddock, cod, and yellowtail flounder off New England; the precipitous decline of king mackerel in the Gulf of Mexico; and the destruction of the Georges Bank herring fishery.

Worldwide commercial landings of fish nearly quintupled from 1950 to 1989, from 20 million metric tons (22,046,244 tons) to 117 million metric tons (128,970,530 tons) in 1998. Much of the activity is by China, which accounts for nearly one-third of the entire world catch. Some 36 million people work in fishing in China, with the fast-growing internal aquaculture fisheries accounting for a quarter of the total. In 1998 the top world producers in descending order were China, Japan, the United States, the Russian Federation, Peru, Indonesia, Chile, and India, all accounting for half the world's catch. The northwest Pacific and northeast Atlantic have been the big producers. Alaskan salmon and Japanese anchovy are the staple items in the northwest Pacific; herring in the northeast Atlantic; and skipjack and yellow fin tuna in the west central Pacific.

The Food and Agricultural Organization (FAO), the basic source of statistics on the industry, believes that as most of the world's fishing areas have reached their maximum potential, it is unlikely there will be much growth in the total catch. (There are three exceptions to the trend. In the eastern and western Pacific, and in the west central part of the Pacific the catch is growing.) Aquaculture, however, presents a distinctly different picture. This business is steadily expanding, especially in China and along the coastal estuaries of Southeast Asia.

Two-thirds of all fish eaten as food comes from marine and inland waters, while the other third is harvested from aquaculture operations. Once fish was sold canned or dried but now it is mostly sold frozen. Shrimp is a prominent item, accounting for 20 percent of the total value of internationally traded fishery products. America's favorite fish—trout, salmon, catfish, and shrimp—come not from the oceans or streams but from fish farms. Like cattle feedlots, these fish farms are breeding grounds for disease, which then can be spread to the wild fish.[72]

Aquaculture is a big growth area for the fishing business, especially in China, which leads the world. Freshwater fish farming in Asia is dominated by different varieties of carps. Shrimp grow in brackish water along the coasts, and mariculture is driven by Japanese kelp. Aquaculture gives landlocked countries a crack at fishing, and in various parts of South Asia from Bangladesh to the Philippines and Indonesia, it offers small farmers a chance to get into the business. Ornamental fish have become a profitable sideline. Singapore is the leader in what is estimated to be a $3 billion business.

However, a Canadian study in 2001 cautioned, "Aquaculture cannot replace wild seafood because so much farmed seafood relies on wild fish for fishmeal." It continues: "Currently a third of all fish landed globally goes into fishmeal and oil. Half is used for aquaculture and half is used for agriculture." The aquaculture component "is increasing rapidly because we are using fishmeal to raise carnivorous fish like salmon. If aquaculture is going to help the situation, you have to raise vegetarian fish—like carp, tilapia and shellfish—and not supplement their food with fishmeals or oils."[73]

In 1990, for the first time since the FAO began conducting annual assessments, catch declined (approximately 3 percent), and world harvest fell below 97 million tons. FAO figures showed stable world harvests for 1991 and 1992. Although overall catch has remained constant in recent years, the increased landings of low-value species (e.g., anchoveta, jack mackerel, and pilchards) used for fish meal have masked the decline of more commercially valuable species. Species with declining catches are for the most part high valued. The FAO in the 1990s asserted that the maximum sustainable yield for the world's fisheries had been surpassed, and showed that 13 of the 17 major global fisheries were depleted or in serious decline.[74] FAO officials at the 1993 UN Conference underscored the paradoxical economics of global overfishing by releasing figures showing that the cost of operating the world's fishing vessels in 1989 was $92 billion, while their catch was worth only $72 billion.

In May 2003 two scientists based at Dalhousie University in Nova Scotia released another groundbreaking study on the impact of industrial fishing on the ocean's big fish over the past 50 years. It showed communities of fish, such as tuna, swordfish and marlin, cod, halibut, and flounder had declined by 90 percent throughout the global ocean. Over-fishing has not only affected numbers of fish, the authors claimed, but their size and weight are also diminishing. The average sizes of some of the large predator fish have been reduced from a fifth to a half of what they once were.

According to the lead author, Ransom Myer, the only way out of this predicament is to cut back the number of fish killed each year by at least one-half—a solution difficult to sell to the world's big fisheries. Myers said, "If stocks were restored to higher abundance, we could get just as much fish out of the ocean by putting in only one-third to one-tenth of the effort. It would be difficult for fishermen initially, but they will see gains in the long run."[75]

The 2001 Canadian report, however, provided another point of view: "The global catch trend is not increasing, it is not even stable, but rather it has been decreasing steadily since the late '80's," stated one of the study's authors, Dr. Reg Watson of the University of British Columbia Fisheries Center.[76] The report also stated that "vast over-reporting by the People's Republic of China combined with the large and wildly fluctuating catch of a small fish, the Peruvian anchoveta, have painted a false picture of the health of the oceans by inflating the catch statistics and implying that business as usual is sustainable."[77]

Flowers

In the global marketplace, the bare necessities of life often become, in effect, luxuries that must be purchased by those who live in poverty in the developing world. At the same time commodities that once may have been luxuries available only to the wealthy become everyday items accessible to the middle class in the more powerful, industrialized trading nations. For example, where once the vast majority of people ate only local, seasonal produce, most middle-class consumers can now choose year-round from a full variety of fruits and vegetables, which are bound to be in season somewhere in the global south, and which can be transported rapidly to markets worldwide.

An even more compelling example of this phenomenon can be found in cut flowers. Once a small, European-based business designed to bring a luxury commodity to the rich, the global trade in cut flowers has been transformed into a booming supermarket industry for the middle classes. Its profitability depends on the speed of airfreight along with cheap labor in the impoverished postcolonial nations of the world. The international flower trade has its roots in one of the more bizarre episodes of early modern European history, but the story of the contemporary flower industry is an all-too-familiar one, as underpaid and disempowered third-world workers labor to produce the Valentine bouquets and dining-table centerpieces of the first world.

The international trade in flowers began in the sixteenth century with the tulip. The rich of Europe grew enamored of tulips and spent considerable sums of money just to import the flowers from Constantinople. The tulip had originated in central Asia, in the Tian Shan Mountains, where Russia, Afghanistan, Tibet, and China meet on the "roof of the world." The flowers then spread westward with the migrating Turks.

By the early seventeenth century tulips were being grown in western Europe, and were the rage in Holland, then in its Golden Age and a major economic power in Europe. Great sums of money were spent to procure and modify tulip stock. All the attention ruined the plant; originally a hardy specimen, domestication into different over-bred strains made the flower helpless against disease. The more beautiful it became, the weaker it grew—and the more valuable.

First the rich, then the growing middle class, in Holland became almost mad for the flowers. In a phenomenon sometimes described as "tulipo-mania," the Dutch abandoned their other businesses to speculate on tulips and their valuable breeding bulbs. Whole fortunes were invested in 40 tulip bulbs. One speculator in Haarlem offered twelve acres of good building ground in exchange for a single tulip. The rare Viceroy tulip, in one account, brought "two lasts of wheat, four lasts of rye, four fat oxen, eight fat swine, twelve fat sheep, two hogsheads of wine, four tuns of beer, two tuns of butter, one thousand lbs. of cheese, a complete bed, a suit of clothes, a silver drinking cup."[1]

Formal tulip markets were established in half a dozen major Dutch towns. There was even a commodities market in tulip futures—likely the first futures market in the world—and soon speculators were rigging bids. Eventually the rich tired of tulips themselves and instead turned to speculating on them. Prices fell. Sellers who had signed contracts for thousands of florins found tulips selling for a few hundred. The market crashed, and despite every effort the local and provincial governments in Holland were unable to agree on any course of action to stabilize the business. It took many years for Holland to regain its equilibrium. By the mid-nineteenth century tulips in London once more climbed in price—a tulip cost more than an oak, and one valuable tulip sold for 75 pounds.

The modern flower business has grown into a large international industry. The hegemony established by the Dutch four centuries ago continues in the present, although it is increasingly being challenged. Globalization has meant an ongoing, progressive shift in supply toward the global south, with its long growing seasons, cheap labor, and looser environmental regulations. To a lesser extent new centers of trade have sprung up to provide direct lines between producers and consumers, especially in the Western Hemisphere.

For few internationally traded goods is time to market as important as for the cut-flower industry. Flowers are very sensitive to the treatment they receive once they have been cut. Strict control of humidity, temperature, and air quality are essential for delivering an attractive product to the market. Growers rely heavily on an efficient post-harvest chain of handlers, storage, and transport. Indeed, in the absence of a "cold-chain" it is practically impossible for even the most efficient producers to sell their produce on the main "northern" markets.

Organization is thus the key to success in this industry. This was clear to the Dutch growers, who nearly a century ago set up the first flower auction, which allowed them to obtain a fair return on their efforts and enabled Holland to become a principal producer and the major cut-flower trading nation in the world. Most flowers physically pass through centralized auction sites, sometimes traveling thousands of miles to reach the sites, only to be promptly shipped out again to markets thousands of miles away. The largest of these sites is the Aalsmeer Flower Auction, located about ten miles southwest of Amsterdam.[2]

The Netherlands remains the world's leading exporter of flowers, though on a declining trend. Colombia is second. Kenya—which boasts the world's largest flower farm—Ecuador, and Zimbabwe have also built up their flower industries. The successful non-European suppliers have favorable climatic conditions, but they are thousands of miles away from the main European and North American markets and have no sizable domestic markets. They have managed to achieve spectacular production growth largely by accessing high-tech cooling systems and fast transportation by airfreight, which allows them to compete with European suppliers that are much closer to the major markets.

The industry is continuously attracting new entrants. Kenya, Ecuador, and Zimbabwe—the rapidly growing exporters of the last decade—are already "established" suppliers compared to their ambitious new competitors in China, India, South Korea, Malaysia, Malawi, Mexico, Palestine, Peru, South Africa, and Zambia, as well as a host of other countries.

Despite the new competition the Dutch retain control of the flower business, in part because they monopolize the thousands of hybrid seedlings or starter plants, which are planted in the Netherlands, and in certain instances, shipped abroad to be grown. In a very real sense the Dutch have reverted to nineteenth-century colonialism.

The Germans buy more flowers than anyone else. But in terms of value the United States and Japan are the largest markets. The American market alone is worth about $15 billion a year for cut flowers and plants. These are sold at 30,000 florists and 23,000 supermarkets nationwide. The biggest American market is in San Francisco; the second largest, in Los Angeles. Although the United States has more land devoted to growing flowers than any other country, most of the U.S. market is supplied from abroad, increasingly from Colombia, Ecuador, and other parts of Latin America, as well as Africa. Japan, Asia's largest market, gets its flowers from Taiwan and New Zealand as well as from Europe. Germany imports almost 70 percent of its cut flowers, most of which it buys from the Netherlands. Indeed, the trade between the Netherlands and Germany accounts for a surprisingly large portion of the world trade. But, even within Europe, African-grown flowers claim a growing market share. And even some traditional Dutch producers are moving operations overseas, to places like Kenya and Zimbabwe.

Roses and carnations are the principal traded products, with the share of the former growing steadily and that of carnations stagnating. In 1995 world rose imports accounted for 23 percent of all flower imports, while carnations had a 15 percent market share, followed by chrysanthemums at 9.5 percent; orchids at 1.7 percent; gladioli at 0.3 percent; and all other flowers totaling 49.9 percent.

The market for flowers is tied to consumer tastes. The wealthy buy special flowers, often professionally arranged; the middle classes buy simple bunches of common varieties. Gift giving is the most-cited reason for buying flowers, for which they must compete with wine and chocolates. But preferences vary. In Italy most flowers go to decorate graves and funerals, while in Japan individuals almost never buy flowers; their sales are institutional.

The prices for cut flowers are generally set in the flower markets of Amsterdam, but in Europe supermarkets are increasingly the major sellers, and they prefer to buy substantial amounts of flowers directly from producers on long-term contracts. "The influence of supermarkets has become much larger, and they are more sophisticated. They are taking more of higher quality product, and there is much more emphasis on quality, not price. Before supermarkets entered the picture, importers sold almost exclusively to wholesalers, with very definite lines as to how the chain of distribution was laid out. You never crossed those lines. . . . Now, supermarkets call importers; supermarkets call Colombian farms." Estimates are that over 50 percent of the flowers sold are by supermarkets.[3]

Meanwhile patterns of ownership are changing, concentrating the industry. In 1998 Dole, the international fruits and vegetables giant, bought out Floramerica, the biggest flower producer. Dole also bought Sunburst Farms, the biggest importer of flowers in the United States.

The changes in the flower business have significant implications for the labor force, both in the long-time supplier countries like the Netherlands and in the up-and-coming supply sites of the third world. The Dutch agricultural economy has been strongly influenced by the flower business, with one-third of all farm income coming from flowers. There are over 1 million hectares (2.5 million acres) of land in Holland devoted to horticulture in general, and more than 125,000 farms. Flowers there are grown by a multitude of small farmers, who earn a decent living and have some power as players in the overall business. More than 5,000 farmers, for example, have banded together in a company to sell roses. Labor in the Netherlands is a key cost—35 percent of operations.

In some parts of the world growing flowers results in turning a large expanse of land into a virtual plantation of greenhouses. The modern industry depends on the existence of a nearby airport and a local labor force. Flowers require long hours of sunlight and a lot of water in a moderate climate. Unlike much of agriculture which can be semi-automated, the growing of flowers is highly labor intensive. The flowers are planted by hand, and the laborer must handle each plant, snipping buds, and trimming stems. Two-thirds of these flower farm workers are women. They are paid minimum wages; since the wages account for as much as one-third of the overall costs, an owner can shift his business from place to place to take advantage of a steady, cheap supply of labor. The workers are drenched with insecticides and fertilizers from the moment they start to "disinfect" the soil in preparation for planting.

Flower workers are at the bottom of the labor pool, and for many this is their first job. In Latin America and Africa they are hired as temporary workers for short, fixed-term contracts. There are no benefits, nor job security. They are paid low minimum wages and expected to work overtime. A worker can end up toiling 50–60 hours a week. Supervisors hover over them, and if they cannot keep up the pace or are complainers, they are fired.

In Africa, men are treated better than women are, often meriting protective uniforms, unlike the women, who are often harassed sexually by supervisors and watched carefully to make sure they are not pregnant. In Colombia it has long been the case that women are made to take pregnancy tests before getting a job. This practice has been judged to be illegal, but many employers do not know about the ruling, and the practice continues. If women workers do get pregnant, they are sacked.

Few workers belong to unions, which in any case struggle to survive in the antiunion atmosphere of many countries, including Colombia. Labor conditions are similar in Kenya, another example of a fast-growing flower-producing nation. Spurred on by European investment, in 1999 it produced $140 million in flowers, 90 percent of which were shipped to the Continent. The business employs 40,000 people on 120 farms, including the world's largest, with 10,000 workers. The work sites are drenched in pesticides, many of them banned in the United States, presenting a constant danger for workers. And the work is always quixotic. In Kenya growing flowers is big business. More than 330 tons of flowers are airfreighted out of Kenya every night, although terrorism has curbed flights from Europe to Kenya and hurt its exports of flowers. Still, horticulture is Kenya's number-three item in terms of exports.[4]

After the Netherlands Colombia is the largest flower grower in the world. Flowers were first introduced there in 1965 by U.S. AID as an antidote for coca. This is ironic because no coca is or has been grown on the Sabana de Bogota where the flowers are grown. The business experienced a rapid growth, due in part to trade agreements that allow flowers to enter the United States without duties under the Andean Trade Preferences Act. In 1990 Colombian flowers brought $230 million in profit; by 2000, the figure was $650 million. There are about 500 companies, and 4,500 hectares (11,120 acres) of land planted in flowers. Eighty percent of the industry's exports are sent to the United States. There are thought to be 75,000 people—mostly women—working directly in the business, with another 75,000 in ancillary jobs. The average pay is about $1.30 an hour. Cynthia Mellon has noted that the current minimum wage leaves Colombian flower workers at around 200 percent below the poverty line for a family.[5]

Drugs

Although seldom viewed as commodities, the opium, cocaine, and marijuana traded on the black market in the United States probably reach total sales of more than $60 billion a year. The United Nations actually places the value of narcotics in international trade at $200 billion. In the year 2000 alone, the United States imported $10 billion of heroin, an opium-based drug.[1]

OPIUM AND HEROIN ▶ Most of the drug trade is illicit. The bulk of the world's opium is grown along a 4,500 mile stretch of mountains—from Turkey's arid continental Anatolian plateau, through central Asia, across Afghanistan and the Hindu Kush, on through the northern parts of the Indian subcontinent, to the mountains of Laos. Peasants and tribesmen of about eight different nations annually harvest some 5,800 tons of raw opium. In 2003 opium production was increasingly concentrated in Afghanistan and Myanmar.

Opium comes from the poppy, which is not difficult to grow. In late summer or early fall the farmer sprinkles seeds on the land. Three months later the leaves of the growing poppy plant have come and gone. The farmer proceeds to lance the seedpod that has appeared, which is roughly the same size as a tulip, and then scrapes up the white sap that oozes out. Once exposed to the air, the white sap congeals. This is opium.

Boiling opium in water removes excess vegetable matter. With repeated boiling in water and acid, the raw opium turns to morphine, a much lighter substance. Heroin is made by combining the morphine base with different ingredients. The main one is a bonding agent—acetic anhydride. Man has known about and used opium for centuries. Speculation is that poppies were first discovered in the mountains of the Mediterranean region during the Neolithic Age. Hippocrates knew about opium, as did the Roman physician Galen. From the Mediterranean opium spread into Europe and later to India and China.

In the eighteenth and nineteenth centuries opium-based medicines were common remedies for colds and headaches. Heroin, actually a trade name for the drug developed by the German Bayer chemical company, was first marketed at the beginning of the twentieth century for bronchitis, chronic coughing, asthma, and tuberculosis. It was sold as an ideal substitute for the addictive morphine and codeine. In its advertising of the time Bayer marketed both heroin and aspirin. "Heroin," proclaimed the blurb, was "the sedative for coughs."

Unrestricted distribution caused an enormous drug-abuse problem, and by the mid-1920s there were thought to be over 200,000 heroin addicts in the United States. In 1924 Congress banned the drug in this country, and soon after, the League of Nations tried to curb production in other parts of the world. An international convention that sought to control opium was signed in 1931—the Convention for Limiting the Manufacture and Regulating the Distribution of Narcotics.

Opium did not become a major problem for society until the nineteenth century. The international trade began soon after Clive conquered Bengal in the 1750s. The British thought they could pay for their colonization by taxing the sale of opium, and from there went on to establish a monopoly in the trade.

The British sold opium to traders, who carried it abroad. In time the revenue the British received from opium amounted to one-third of their total Indian treasury. That treasury financed the British conquest of India and its subsequent administrations.[2]

The British used Indian opium to develop a trading network between Britain, India, and China. Before opium the British bought tea from China with silver, which meant a continual outflow of the precious metal. Eventually, the British sent their ships laden with cloth to India, where the cloth was unloaded and sold and the proceeds used to buy cargoes of opium. The ships then proceeded to Hong Kong, where the opium was offloaded onto speedy coastal cutters, which sold it at many ports along the Chinese coast. Once the opium was unloaded, the British ships took aboard tea before starting on the long voyage for home.

In China the British became the biggest merchants of opium the world has ever known. But the British trade had declined by 1910 as China's domestic production began to fill demand. From China the trade gradually fanned out into Laos, Thailand, and Burma.

The current illicit heroin trade in Southeast Asia can be traced directly to the chemists of Shanghai and their descendants, who under the British were at the center of business. In 1951 two nationalist Chinese divisions, including descendents of the Shanghai chemists, fled from the communists into Burma, bringing the heroin business with them. The Nationalist Chinese, who by that time had set up their government in Taiwan, reequipped these two divisions in Burma, as did the American CIA. Later many of the soldiers who had fled to Burma were repatriated to Taiwan, but by the 1970s Southeast Asia accounted for roughly one-third of the world's illicit heroin. Most of it came from Burma. Thailand and India were also major producers.

The distinction between legal and illegal opium is a political one. A series of conventions dictate which nations can control opium, how much can be produced, and so on. A 1951 UN convention set the most recent legal limits.

That convention permitted Turkey to grow 100 tons of opium a year. President Richard Nixon undertook a campaign to stop the international trade in heroin in 1972 when he used U.S. military ties to Turkey to persuade that nation's government to stop production of opium. At the same time he successfully persuaded the French to knock out the Marseilles drug laboratories run by Corsican gangsters that refined the Turkish crop. It was a success for a short time, then Turkish peasants soon began growing the poppy again.[3]

When Nixon pressured Turkey to stop growing opium, heroin began to crop up in Mexico. While Mexico produced just 2 percent of the world's supply, almost all of it went to the U.S. market through an intricate maze of traffickers. Eventually the Mexican crop was curtailed by aerial spraying of poppy fields with the deadly Agent Orange. That slowed Mexican production, but heroin then began to come in substantial amounts from Bolivia and Colombia. In 2001 the White House reported that Colombia provided 62 percent and Mexico 38 percent of all the heroin sold in the United States. There was also some poppy growing in Venezuela and a little in Peru.[4]

The major opium producer today is Afghanistan. Until the Taliban slapped a ban on growing opium in 1991 Afghanistan produced 75 percent of the world's supply. If the Afghan crop were priced at market value, total revenues would run in the neighborhood of $100 million. Estimates are that the Taliban's annual revenue from opium during the 1990s ranged anywhere from $10 to $75 million, much of which was used to finance their march to power. Just as in Indochina, where heroin profits fueled the French colonial system, in Afghanistan opium money helped fund the CIA's not-so-secret war against the Soviet Union. But even though farmers do not make much compared to the distributors of the finished products, they still get as much as five times more for their poppies as they would for raising other crops like wheat or rice.

The real money in the business is made by the traffickers, who operate along the borders of Afghanistan. These people usually are not Afghans. They include Nigerians, Turks, Chinese, and Russians. For years the Russian army stationed in Tajikistan played a big role in the smuggling. Opium was run over the border into Russia, and from there worked its way to the Baltic states or Europe. The traffickers are able to mount well-financed and modern military operations, fighting national security forces in the region. In Iran 30,000 troops have been deployed along the Afghan border over the last 20 years in an effort to stop drugs from coming into Iran's own huge drug market, through which Afghan heroin passes on its way to Turkey and Europe. By 2002 3,000 Iranian soldiers and police had been killed in the fighting. The industry responds to demand from Russia and western Europe. Eighty to ninety percent of heroin in Britain and on the Continent comes from Afghanistan.

The U.S. war on drugs in this region is fraught with contradictions. Up until the Al Quaeda attacks on the World Trade Center in New York and the Pentagon in Washington on September 11, 2001, the U.S. government urged as part of its war on drugs that the Taliban (which the United States never recognized) stop growing poppies. In at least one report in 2001 the State Department's narcotics officers reported after a firsthand inspection trip of Afghanistan that the Taliban appeared to have stopped growing opium. While the United States would not recognize the Taliban, the federal government seemed to reward the production decline with aid extended through the United Nations. However, after September 11, the Bush administration turned hard against the Taliban, supporting its Northern Alliance opponents, whose opium business reportedly flourished under the Taliban ban as farmers shifted their crops northward. At least for the time being the United States has abandoned its drug war in Afghanistan for its war against terrorism. With a new Afghan government installed at the request of the United States, opium and narcotics trading once again flourished.

Although consistent figures are hard to come by, all central Asian governments have said they are worried about the growing involvement of women in drug trafficking, particularly as couriers or so-called "camels" or "mules." In Kyrgyzstan, for example, an estimated 30 percent of drug addicts and drug traffickers are women; in Tajikistan, the proportion of women traffickers is estimated to be higher and on the rise. Concerns in other central Asian countries have led to the fear that the drug business there is becoming feminized.

In 2000 a kilo of opium sold in Afghanistan for $30. A kilo of heroin (which consists of 10 kilos of opium) went for $30,000 in Moscow, but $150,000 in western Europe. In New York City in 2000 heroin sold for anywhere from $60,000 to $74,000 a kilo.

COCA AND COCAINE ▶ Almost all of the world's cocaine comes from the Andean region of South America, i.e., Colombia, Peru, and Bolivia. Historically the cocaine base was produced mostly in Peru and Bolivia and then transported by the Colombians. By 2003 production in Colombia expanded, but it declined in Peru. The collapse of some large Colombia drug cartels and possibly the civil conflict in the country have fueled coca leaf production. Peru's coca crops suffered the effects of a fungus in the 1990s. By 2003 Colombia controlled 68 percent of all coca leaf production, thereby lessening the need to import from Peru and Bolivia. Half of Colombia's cocaine comes from one province—Putumayo. Little of this cocaine is bound for Europe. As much as 90 percent of it, however, ends up in the United States.[5]

Cocaine is a far more lucrative end product for growers than coffee. Coca harvests can bring in ten times more money than coffee. This fact led an estimated 1,000 Colombian farmers in 2001 to convert their coffee farms to coca farms. Colombian coffee growers earn $50 for 100 pounds harvested once a year, while coca brings them $160 per 100 pounds three times a year.[6]

Coca farmers can sell the leaves for processing, or can get more money by making coca paste themselves. The coca plant leaves are reduced to an alkaloid paste by soaking them in a solvent such as kerosene. The farmer must then decide to whom he will sell the paste—the paramilitaries who pay $860 per kilogram in 2001, or leftist guerrillas who offer $180 or so. He must factor into the equation the knowledge that the guerrillas have killed peasants who sell their paste to the paramilitaries. Many solve the dilemma by selling part of their paste to the guerrillas, and then holding back the rest for sale to the paramilitaries.

The paste is then transported to laboratories, where the cocaine is isolated from the other alkaloids by using hydrochloric acid. A lab worker can make $350 a day. The processing goes on after dark using chemicals like sulfuric acid, potassium permanganate, ammonia, and acetone to remove unwanted alkaloids. The cocaine crystal is dried in microwave ovens or put under heating lamps, then compressed into 2.2-pound packets wrapped in plastic and latex. The packets are marked with common recognizable logos for Coca-Cola, McDonalds, or cartoon characters like Pikachu and Popeye to signify the drug's owner and its destination. From the labs the finished cocaine goes to airstrips located near the processing spots and flown to Pacific or Caribbean coasts. There it is placed on fast boats of up to six-tons burden, manned by crews of five or six. The boats either make the long haul—50 hours—to Mexico with one refueling stop or meet up with larger ships at sea where cocaine shipments from several small boats are combined and then shipped to Mexico. There the country's powerful drug cartels take over.[7]

Delivered in Latin America a kilo of 90 to 98 percent pure cocaine costs between $4,000 and $8,500. Kilos of coke in New York, where they are by then less pure (containing less cocaine and more "cut"), sell for over $30,000. The cocaine trade, obviously then, is of immense value to the producers and their distributors. Authorities in Colombia concede that an estimated $8 billion illegally comes into their country alone through the illicit drug trade. The size of this figure, together with coca's general importance to the population, has somewhat stymied the efforts of the United States and the United Nations to stem exports. Drug exports have also created unexpected benefits for the governments of producing nations: U.S. interest in stamping out cocaine traffic has resulted in a rising tide of aid funds and cash for equipment, training, and agricultural assistance that in the end run bolster the military and security forces deployed in the war on drugs.

For American government officials on the spot in the affected countries such as Colombia the situation is sometimes problematic. They are unable to make much of a dent in either the production or the distribution of cocaine, but they are unwilling to legalize its use in the United States. It is thus likely that coca growing and cocaine production will remain an expanding and profitable industry for some time to come. Plan Colombia is supposed to dry up cocaine on the streets of New York and other cities by cutting off the supply at the source. That means reducing by half the 300,000 acres of coca fields in Colombia over five years. The United States pledged $1.3 billion in 2001 to support the $7.5 billion scheme with army antinarcotics training and helicopters.

In 2001 the war was bogged down. Over 38,000 hectares (94,000 acres) had been sprayed in one year alone, but coca production shifted to other parts of Colombia and spread into Ecuador. The program led to a Vietnam-style counterinsurgency in which U.S.-trained units of the Colombian army linked up with paramilitary death squads in a bloody drive against guerillas. U.S. Special Forces, who are doing the training, are kept out of the fighting, but U.S. civilian contractors who fly the spray planes have been reported in the thick of firefights.[8]

The cocaine business can result in substantial pollution. In Colombia alone, U.S. State Department reports indicate that producing cocaine results in large amounts of sulfuric acid, acetone, and kerosene being dumped across the Andean region of that nation. The pollution kills marine life in the rivers, and in the Caquetá River basin in southern Colombia, the primary growing area, there have been reports of people and livestock falling ill from the water pumped out of the river and wells.[9]

Meanwhile the rural peasantry was getting drenched with the herbicide RoundUp Ultra. The herbicide has been linked to illness and injury; in one five-year study in the 1980s, California doctors reported that its active ingredient, glyphosate, ranked third out of 25 chemicals that cause harm to humans. Some observers say the aircraft blitzing Colombian coca fields are flying too high to ensure surrounding villages and farms are kept safe from the spray. To fly lower would mean risking a direct hit by rebel troops on the ground, however. Alberto Saldamando, a member of the International Indian Treaty Council based in San Francisco and a member of an EPA advisory committee, in 2002 sought to persuade the U.S. government to stop spraying herbicides: "Our concern is the longevity of the effects of the spraying: If the farmers can't plant, they can't grow or eat." He noted, "This is going to affect the whole Agricultural economy. We think it's a very serious health-damaging case. We are talking about indigenous people. They are poor, they are not aware of what can happen to their health."[10]

RoundUp is sold widely in the United States, and the Environmental Protection Agency says it is safe for most commercial uses. In an out-of-court settlement its St. Louis–based manufacturer, Monsanto, admitted to certain reservations about such glyphosate-based herbicides. It withdrew claims that RoundUp is "safe, nontoxic, harmless, or free from risk" and signed a statement that said "absolute claims that RoundUp will not wash or leach in the soil are not accurate." The company admitted the chemical "may move through some types of soil under some conditions after application." RoundUp Ultra, the product used in Colombia, is a concoction boosted by other powerful chemicals manufactured by ICI and Exxon Mobil.[11]

Plan Colombia has a short but dubious history. In 1999 the General Accounting Office concluded that "U.S. and Colombian efforts to eradicate enough coca and opium poppy to reduce the net cultivation of these crops have not succeeded to date." Despite fumigating 65,938 hectares (162,933 acres) of Colombian coca in 1998, the office wrote, the total number of hectares of coca under cultivation in Colombia grew from 101,800 (251,548 acres) to 122,500 (302,698 acres).[12]

Defoliation merely sends production elsewhere. Successful eradication programs in Bolivia and Peru in the 1990s led to a sharp rise in production in Colombia. And as the spraying concentrated in one part of Colombia, coca growing sprang up in another. "The pattern has been that fumigation 'chases' Coca cultivation from one area to another, while overall cultivation levels rise," noted a 2001 report by the Washington Office on Latin America. Fumigation does result in a short-term increase in cocoa prices, but, according to the Drug Enforcement Agency, has not resulted in any change in the price of cocaine in the United States. And, the report stated, while the military aspects of the plan were in full effect, promised alternative assistance to farmers had not begun.[13]

In 2001 Democratic congresswoman Jan Schakowsky, who represents the Chicago suburbs, offered a measure—cosponsored by Democrats John Conyers Jr. of Detroit and Cynthia McKinney of suburban Atlanta—to stop funding for the fumigation project. In February Schakowsky made a fact-finding mission to the Putumayo province, where she met with health ministers, governors, mayors, and police and military officials, all of whom reported RoundUp's devastating effects. "People told of rashes and intestinal problems," Schakowsky said. "There are an increasing number of internally displaced humans. It has destroyed legal crops and livelihood." As for the overall effectiveness of the program, said the congresswoman, "We've seen no change in the availability or price of cocaine. It is pretty much the same. Coca production simply moves. It doesn't take a genius to figure out that if demand is strong you move your operation. Fumigation is never going to get ahead of that. It is just going to hurt individual people and some of the peasants who are involved in it."[14]

Most of the cocaine that reaches the United States arrives by ship. But sometimes it is flown in, or carried by human "mules" who swallow pellets filled with cocaine. Sometimes they come with cocaine sewed into their clothing or hidden on their body.

MARIJUANA ▶ The *Cannabis sativa* plant has long had economic importance as the source of hemp fibers for use in textiles and rope and pulp for paper, but the trade value of these products is small in comparison with that of the plant's drug derivatives—marijuana, hashish, and liquid concentrate.

The economic significance of marijuana is no longer just that of a cash crop for small farmers, but as a highly profitable commodity in world trade. In the Canadian province of British Columbia marijuana competes favorably as an export item with timber, which has been hit with high U.S. tariffs. The profits—as much as $6 billion—are a major contributor to the province's economy, as they are reinvested in the purchase of various consumer items.

According to the U.S. government's own statistics, nearly one-third of all Americans have smoked marijuana sometime during their lives. It is the most widely used of illicit drugs. The business is thought to be worth as much as $10 billion a year, ranking it in the top ten American agricultural crops.[15]

The marijuana trade begins with the harvest of the cannabis leaves, which are dried and pressed into bricks for transit. An acre yields six or seven tons of marijuana. Hashish is made by extracting the plant's resin through scraping, shaking, or pressing the leaves or by use of solvents; the resin is then formed into slabs. Further processing yields a liquid concentrate with a very high percentage of tetrahydrocannabinol (THC), the chief psychoactive ingredient in cannabis.

Much of the marijuana consumed in the United States comes from Mexico. Canada provides a high-potency strain as well. One-third of all marijuana is domestically produced—this despite the government's continuing effort to stamp out the business. The government's drug war within the United States, with its use of paraquat sprayed from the air to kill marijuana plants, is often credited with increasing—not decreasing—marijuana production. Threat of airborne attacks drove users indoors to grow pot in greenhouse arrangements that could not be detected from the air. The marijuana that is grown in this way can be very pure and potent. States with the biggest marijuana production include California, Florida, Oregon, Alaska, and Kentucky.

The Department of Justice reports that in addition to the heavy trade from Mexico and Canada small amounts of marijuana are shipped in from Colombia, and that traffickers from Jamaica and the Bahamas are active in the southeastern United States. Marijuana grown in Thailand and Cambodia enters the country from the West Coast.[16]

The Mexican drug operators distribute the crop through numerous associates in southwestern border cities, sometimes mailing small quantities through package services. Jamaican gangs, which control much of the distribution on the East Coast, buy substantial amounts from Mexican and Colombian gangs at the U.S. border and ship it east.

Prices for commercial-grade marijuana have been generally stable. They range from approximately $400 to $1,000 per pound in the American Southwest border areas to between $700 to $2,000 per pound in the Midwest and Northeast, according to the U.S. Drug Enforcement Agency.[17]

Cannabis is thought to have originated in Asia, but it became an important trade item throughout the Near East. In the tenth century B.C. it was used in religious and secular ceremonies as an intoxicant, in medicine as an ointment for treatment of burns and pain, and in commerce as a source of fiber for blankets, sailcloth, and rope. It was an important crop in empire building, cultivated by the Spanish colonists in Latin America and British colonists in North America, where it had become a staple crop by 1630. The British used colonial hemp to make clothing. American hemp cultivation died out with the advent of the cotton gin, reappearing briefly during the Second World War, when the supply of fibers from the Far East was cut off.

The major cannabis hemp-producing countries today are Russia, Italy, and the former Yugoslavia, all of which use the fiber domestically. Hemp is also widely recognized as an economically and ecologically more efficient source of paper pulp than forest wood; it is sometimes used in making paper money. Its seeds are an abundant source of oils for use in paints and soaps. Because of the stigma surrounding and laws against cannabis, however, such uses have not been explored very extensively.

While the demand for cannabis products in the United States is largely

limited to marijuana, the market in Europe centers on hashish and cannabis oils. This is probably because of the area's proximity to the hashish-
producing countries of Lebanon, Afghanistan, Pakistan, Morocco, and other
parts of the Near East. Statistics on the volume of the European hashish
trade, based on border seizures, are even less reliable than those for the
United States, as few European countries have made concerted efforts to
interdict cannabis traffic.

Hashish (cannabis resin) is mostly smuggled into Europe by European-
based gangs, according to a 2000 report by the UN Office on Drugs and
Crime. It comes from Morocco via Spain or from Southwest Asia. Afghan
hashish also arrives in Europe, carried by sea from Pakistan or overland
through Iraq and Turkey. Overall demand seems to be increasing. The
growth rate in hashish trafficking in the 1990s, measured by numbers of
seizures, was twice that of marijuana.

TOBACCO

Smoking tobacco constitutes the most dangerous form of substance abuse in
the world. Damage from it dwarfs that of marijuana, cocaine, and heroin. By
the end of the twentieth century 1.1 billion people smoked 5.3 trillion cigarettes every year. This resulted in 400,000 deaths annually in the United
States alone. It is estimated that by 2030, if present trends continue, tobacco
will be the biggest cause of death in the world, with 10 million fatalities a
year. The World Health Organization reported that tobacco causes more
deaths than all other forms of substance abuse combined, and represents 20
percent of all deaths in developed countries.[18]

It might be argued that, compared to the international petroleum cartel,
the tobacco cartel dominated by U.S., British, and Chinese companies, has
succeeded against all sorts of odds in protecting and expanding its $200
billion a year business.

Despite tobacco's well-publicized adverse effects to health and the efforts
to curb its use, especially in the United States, the industry continues to
grow. Its growth will be dependent on youngsters in developing countries.
Persuading kids to smoke is the surest way to increase the industry's profitability. Indeed, during the 1990s, Camel, Marlboro, and Newport brands of
cigarettes dramatically grew because of their appeal to young people. They
captured more than three-quarters of the adolescent market.

The tobacco business is an excellent example of the emerging globalization in trade, where national markets are subsumed within an international business scheme. So, as New York City bans smoking in restaurants and other public places, the companies can shift their marketing efforts to women and children in the developing world. Marketing cigarettes is the single most cynical expression of the advertising industry in action. While the. United States is conducting its highly publicized war on heroin, cocaine, and marijuana, it continues to subsidize the growth of tobacco on American farms and has been assisting the industry boost exports.

Cigarette marketing is a bizarre example of industrial society's screwy values. During the early part of the last century heroin was advertised for its medicinal uses but was eventually replaced by aspirin and finally criminalized. Like heroin tobacco was widely consumed, then slowly restricted in use, with marketing redirected to the third world. Where the trade in cocaine and heroin has been driven underground in much of the industrialized West, the tobacco industry operates in the open, enjoying its image as a patron of the arts and a reputation for its humanistic role in helping to finance the campaign against AIDS. The money for these charitable enterprises comes from sales of cigarettes in the poor countries of the world, where people who make as little as $100 a year end up squeezing some of their earnings into a pack of cigarettes.

Statistics etch out the bare outlines of this huge market: One-third of the world's adult population smokes. In the third world, half of the men smoke, while 9 percent of the women smoke. But in developed countries 35 percent of the men and 22 percent of the women smoke. The Asia-Pacific region consumes the most cigarettes—about 2.8 trillion a year. China is especially important. "One in 3 cigarettes smoked in the world today are smoked in China," reported the World Health Organization. The Americas are the next biggest consumers of cigarettes with 722 billion cigarettes a year. These two are followed in rank by eastern Europe and the former Soviet Union countries with 681 billion, the European Union at 617 billion, the Middle East at 297 billion, and Africa at 167 billion cigarettes a year.[19]

Since the first Surgeon General's report linking cigarette smoking to cancer appeared in 1964, the major tobacco companies have gone through twists and turns to keep going. At first they diversified into other fields— department stores, canning fruits and vegetables, selling beer, drilling for oil, operating ship lines, and selling dog and cat foods. Still cigarettes remain at the heart of their operations. Tobacco seems to one of the few industries around the world that is recession proof. By the end of the twentieth century these companies had mostly pulled back, concentrating on selling cigarettes and shedding the other products.

China is the smoking capital of the world, with 60 percent of all men smoking. That's 300 million people. (Only 8 percent of Chinese women—45 million—smoke.) A government monopoly, the China National Tobacco Corporation, is the major factor in the Chinese market. In 1995 China produced 1.7 trillion cigarettes, roughly one-third of the entire world market. Most Chinese cigarettes are sold within the country.

Tastes in tobacco have changed dramatically during the twentieth century. In 1900 cigarettes in the United States accounted for only 3.4 percent of all leaf tobacco consumed there. A century later they represent 92 percent of total tobacco consumption. (Cigars represent 4.3 percent, with snuff and chewing and smoking tobacco accounting for the remainder.) Almost all cigarettes sold today have filter tips. Since most filter tips have a shorter tobacco column than nonfilter brands, and because there has been a trend toward lengthening the filter and reducing the circumference of the cigarette, there has been a significant reduction in the need for leaf tobacco.

Leaf tobacco is grown in 120 countries, literally all over the world except Europe. Tobacco can grow in a wide range of soils and climate, and it is an ideal crop in poor countries because it can take root in soils with low fertility. The business is thought to involve some 20 million people worldwide. Only a few nations produce most of the world's tobacco. They are China, India, Brazil, Turkey, and Zimbabwe. In terms of finished product, China, the United States, and Brazil account for 60 percent of the total. Russia, Japan, and Germany are the largest importers.

The United States itself produces a mere tenth of the world's tobacco crop, and exports 30 percent of what it grows. Two-thirds of American tobacco is grown in two states: North Carolina and Kentucky. An American corporation, Philip Morris, is the largest cigarette company in the world, accounting for 16 percent of the world market. Today it receives more than one-half of its cigarette profits from sales abroad.

Growing tobacco does not necessarily improve the national economies of poor countries, but just the reverse. Two-thirds of the developing nations around the world spend more on importing tobacco than they gain from exporting it. Thus, tobacco production actually reduces export earnings. And this situation is likely to grow worse. As one nation after another institutes tobacco-control programs, tobacco will be in oversupply, causing prices to small holders to drop. Already tobacco farmers make a tiny share of the profit from cigarette sales, with the manufacturers taking the lion's share.

Few nations depend on tobacco as a means of income. The United States is at once the largest exporter and the largest importer of tobacco. There are ten major tobacco-exporting nations: the United States, Turkey, India, Brazil, Bulgaria, Greece, the Philippines, Canada, Malawi, and Zambia. The major importers are the European Union, United States, and Japan. The United States exports most of its tobacco to western Europe and Japan.

Almost all the tobacco in international trade is handled by a handful of companies, all of which function similarly. They buy the tobacco after harvest, usually at auction, have it packaged in hogsheads, and ship it to the manufacturer. The buying company is reimbursed by the manufacturer for the price it paid for the green tobacco and is provided with a fee for service rendered.

A handful of transnational companies account for close to half the world market. The big companies are Philip Morris (now Altria Group, Incorporated), British American Tobacco (BAT), Japan Tobacco (JT Group), Imperial Tobacco, Gallaher Group, R. J. Reynolds Tobacco Holdings, Incorporated, and Loews Corporation.

The industry leaders frequently merge to further consolidate their power and tend to be involved in a range of other industries and ventures.

— The Altria Group: This conglomerate is the biggest tobacco outfit in the world and is the parent company of Kraft Foods, Incorporated, Philip Morris USA, Philip Morris International, and Philip Morris Capital Corporation. It is the largest shareholder in SABMiller, PLC, the second-largest beer company in the world.

   Key cigarette brands in the United States include Marlboro, Virginia Slims, Parliament, and Basic. Brands sold overseas include Marlboro, Lark, Chesterfield, and L & M.

   Kraft Foods produces, among other things, Kraft cheeses, Maxwell House coffee, Oreo cookies, Philadelphia cream cheese, and Milka chocolates.

— British American Tobacco (BAT): The second largest tobacco group (accounting for 14.6 percent of the market), BAT acquired Rothman's Group, another large tobacco group, in 1999. By 2003 BAT was selling 300 brands, among them the popular Dunhill, Lucky Strike, Kent, State Express 555, Peter Stuyvesant, and Benson & Hedges.

- Japan Tobacco Group (JT): Japan Tobacco sells Camels, Mild Seven (the leading brand in Asia), Salem, and Winston cigarettes. In Japan it sells nine out of the top ten brands.
- Imperial Tobacco: Imperial Tobacco dominates the British market, accounting for more than 40 percent of it. The company makes cigarettes and pipe tobaccos, and roll your own tobacco, rolling paper, and tubes. It makes, markets, and distributes the Sina 2001 brand, and distributes Marlboros in Britain for Philip Morris. It also owns Lambert & Butler, the single biggest brand name in the United Kingdom. Its brands include Richmond, Golden Virginia (roll your own tobacco), Rizla (papers), and Classic (cigars).
- Gallaher Group, PLC: Some of the company's brands include Benson & Hedges, Silk Cut, Mayfair, Sovereign, and Sobranie. Gallaher is a leading manufacturer of cigarettes in Britain, with marketing across Europe and in Kazakhstan.
- R. J. Reynolds Tobacco Holding: R. J. Reynolds Tobacco Holding owns R.J. Reynolds Tobacco Company, the second-largest American tobacco company, with brands including Camel, Winston, Salem, and Doral. It also owns the Santa Fe National Tobacco Company, Incorporated, which makes American Spirit cigarettes and other tobacco products.
- Loews Corporation: Loews Corporation owns Lorillard, Incorporated, the American Tobacco Company, CNA Financial Corporation, Loews Hotels, Diamond Offshore Drilling, Incorporated, Texas Gas Transmission, LLC, and Bulova Corporation.

LEGAL SUITS BROUGHT by six Florida smokers against the five big American tobacco companies were organized into a class action in the name of the state's 700,000 smokers. It eventually led to the Master Settlement Agreement, signed in 1998, which involved 46 states. There are separate industry state settlements in Florida, Minnesota, and Texas. All told, the settlement requires the industry to pay $246 billion. The original class action suit was brought against the 5 big tobacco companies: Philip Morris, Liggett Group, Lorillard Tobacco, American Tobacco, R.J. Reynolds, and Brown & Williamson. At first attorneys for the plaintiffs sought to include all American smokers in the class, but it was eventually narrowed to represent just Florida smokers. The trial lasted two years and resulted in a decision against the companies and the largest legal award for damages in U.S. history—$145 billion. In May 2003, however, a Florida state appeals court judge threw out the damage award on grounds that the state smokers' cases were too dissimilar to be combined in a class action, and ruled that the trial had become so emotional that the verdict was issued by a "runaway jury."[23]

MEDICINAL HERBS

Interest in Eastern medicine as a supplement and even substitute for existing modern medical practice has seen a dramatic growth in the business of producing and selling herbs. Where small firms at one time produced those herbs, today the giant pharmaceutical companies dominate a billion-dollar business. The U.S. nutrition industry, which includes herbal medicines as its top category, grew at a rate of 8 percent in 1999, to $44.5 billion. Herbs and botanical products represented $4.3 billion of that total. The top companies are American Home Products, Leiner Health Products, Rexall Sundown, Pharmavite, and General Nutrition Centers, Incorporated.

Top-selling herbs in 2000 were gingko bilboa ($250 million), echinacea ($208 million), garlic ($174 million), and ginseng ($185 million). The herbal business in general dropped on publication of a study showing that Saint-John's-wort had little effect on depression.

GINKGO ▶ Ginkgo is touted as an antiaging herb. The gingko bilboa tree is the oldest known tree species. The tree, which may live for as long as 1,000 years, is native to Asia but has been planted in North America for ornamental purposes for almost two hundred years. Ginkgo is supposed to have beneficial effects on memory, other brain functions (particularly in the elderly), and circulation. European physicians also recommend it for tinnitus, dimming peripheral vision, and arterial disease. Gingko fruit and nuts have been used for medicinal properties for centuries in Asia, but the use of its leaves is more recent, stemming from studies conducted in 1950s.

GINSENG ▶ The ginseng plant, a small perennial, is the king of herbs. It had been used in Asia for 5,000 years and was valued in China sometimes more than gold. It goes into hundreds of products, from chewing gum to gin. It often appears in tonic form meant to boost energy and stamina. Many people drink ginseng in various liquid forms to enhance endurance, reduce fatigue, and improve coordination and reaction time. In 1904 ginseng was reported to have been widely consumed in China because it promoted health, virility, and longevity.

GARLIC ▶ At least 5,000 years old, garlic is a medicinal food that is claimed to have a protective effect against leading diseases of the world. Garlic supplements are the second most popular herbal supplements sold in the United States. It is believed to help reduce cholesterol levels, lower blood pressure, reduce the risk of arteriosclerosis—the hardening of the arteries that can lead to stroke and heart attack—and improve heart health in general.

ECHINACEA ▶ Echinacea, the purple coneflower plant, has long been America's best-selling herbal remedy. Widely used today to stimulate functioning of the immune system, echinacea was the major medicinal plant of Native Americans of the Great Plains. With the introduction of antibiotics, echinacea was all but forgotten, but now with questions being raised about the efficacy of antibiotics, echinacea is back. Many people use it as therapy for colds, flu, and minor infections.

SAINT-JOHN'S-WORT ▶ Sales of Saint-John's-wort were hurt by studies that showed it had negative counteractions with other drugs. It had been widely used in Europe for depression before becoming a fad in the United States.

GINGER ▶ In Germany ginger, a plant native to Europe and Asia but grown around the world, was one of the most frequently prescribed remedies for mild to moderate depression. Today it is one of best-selling dietary supplements in the United States.[25]

TRADE IN BASIC commodities is international and it can be strongly influenced, even dictated, by one corporation or organization. Consider the example of Premarin, the biggest selling drug in America for estrogen replacement. It is based on one commodity: the urine of pregnant horse mares. This unusual situation led to the creation of an intricate market mechanism.[26]

MARES' URINE ▶ One estimate has about 45,000 pregnant mares working to produce urine for Wyeth-Ayerst Laboratories. Most of them are concentrated in the prairie provinces of Canada (Manitoba, Saskatchewan, and

Alberta), with Manitoba earning the sobriquet of "the urine capital of the world." In addition to their daily flow of urine, the mares eventually give birth to foals, about 35,000 of them. The company does not own the mares directly but subcontracts with farmers and ranchers, who sometimes offer free boarding for pregnant mares over the winter to keep them pregnant. The exact revenues for urine are unknown, but in Manitoba in 1998 20,364 pregnant mares brought in $43 million (Canadian). The mares produce three-quarters of a gallon of urine a day—100 gallons per season—and each mare nets $1,817 in urine sales. While most of the business is in Canada, 40 operations have sprung up in the United States to supply Natural Biologics in Albert Lea, Minnesota. If it is not used to make Premarin in Canada, mares' urine is shipped to Italy, Switzerland, and the United Kingdom, where it goes into various types of Premarin sold there.

As for the progeny of the mares, the foals face short brutal lives. Soon after they are born the foals are fattened and slaughtered, and their meat sent to Europe, where it appeals to consumers frightened away from beef because of mad cow and foot and mouth diseases. Foal steaks are sold in Paris butcher shops for $1 a pound. Because the Japanese like to sell fresh horse meat, the foals are stowed in the holds of ships and transported live to Japan from Seattle and other West Coast ports. In Canada the often-emaciated and injured foals bring anywhere from $70 to $100 a piece at auction. There are three foreign-owned slaughterhouses in the United States dedicated to handling foals.

Animal-rights activists oppose the practice, and United Animals Nations sends agents to Canada foal auctions to buy the young horses and find them homes. In Europe a campaign to persuade women to shift from Premarin to alternative natural formulas has met with apparent success. Animal rights groups there and elsewhere encourage women to use alternative estrogen replacement methods. Most of the operations are in Canada, where the industry regulates itself. In the United States one might suppose that the Department of Agriculture should oversee the mares' urine business. But so far it has claimed that the horses do not fall under the Animal Welfare Act since they are used for neither research nor teaching.

The foal market roughly depends on the price of hay. If it becomes too high, farmers sell their horses for slaughter rather than go to the trouble and expense of feeding them.

Human Beings

SLAVES ▶ More slaves exist in the world today than ever before in history. Some 27 million people currently live in bondage. At least 800,000 people—mostly women and children—are bought and sold on the world market each year. They are made to toil in sweatshops, fields, and brothels, and on construction sites in both developed and developing countries. Trading in human beings is high profit, and low risk, "because unlike other commodities, people can be used repeatedly, and because trafficking requires little in terms of capital investment."[1]

The United States is both a transit and destination point. The U.S. State Department estimated in 2003 that 18,000–20,000 people, again primarily women and children, are trafficked to the United States annually.[2]

Children are traded in large numbers because they are a source of low-cost labor and particularly desirable in the sex business. One account from Advocates for Free the Children reports sexual exploitation of children affects 1 million kids a year. Most of the children involved in the sex business are between 13 and 18, although there are cases involving some younger than 5 years old.[3]

For an American citizen, educated to believe slavery is outlawed in most places, the statistics seem almost unbelievable: 30,000 children in India; anywhere from 80,000 to 800,00 in Thailand; 25,400 children in the Dominican Republic; 3,000 in Bogota; 5,000 in Mexico; 70,000 women and girls in South Africa; 185,000 prostitutes in Vietnam, 30 percent of whom are under 16.

Many of these children become infected with AIDS. One report found that at least two-thirds of child prostitutes in Thailand are HIV positive.[4]

In a world seeking low-cost labor, children become virtual slaves in any number of work-related situations. The United Nation's International Labor Organization calculated in 1996 that 250 million children from 5 to 14 years old were employed, half of them full time. This was much higher than previously thought. Earlier estimates totaled only 73 million.

The most common form of slavery is debt bondage or bonded labor in which a person becomes collateral against a small loan. The loans range from $10 to over $200, and are usually incurred to pay for basic necessities of life, such as food, medical treatment, emergency needs, a marriage dowry, funeral expenses. Often the loans cover the amount the buyer paid to enslave them or the costs of transporting the unwitting slave to another country or destination under false pretenses. To pay back these debts and loans people work as slaves for their entire lives, and still find it impossible to repay loans at exorbitant interest rates of 60 percent or more, usually inflated by sketchy accounting. In the end, if still enslaved, the victim may pass on the debt to future generations. Human rights groups have estimated that there are anywhere from 15 to 20 million slaves in bonded labor in India, Pakistan, Bangladesh, and Nepal. Adults and children alike are enslaved. In India there are thought to be at least 5 million children in debt bondage in every conceivable industry: agriculture, prostitution, and manufacturing of silk, leather, salt, cigarettes, fireworks, soccer balls, apparel, and carpets, to name a few. Child bondage and even child labor are formally banned in India, and have been for years, but the government fails to enforce the laws. In the fishing industry crews are recruited through what amounts to press gangs. Modern slavery can be viewed as just another industry—in this case, estimated to contribute $13 billion to the global economy every year.[5]

In April 2002 a glimpse of what it is like to be a slave in the Chinese fishing industry became public in a Hawaiian case involving a mutiny aboard a Taiwanese fish factory boat called the *Full Means No. 2*, owned by a Taiwanese firm and registered in the Seychelles. The crew—all young, unmarried men—was recruited from rural villages in China, where local Communist Party functionaries rounded them up. The officials were rewarded by the Taiwanese company with finders' fees in the form of a cut taken from the crew members' salaries. Attorneys for the crew said in a three-year deal they were to get $50 a month while at sea, and on returning to China, $80 for each month worked. There would be enough money for each crew member to buy some land and a house or get married. Wages, however, were depleted by employment commissions, board, and other costs.[6]

The boat was at sea for 18 months. "It is a very strange and very unhappy life," Pamela Byrne, a federal public defender, told the *Washington Post*. "They're never paid. No contact with the outside world. Never allowed to phone home. Kept at sea for three years. Never allowed to touch land." Eventually one of the crew members staged a mutiny, killing the captain and first mate. After a couple of days the rest of the crew overpowered him, and set sail for Honolulu where they were taken into custody. One man was charged with murder, and the others were held as material witnesses. According to their attorneys, none of the crew ever was paid anything.

Workers landing in frontier towns along the Amazon wilds in Brazil cutting timber or working on cattle ranches are offered good pay, free lodging, and food. But the situation quickly deteriorates. "It was 12 years before I was finally able to escape and make my way back home," Bernardo Gomes da Silva told the *New York Times*. "We were forced to start work at 6 in the morning and to continue sometimes until 11 at night, but I was never paid during the entire time because they always claimed I owed them money."[7]

War in the Balkans during the 1990s was a boost to the sex business and helped swell the ranks of indentured servants who worked in it. UN workers and peacekeeping troops on R & R beat a path to the nearest brothel. The employees of one company hired to set up police operations were accused of selling women and children for prostitution.[8]

The town of Velesta in Macedonia became a hub of the trade. Many women from former communist-bloc countries were lured into prostitution and held against their will. As many as 2,400 to 2,600 women slaves may be in Macedonia at a given time. One woman said she was lured from the Ukrainian Black Sea port of Odessa by Serbs who offered her unspecified work abroad. She was driven to a town in northern Macedonia and sold to a bar owner. She was taken to his bar, held under guard, and beaten. "I bought you and you can say nothing," she recalled a former boss telling her.[9]

In the Punjab province in Pakistan women's bodies have been treated as pawns in rituals of trial and punishment. "What happens in war?" asked

Attiya Inayatullah, Pakistan's minister for women's development. "Rape is used as a tool of war. Similarly here, rape has been used as the ultimate humiliation." She was commenting on the gang rape of a 28-year-old Pakistani woman, inflicted in revenge for her supposed act of illicit sex. She had been raped by four men at the direction of the tribunal council.[10]

A 2001 U.S. State Department report cites all Macedonia neighbors— Greece, the former Yugoslavia, Romania, and Bulgaria—along with Lebanon as countries with records in trafficking in women. The report singled out places like Bosnia, Greece, Saudi Arabia, Israel, and Pakistan, but downplayed the role of such countries as Moldova, Costa Rica, and Japan. Human Rights Watch said the State Department report, "concentrates too much on trafficking for 'sexual exploitation' to the exclusion of trafficking into other forms of forced labor, among them sweatshop labor, domestic servitude, and enforced agricultural and construction work."[11]

In Costa Rica the government actually facilities the trafficking of women, according to Human Rights Watch. The Japanese government treats trafficked women as illegal immigrants or criminals, who are often placed under arrest and deported. Israel criminalizes trafficking for forced prostitution, but excludes all those who are brought there to engage in other forms of forced labor.[12]

The situation is no better in South Asia, according to a report issued by Amnesty International in 1998 highlighting the use of bonded laborers and the "trafficking of huge numbers of girls from Nepal and Bangladesh to work in the sex industry in India and Pakistan, often with the acquiescence of state officials."[13]

In Southeast Asia hundreds of thousands of girls as young as eight years old—and also boys—from Burma, China, and Cambodia, work in a sex industry aimed primarily at servicing Western and Japanese men.

A steady stream of migrating job seekers plies the route from Thailand to Japan. Because Japan has tight immigration laws, this trade operates illegally, sometimes under the auspices of the Japanese gangsters. Much of this stream is made up of Thai women who end up as forced prostitutes in Japan. Human Rights Watch relates the story of Thip, a young woman who came to Japan in 1999, supposedly to take up a job as a waitress in a restaurant. On arrival she was told she actually owed $38,500 for the cost of job placement and travel, and instead of the restaurant she was put to work in a brothel. "The customers paid 12,000 yen (approximately $100) for eight minute sessions, but Thip's share was only 2,000 yen. From this amount, Thip was expected to pay 34,000 yen a day for rent and protection money. This meant she had to serve 18 clients each day before any earnings were applied toward her debt." In fact Thai women who end up as prostitutes in Japan find their debt rising every day, supposedly representing room and board as well as protection costs.[14]

Because of the availability of young women, prostitution has become a magnet industry, with organized sex tours bringing men to the prostitutes. "Are you seeking a nymphomaniac, an expert in massage, an innocent in need of seduction, or a mature skilled loving that is considerate, gentle and very patient? Whether you want to seduce, be seduced, or just enjoy, we can help you find your desire," reads one Web come-on for "love tours" in the Philippines, Thailand, and Cambodia. "In Bangkok alone, if you went to a different erotic establishment every night including bars, nightclubs, short time hotels, bordellos, massage parlors, barber shops (that's right barber shops), beer gardens, outdoor pickup bars, strip-bars, it would probably take you over 3 years. We steer you to the best, and away from the worst." One tour advertised 12 nights in the Philippines with introductions to one or more companions for $2,195.[15]

In the worldwide sex industry men can take advantage of differing wage rates. A night in the United States will cost more than $200. In India a young girl costs $10.

Congresswoman Carolyn B. Maloney of New York City and her staff actively campaigned against the sex trade. "Americans frequently travel to foreign countries to engage in sexual activities with children, and children from foreign countries are brought back into the United States as sex slaves by Americans visiting these countries, according to *Newsweek* and AP reports respectively," she stated.[16]

THE BUYING AND selling of human beings formally ended in the West in the nineteenth century. But in certain parts of Africa, particularly Sudan and Mauritania, it thrives today. In Mauritania, a Muslim former French colony in West Africa, 100,000 black Africans are enslaved and used as property, traded to repay debt, forced to work long hours with no pay of any kind, refused the right to marry or associate with other blacks, and are used for breeding. They can be exchanged for camels, trucks, guns, or money. They are denied any education. The slave status is hereditary. Forty percent of Mauritania's 2.5 million population are either slaves or former slaves. Slaves raise their own children but are the property of their masters, who feed them and lease them out. The American Anti-Slavery Group related in a report the story of a former slave named Aichana Mint Abeid Bolil. During her time in slavery she was loaned out to her master's friends or sent to the city and put up for hire as a servant. On the marriage of the master's daughter, he gave Aichana's 12-year-old daughter as a wedding present. "In the case, where say a 60 year old man essentially buys the services of a 12 year old girl from her family, and then dies, the girl is inherited by the dead man's brother or some other family member." If they are caught trying to escape, slaves often are beaten and tortured; in one case, "his master's brother slashed his heel with a sword to prevent him from running again."[17]

Yet another slave's story was recounted by the Anti-Slavery Group: "I was raised to serve my master's every need, often without regard for my age or my abilities. I had to haul water from a well, shepherd cattle, travel with my master to care for his camel, and take care of my master's children. My only reason for being was to care for the master's family's every need."

In Mauritania, slavery has existed since the thirteenth century. Possession of slaves enhances an owner's status. Animal husbandry and agriculture there depend on slave labor.[18]

Mauritania officially banned slavery, first in 1905, then in 1961, and again in 1981. These measures were never enforced. Human Rights Watch in Africa has documented the existence of 100,000 slaves. Nonetheless the Mauritania government says slavery does not exist. And the U.S. State Department, the keeper of so many records, has been of little help. In 1994 it documented 90,000 slaves in Mauritania, but a year later the department claimed these same slaves had disappeared.

In the Sudan children are sent to camps that function as slave markets. In 1989 a person could buy a woman or child for $90. But by 1990, amidst a great flux of refugees created by war, the price fell to $15. Amnesty International reported in 1997 that in northern Uganda 8,000 children, some of them as young as 11, had been abducted and forced to become sex slaves and child soldiers. In the civil war in Sierra Leone thousands of women and children have been killed, while others have suffered crude mutilation. Girls and women have been forced into sexual slavery.[19]

In Ghana there is a practice called *trokosi* or slavery to the gods. "Yes the girls are my slaves," said one priest. "They are the property of my shrine. They are brought here as virgins to be married to the gods. So if a man from the village wants one for himself I have the power to give her to him."

Trokosi means never-ending penance. Should a woman die, her family must give the priest another girl. They can be as young as 10 years old. There are thought to be some 3,000 women in slavery in Ghana. Said one slave girl: "My grandfather had illegal sex with a woman; the gods punished our family. I was the virgin daughter, so I was brought to this village and given to the priest to stop the disasters happening." Human rights attacks on trokosi are seen as attacks on African culture.[20]

In this region, where one-quarter of the world's children live, armed bands have captured, tortured, and forced children to fight as soldiers.

The Canadian police in 2000 began an investigation into charges that international diplomats were bringing children into Canada, claiming them as their own, to be used as menial servants at embassies in Ottawa. In some cases the children suffered sexual assault.[21]

IN MARCH 2002 a federal judge sentenced a Silver Spring, Maryland, couple to 9 years in prison and fined them $105,306 in lost wages for the enslavement of a teenager from the Cameroon. The teenager said the couple brought her to the United States from Cameroon in December 1996. She was expected to work as a domestic while attending high school, but as it turned out, as the *Washington Post* reported, "she worked round the clock, cleaning, cooking and caring for the couple's three young children." After three years of this the young woman ran away.[22]

In Afghanistan opium farmers in the north displaced by the closing of opium fields have negotiated with operators to carry them through Afghanistan and into northern Iran at high prices. Because these desperate men cannot afford the price, they pawn their women to the truck drivers for use as wives and sex slaves until they are able to raise the money to pay off the debt. In March 2002, in the aftermath of major combat against the Taliban in Afghanistan, the *New York Times* reported children were traded for bags of wheat. In one instance a father sold two of his boys to a restaurant owner with the promise that they be well fed. He received $5 a month for the boys over 2 years, after which the buyer would obtain complete ownership. "It is cheaper to buy boys than hire boys," one buyer said. One Afghan father ran across the son he sold in a street. "I felt bad that I was sold," the boy said, adding, "I cried. Sometimes I still cry. I cry at night. But I understand why the selling of me was necessary."[23]

In Iran, where the right-wing Muslim clergy enforces rules against women, they themselves take women into virtual servitude as "temporary wives" used in rotation for sex and breeding. When they are finished with the women, the holy men cast them and their children aside to go on to another. In the Persian Gulf nations of Qatar and United Arab Emirates, sheiks made wealthy from oil purchase little boys from Bangladesh, India, and Pakistan to become "camel jockeys." Racing camels is a popular sport. The boys are lashed atop the camels with Velcro straps and scream in fright as the camels race, supposedly making the animals go faster. It is not unusual for a child to slip under the camel, where he eventually is seriously hurt or dragged to death. Boys who do not please their owners are taken into the desert and left to die.[24]

THE SEX TRADE is particularly virulent on the subcontinent. About 3 million girls and women are trafficked for prostitution and cheap labor every year, according to a UNICEF report of 2000. The greatest global trade in human beings today is in girls from 7 to 15 years old for prostitution. This is an intricate business. A procurer will go to a village in Africa or Asia and purchase a girl for $30 to $50. He takes her across the border to a neighboring state; for example, a girl purchased in Nepal will be taken to India. There the first procurer sells her to a second trader for $80 to $90. This procurer locks her up or may give her training to become a prostitute before transporting her to one of the "boomtown" markets like Bombay, where he sells the girl to the madam of a brothel. The girl is put to work, servicing anywhere from 10 to 25 men a day at prices as low as $1.50 for half an hour to 45 minutes. The same girl might bring in $800 to $5,000 in New York City, which might seem high at first, but, because this is an underage girl, her pimp must employ a web of protection around his prize catch, and bodyguards, lookouts, and corrupt policemen must all be paid off.[25]

For her first five years in India she gets nothing for this servitude save for room and board. In the second five years she receives half of what she makes. During her stay in the brothel the girl may become pregnant, which the madam encourages because having a baby will keep the girl working for her. If the young prostitute has a girl, then that child grows up to be a prostitute. If it's a boy, sooner or later he is forced out into the street, joining one or another of the street gangs. Girls continually work to pay off their purchase price. But since they do not know what that was, they cannot tell when to stop working.

By the time the young prostitute from the village has spent ten years in the brothel, she is in all likelihood stricken with disease, often with AIDS. Her body is run down, and men are no longer interested in hiring her services.

She then becomes what amounts to a slave to the other prostitutes, cleaning the brothel and doing household chores. Then she dies.

Ruchira Rupta, a UN employee who has worked as a journalist and film-maker tracking slavery of women in India, said there are at least 100,000 Nepalese women working as prostitutes there.

The sex trade exists around the world, but it is concentrated around a relatively small number of "boomtowns" where the girls are sold. These big cities include: San Francisco and New York in the United States; London, Paris, Amsterdam, Prague, and Zurich in Europe; Bombay, Bangkok, Manila, and Kuala Lumpur in Asia; Johannesburg in South Africa; and Tel Aviv in the Middle East. These markets are supplied by various regions. Girls bought in Burma, Thailand, and Cambodia are sold in Bangkok, Manila, and Kuala Lumpur. Here many of the clients are Australian and Japanese businessmen. Girls from Bangladesh and Nepal also go to these cities. Western Asian establishments and those in the old Near and Middle East procure girls from Sri Lanka and Pakistan. Girls from central Asia end up in brothels in Hong Kong, Calcutta, and Bombay. Nepalese girls often are sold in New York; Indian girls in San Francisco. Balkan girls are traded in Albania and Italy before being shipped to markets in Europe. Girls from Costa Rica are sent to the United States. The sex markets often thrive around military bases. In South Korea, for example, there is considerable trafficking in Russian and Latin American women at military bases along the DMZ.[26]

The market in children, of course, is not confined to the sex trade. Young girls and women are also enslaved as domestic servants. Others are put to work in sweatshops and employed in contract labor. Many end up in the entertainment business (pornography); others are sold for adoption; and still more are forced to become child soldiers. One gang of kidnappers bought children from poor Pakistani parents or stole them from hospitals where they had been abandoned by their parents, transported them to Malta, and resold them at a profit.

The United Nations reported that western Europe has an estimated 500,000 women from other nations who have been brought in for prostitution or human slavery. And there are other ways slavery works in the West. In the United States, for example, professional staff of such international organizations as the International Monetary Fund, World Bank, and United Nations are permitted under the immigration laws to bring home with them personal domestic servants, maids, and nannies. In several different legal actions in Washington, these servants have argued they are serving in virtual slavery. Their passports are taken away, and they are made to work long hours, and, in some cases, labor in the employer's second business for no money.[27]

BODY PARTS ▶ In a sense the wealthy have always possessed the bodies of the poor by controlling their labor in various ways. Over the last few centuries this relationship has become global in scope, as the wealthier nations exploit the labor of poorer countries. Only recently, however, have advances in medical science turned human body parts literally into commodities. Today a booming if unorthodox international business exists in human kidneys, eyes, skin, and much more. And the flow of these human commodities follows the usual pattern—from the poor to the rich, from the third world to the first world.

This commodification begins with the smallest unit of human biology—the cell.

In July 2000 the U.S. House of Representatives banned human cloning even for research. (Almost immediately three scientists announced they intended to push on with cloning experiments—despite warnings from numerous scientists that these experiments would lead to the birth of babies that would quickly die or be deformed.)[28]

While politicians found it relatively easy to agree on cloning, they engaged in prolonged debate on the related issue of the use of stem cells for medical research. Stem cells are highly mutable cells obtained from embryos as young as a few days old. These cells can divide over indefinite periods of time, evolving into liver, muscle, blood, and other specialized organ cells. Embryo cells are especially valued by researchers, and embryos set to be trashed by fertility and abortion clinics can be used. Under the law cells must be derived by privately funded scientists, who can then pass them on to federally funded colleagues. The debate over what to do was protracted and emotional. Christopher Reeve, actor and quadriplegic, argued for the research: "You don't really have an ethical problem because you are actually saving lives by using cells that are going to the garbage," he told CNN. "I just don't see how that's immoral or unethical. I really don't."

The pro-life movement was vociferously opposed. They could look to Pope John Paul II who opposed the research. The Pope warned of "a tragic coarsening of consciences" that starts with abortion and goes on to an "acquiescence in related evils such as euthanasia, infanticide, and, most recently, proposals for the creation for research purposes of human embryos."[29]

After considering the matter for several weeks President George W. Bush sought to carve out a middle ground, allowing the continued use of existing stem cell lines. The National Institutes of Health sponsored $19 million in fetal-cell research and is in charge of the current rules. What was largely ignored in these public morality debates were any questions regarding the private companies that are spearheading the research and stand to profit from it. They have created the worldwide market for stem cells, permitting some research to go forward, whilst banning other research. In the end the stem-cell research understandably would almost surely continue in other nations even if the United States banned it, and it would be sponsored by the same international pharmaceutical companies that were providing financial support to American scientists. Australia currently works on stem cells from Singapore. Great Britain is gung ho. France, Germany, Japan, and Canada remain undecided.[30]

The science utilizing stem cells is closely held. Johns Hopkins University holds patents to advanced techniques for researching fetal germ cells; likewise the University of Wisconsin Research Foundation (WARF), an affiliate of the University of Wisconsin, holds patents for techniques with embryonic stem cells. The Geron Corporation, of Menlo Park, California, has licenses from both Hopkins and WARF. As of August 2001 two Hopkins medical school doctors—John D. Gearhart and Michael Joseph Shamblott—owned an undisclosed amount of stock in Geron.[31]

Frost and Sullivan, a consulting firm, reported that "the worldwide market for cell lines and tissue cultures brought in nearly $428 million in corporate revenues in 1996," and could be expected to grow steadily over time. Federal law prohibits the sale of fetal tissue, but clinics can charge reasonable fees for gathering and ferrying it to researchers.

Stem cells occupy but a niche in the big new market in human organs. By 2003 websites carried advertisements from people wanting to sell their kidneys. Numerous individuals scour foreign markets for various types of organs. In Pakistan and the Philippines kidneys could be easily purchased, and implants can be legally purchased and installed in modern offices.

With about 50,000 Americans waiting for kidneys, Richard Epstein, a law professor at the University of Chicago, told the Canadian National Post in 2001 that little can be done to prevent the trade. "When you have willing buyers and sellers, they will always find a way to get together," he said. "The key is to institutionalize the arrangement to prevent abuse from occurring."[32]

Selling body organs is illegal in the United States and roundly condemned by the World Health Organization and the International Transplant Society.

The National Organ Transplant Act calls for a maximum $50,000 fine and five years in prison if a person is convicted of buying or selling organs.

The trade, however, goes on. In the Philippines brokers can make $20 for every organ they procure—often from slum dwellers—for wealthy patients from Saudi Arabia, Qatar, the Persian Gulf countries, and on occasion American citizens who attempt to disguise their purchase by pretending to be Filipino. People sell their kidneys to wealthy foreigners for anywhere from $2,000 to $2,500. The business is meant to be illegal in the Philippines, but is so open that people wanting to sell their kidneys and kidney agents prowl the hospital waiting rooms. According to a June 2001 report in the *Canadian National Post*, "Some transplant surgeons will even sell foreign patients a package deal for $30,000 to $40,000, arranging everything, from the donor to a private recovery room, doctors in Manila say. One man bought an ice machine and a pig-farming operation" with the proceeds from the sale of one of his kidneys.

The director of NYU's renal transplant program at the NYU Medical Center disclosed in a *Village Voice* article by Erik Baard and Rebecca Cooney that several patients, often Chinese-American women, visited him. They had transplanted kidneys which had been removed from Chinese prisoners after they were executed. It was well known that patients in Asia almost routinely obtain organs from executed Chinese prisoners, but the NYU director's disclosure marked the first time American patients admitted to procuring such organs. According to Baard and Cooney's article, Chinese government regulations allow prisoners to be donors with the prior consent of themselves or their families, unless the body goes unclaimed. Human-rights groups point out that since prisoners are often held incommunicado, their bodies do remain unclaimed.[33]

"Several patients were very up-front and candid about it, that they bought an organ taken from an executed convict for about $10,000," the NYU director told the *Voice*. "Most of the patients are ecstatic to be off of dialysis, and none has seemed particularly perturbed regarding the source of the organs." An FBI sting operation in New York, which failed when a crucial witness fled the country, nonetheless revealed that patients could obtain kidneys and corneas in China, and that organs were advertised by a man describing himself as an organs "broker" in a Chinese-language newspaper published in the United States.[34]

The Chinese execute more prisoners than all other countries combined—over 1,200 in 2001, according to Amnesty International, which cited 1999 figures gathered from Chinese government sources. (The *New York Times* on 28 December 2001 reported the volume of executions in that year was "estimated at 5,000 to 10,000 by people who study the subject.") The Chinese judicial system leads the world in executions for such crimes as stealing money and drug trafficking. The money spent by patients to get organs goes to those who handle the bodies. Judges receive remuneration for alerting hospitals when a likely donor is sentenced to death. One Chinese man from Columbia University's Human Rights Center testified to Congress in 1998 that when he was on death row, a guard told him that organ removal is frequently the means of execution. "There are almost no exceptions," the man told Congress. "They first are given anesthesia. Just the same as killing a pig. . . . We use cloth to wrap them up and bring them to the execution ground. No one cares if they are alive or dead." Observers claim that prisoners are shot in the head when a liver is wanted and in the chest for a cornea. Apparently healthy prisoners undergo blood tests and medical exams to determine which patients they might be partnered with. The executions then are scheduled to accommodate the arriving patients. Because of international criticism of their numerous public executions, Chinese officials claimed they were switching to lethal injection as a more humane means of killing criminals. But the switch may also have been made with organ harvesting in mind. Drugs would not damage vital organs wanted in transplants, and an execution schedule allows for more control over the organ-removal process than trying to rip a person's liver out in the back of an ambulance on the way from the execution grounds.[35]

One Chinese doctor applying for political asylum in the United States testified before a Congressional committee in 2001 that he removed the skin for transplant from about 100 executed prisoners. The doctor said that he began slicing skin right after the execution. In one case in 1995 the doctor said a man who was shot did not immediately die, whereupon surgeons harvested his kidneys while his heart was still beating. Organs from executed prisoners are doled out according to a pecking order, with top military, government officials, and foreigners who pay $15,000 getting first pick, followed by the general public.[36]

In Great Britain a scandal erupted at hospitals in Liverpool and Birmingham in 1999 when it was revealed that they had been storing body parts of children in their basements. The hospitals admitted regularly giving drug companies body parts from living children in return for financial donations.[37]

The body-organ business had its modern origin in South Africa, where Dr. Chris Barnard made the first heart transplant. While no one accuses Barnard of being a racist, "race was always at issue in South Africa's organ transplant program and it continues to haunt the practices of transplant surgery to this today," writes Nancy Scheper-Hughes, a University of California, Berkeley, anthropology professor who has studied the business and created Organs Watch, a field-based medical human rights and documentation project funded by the University of California and the Soros Foundation to track the industry. "During the heyday of apartheid, transplant surgeons were not obligated by law to solicit family consent before harvesting organs (and tissue) from cadaver donors."[38]

Scheper-Hughes explains that there is no lack of poor people in the world anxious to sell their organs; the real obstacle lies in finding enough wealthy and well-insured patients who are willing to travel to buy. Religious practice sometimes helps to establish trade routes. In the Middle East fundamentalist Islamic and Orthodox Jewish reservations about tampering with the body lead patients in the Persian Gulf and Israel abroad—to Iran and Iraq, India (a poorer option), the Philippines, and the United States. Israelis go to eastern Europe, Russia, and the United States. There is even a secondary market in organs, with first-world doctors—from the United States in particular—dumping such things as old or dated and poor quality corneas in parts of Latin America. Growth hormones in the United States are said to come from pituitary glands of dead poor people: one doctor in Recife was prosecuted for selling inner ear parts from pauper cadavers to NASA for space research. Heart valves were procured from a police mortuary in South Africa to go to medical centers in Germany and Austria.[39]

The business has led to the kind of body-organ brokers that strive to bring buyer and seller together. This can be Internet-based, as in the United States, or in other countries people who call themselves "International Transplant Coordinators" simply set up businesses. They solicit organs from people in debt or in need, poor people, prisoners, and the jobless waiting in employment lines, for example. "Don't think of me as an outlaw," one told Organs Watch. "Think of me as a new version of the old-fashioned marriage broker. I locate and match up people in need; people whose suffering can be alleviated on either side."[40]

Another booming aspect of the business is to be found in the merchandizing of human eggs and sperm. The exchange is sometimes pictured as taking place between a hard-pressed college student and an infertile couple wanting to have a baby. Most of the women selling their eggs are between 18 and 32. The donor is first given drugs to induce production of eggs, which then are extracted from the ovary by means of a needle. The eggs are joined with the sperm of a male partner and implanted in the purchaser's uterus. In 1998 eggs of more than 5,000 donors got to the implant stage, and they produced live births in 40 percent of the cases, the *Washington Post* reported. The purchasing couple usually pays for the donor's medical expenses, and provides her with short-term life insurance. Donors have been reported to receive large amounts of money, in one case $18,000. But for the most part fees range below $5,000. In the Washington area a usual price is $3,000, although in the New York metropolitan area prices sometimes reach $7,000. The cost of eggs is not all that is involved, as the infertile couple also has to spend anywhere from $8,000 to $20,000 for in-vitro fertilization.[41]

CADAVERS ▶ While many aspects of the body-parts business are illegal and raise ethical questions, little attention has been paid to the traditional and accepted business of trading cadavers and parts of cadavers for medical research. In early 2004 journalists at the *New York Times* and elsewhere published lengthy exposés on this subterranean business. The *Times* described how the director of the University of California at Los Angeles campus cadaver laboratory routinely, and apparently with the university's knowledge, transferred dead bodies and parts to over 100 research institutions and private companies. Although it is generally held to be illegal to sell dead bodies, brokers can get a "facilitator" fee for arranging the transfer. The going rate for a whole body at the time the article was written was $1,000 and up, but specialists who were looking for a good head might pay $500 in processing fees. A torso could cost $5,000, and a spine, $3,500. In 2002 a pharmaceutical company paid $4,000 for a box of fingernails and toenails. The business is not regulated, and as one medical school official said, "It is easier to bring a crate of heads into California than a crate of apples." Among other things these articles described how one crematorium operator took and sold heads, hands, spines, and knees from bodies he was supposed to burn.[42]

BLOOD ▶ Human blood is clearly a vital commodity—the fluid of life, necessary to countless medical procedures. One might expect that such a precious substance would be handled with the utmost of care, and receive a high level of attention from governing bodies on local, national, and international levels. Yet, as a practical matter, blood enters global commerce with shockingly insufficient regulation. The result is a system of trade and distribution that has often been disorganized, poorly monitored, unjust, and, at times, deadly.

Blood occupies an unusual position in the marketplace, in that it has long been viewed as both a service and as a commodity, as a gift and a money-making product. The blood supply has been caught in a tug of war between nonprofit service organizations such as the Red Cross and moneymaking pharmaceutical firms.

The advent of blood as a commodity dates from the mid-seventeenth century, with the first experiments aimed at transfusing blood, first among animals, and then from animals to humans. There were also other medical practices involving blood—for example, bloodletting as a purported cure for certain ailments, a treatment that helped kill George Washington, and probably many others. The first transfusions among humans took place in the early nineteenth century, and transfusing blood grew in popularity over time.

By the twentieth century people began collecting and distributing human blood in various ways. Londoners organized societies of donors to give blood. In the 1930s the Soviet Union formed transfusion centers and began to pay workers for their blood. During the Spanish Civil War doctors collected and stored blood before using it. As the Second World War began the British had established four large blood centers where thousands lined up to donate their blood. During the war transfusing became a mobile operation, with doctors traveling across the front, followed by refrigerated trucks loaded with blood.

In the United States in the 1930s the federal government through the Federal Trade Commission declared blood to be a commodity in interstate commerce, where the seller had to guarantee the safety of the product or be open to lawsuits. Among other things this system suddenly transformed into apparent conspiracies the innocent-seeming arrangements among doctors for swapping blood. The doctors had generally claimed the provisioning of blood was a service and that the vital fluid was distributed fairly, based on need. In some cases this probably was true—but in others, high payoffs were undoubtedly involved. With the FTC ruling, for better or worse, blood was formally turned into a commodity, and these small-scale private arrangements began to be replaced by large-scale trade operations.

Blood banking became a serious business in the 1950s. By the middle of the decade 150 blood banks existed in New York City alone, charging anywhere from nothing to $60 a unit. Blood, like oil, was an entrepreneur's dream come true—an unregulated and profitable new industry. In Kansas City, Missouri, entrepreneurs created an insurance scheme in which, for a fee, members of a family could donate blood into a bank and then withdraw it when needed. This type of scheme eventually was replaced by nonprofit community blood banks. But entrepreneurs fought for a slice of the business, challenging the blood bank monopolies. Blood was traded in interstate commerce just like a barrel of oil or a rod of steel.

The actual blood industry has come to consist of complex networks involving both private companies and nonprofit organizations. Today the Red Cross, a government-sponsored nonprofit organization, collects about half the whole blood collected in America. It collects blood from donors and transfers it to the hospitals, which repay the costs involved by passing them on to the patients.

Whole blood is made up of several different parts, some more valuable in the commercial marketplace than others. Plasma is the liquid part of the blood—a clear, amber-looking fluid containing red blood cells. White blood cells defend the body against infections and other foreign agents, and platelets are involved in blood clotting. Whole blood can only be stored for transfusions for about three weeks, while separated plasma can be frozen and stored indefinitely.

Gathering plasma and making it into various products is generally a commercial business, dominated by four firms: Cutter Laboratories, owned by Bayer A.G.; Alpha Therapeutic, owned by the Japanese; Armour, owned by Rhone-Pulenc; and Hyland, owned by Baxter TraAmerican. These companies trade on an international level.

One reason blood became an attractive business was because of the extremely low costs involved. By drawing blood from the poor in the city slums or around military bases, and later in prisons, the blood entrepreneurs could buy the product for almost nothing from desperate people who had virtually nothing else to sell, then jack up the price many times over for the mainstream market. Blood collection became "part of the weary landscape of America's skid rows, with winos and drug addicts lingering outside and shady practitioners within," writes Douglas Starr. While nationwide little blood came from these sources, they were the heart of the business in big cities like New York. With blood from the slums came the dangers of infection from hepatitis and malaria. By the mid-1960s only seven states licensed blood banks.[43]

The invention of processes for separating and storing plasma was a boon to the business. Large pharmaceutical companies got involved, and wildcatting blood prospectors went searching for blood among the poor in villages and cities from Nicaragua to Haiti. Some entrepreneurs captured blood from dead people and sold it on the market. Infected blood became a large enough problem to attract national attention. In 1972 President Nixon asked for an investigation into the blood business. The FDA took control, and the industry was encouraged to set up voluntary standards.

Nevertheless the trade in third world blood grew through the 1970s, with the United States occupying center stage. During the 1980s blood businessmen took advantage of lax U.S. regulation and a growing demand for blood to buy blood cheap from a captive population in state prisons, then sell it across the world. As it happened, much of this blood was tainted, infected with hepatitis and other diseases. Soon HIV was added to this list of diseases, rendering contaminated blood even more deadly. Its sale led to a rolling crisis all across the world, with hemophiliacs dying from bad blood.[44]

The state of Arkansas during the governorship of Bill Clinton in the 1980s provides an example of how easy it was to obtain and sell blood in the United States, and how blood trade originating here could infect people around the world. In the early 1980s the Clinton administration awarded a contract for prison medical services to Health Management Associates (HMA), a company set up by Francis Henderson, an Arkansas doctor. Later, Leonard Dunn, a friend of Clinton's and a campaign fundraiser, became its chief executive officer.

Until then the Arkansas prisons, as well as prisons in other southern states, had been making a profit selling inmate blood. But in 1982 a glutted blood market crashed, threatening the program. "I called all over the world," Henderson subsequently told state police investigators, "and finally got one group in Canada who would take the contract." The group was Continental Pharma Cryosan, Limited, a Canadian company notorious in the blood trade for such practices as importing blood from Russian cadavers and relabeling it as Swedish. Cryosan never checked out the plasma-collecting centers in the United States from which it obtained blood, depending instead on the licensing procedures of the Food and Drug Administration—which in turn were quite lax.[45]

Little was known about AIDS during this period, and Cryosan president Thomas Hecht said there was a "strong feeling" that prison plasma was safer than that taken from the population at large—though he does not explain his reasons for this unlikely conclusion. Here is how one former inmate, appearing on the Canadian television program *The Fifth Estate*, described giving blood in prison: "Have sex in the fields on your way going to the plasma, you know, anybody in the dormitory, going to take a quick bath, run and have sex in the showers, then go to plasma. Go shoot up and go to plasma."[46]

In Canada the tainted blood was turned into clotting factor and sold to the Red Cross. When in 1983 Canadian officials discovered the source of the blood, they canceled the contracts. An international recall followed—blood from Arkansas had gone to Europe and Japan, and in at least one instance was sent back to the United States—but it was too late. By then most of the blood that had been sent to Canada had been used by hemophiliacs.[47]

The recall did not stop HMA's prison blood business, which continued until 1994. According to one prison subcontractor, officials knew that hepatitis was rife in the 1970s, and by 1980 were concerned about a "killer" hepatitis strain, which became known as hepatitis C. In 1985 there were press reports about AIDS in the prisons. That same year a group of inmates filed suit in federal district court to require AIDS testing.[48]

In 1986 Governor Clinton called for an investigation of HMA after it was accused of negligent care. The investigation eventually cleared HMA of criminal wrongdoing, but a second inquiry, by an independent California firm, concluded that HMA had violated its contract in forty areas, and put much of the responsibility for its poor performance on state prisons chief Art Lockhart. Asked by reporters whether Lockhart should resign, Clinton said, "No. I do not think that at this time I should ask Mr. Lockhart to resign." The contract was renewed.[49]

EXCREMENT ▶ Human manure has played a role as a fertilizer for centuries, and continues to do so today. Traditionally, small farmers collected human feces—more pleasingly referred to as "night soil"—from the outhouses of their own families and communities, and used it to enrich the soil on their farming plots. The commodification of excrement parallels the transformation of the agricultural business, along with the growth of cities and the resultant need to dispose efficiently of large concentrated quantities of human waste.

Our modern system of sanitation traces back to the early days of the Industrial Revolution in Great Britain, when thousands of laborers were crowded into cities and large towns to work in the new factories. Their living conditions were abominable and led to a high death rate. The Utilitarians, anxious to find a more efficient and useful way to increase the productivity of the laboring poor, undertook an inquiry into the sanitary conditions. Led by Sir Edwin Chadwick, a Benthamite, a group conducted an inquiry across the country and on the European continent as well. The review led to the concept that still governs sanitation—namely, that instead of dumping foul wastes in back alleys and courtyards where it contributed to pestilence, towns and cities should be encouraged to collect sewage and drain it into running bodies of water, where it could dissolve and be naturally transported away. But Chadwick wanted to go much further. Instead of simply washing it away, he wanted to collect human waste and use it as manure to fertilize crops. An unexpected development in the sanitation program in the city of Edinburgh provided him with an idea of what might be done:

A practical example of the money value which lies in the refuse of a town, when removed in the cheapest manner and applied in the form best adapted to production viz, by a system of cleansing by water, is afforded in connection with the city of Edinburgh. It appears that the contents of a large proportion of the sinks, drains and privies of that city are conveyed in covered sewers to the eastern suburb of the town, where they are emptied into a stream called the Foul Burn, which passes ultimately to the sea. The stream is thus made into a large uncovered sewer or drain. Several years ago some of the occupiers of the land in the immediate vicinity of this stream diverted parts of it, and collected the soil which it contained in tanks for use as manure. After this practice had been adopted for a long period, the farmers in the vicinity gradually found that the most beneficial mode of applying the manure was in liquid form, and they conducted the stream over their meadows by irrigation. Others, perceiving the extraordinary fertility thus obtained, followed the example and by degrees about 300 acres of meadow, chiefly in the eastern parts of the city, but all in its immediate vicinity, and greater part of it in the neighborhood of the palace of Holyrood, have been systematically irrigated with the contents of this common sewer. From some of this land so irrigated, four or five crops a year have been obtained; land once worth from 40s to 50 sh per acre now lets for very high sums.[50]

In the modern era the industrial nations of the West have largely turned away from the practice of using night soil, but it remains a staple fertilizer in parts of eastern Asia and the western Pacific. In Asia aquaculture ponds have been fertilized with both human and animal wastes for centuries. According to one estimate, at least two-thirds of all farm fish in the world come from ponds so fertilized, with China producing the bulk of those fish. Fish produced in these ponds are the cheapest source of animal protein available.

In China night soil has historically been used to fertilize crops as well as to feed fish, although in recent years the introduction of chemical fertilizers, along with a change in collection systems, has contributed to a decline in the practice. With fertilizer prices rising, however, and water for irrigation growing scarcer, night soil is regaining its competitive position. According to one estimate, about 164 million tons of night soil are produced in China (equal to 4 million tons of commercial fertilizer). Only one-third of this is utilized. Currently night soil is mixed with garbage and straw and sold to farmers. In addition there are some experiments in producing methane from human manure.

In December 2000 Beijing called a halt to the historic ritual of collecting night soil in the capital. From the beginning of the twentieth century numerous desperate people coming into Beijing from the suburbs collected night soil as a first job. In the heyday of communist China night soil collectors were celebrated as model workers, and the late chairman Mao Ze-dong went out of his way to make friends with a couple of them. A statue of one collector was erected near Tiananmen Square. This by no means signals the end of China's use of night soil, however, for now little green trucks race about the city sucking up sewage from septic tanks fed by hotels and residential dwellings. The trucks haul the sewage to the suburbs, where it is spread on cabbage patches. Xinhua news service observed that the collecting of night soil by hand "is now in disharmony with Beijing's modern image."[51]

Night soil is used by countries outside Asia, as well. For example Australia and Germany use wastewater in agriculture, along with India, Mexico, and Tunisia. Human excrement is employed in China, Guatemala, India, and the United States. India and Indonesia employ both wastewater and excrement in aquaculture.

In Kano, northern Nigeria's commercial center, there is a well-defined market for human excrement. The contents of the city's numerous pit toilets are shoveled into drums that are taken by pickup trucks to the outskirts where they are dumped out. During the night dealers come to claim these prized goods. "We collect the excrement here for sale," Isa Idi, one of the excrement merchants told the BBC. "When we collect it, we sell it for money and we collect the money. We sell a measure for between 50 and 60 naira (about 50–60 cents) and collect the money," he explained. The traders transport the excrement by donkeys out into the countryside, where farmers in villages buy it for use as fertilizer. Poor farmers use human waste because they cannot afford chemical fertilizers. And some of them prefer it. "You can see that farm there, they applied it on the farm, but they did not apply it on this one." one farmer explained to the BBC reporter. "You can see that that farm is more productive than this one here; the crops there are growing better. This is how we judge its effectiveness." Nigerian environmentalists argue using human excrement is counterproductive, since it may cause disease, including dysentery.[52]

In the United States for a time a train hauled New York sludge and industrial waste to the small town of Sierra Blanca, Texas, where it was spread on the desert. But because of the high cost, New York in 2001 instead began sending sludge to New Jersey and Pennsylvania. Lancaster County, Pennsylvania, has received 225 tons of New York sewage sludge every day at a private composting plant.

HAIR ▶ Human hair is a valued commodity in international trade, and a growth industry. The hair market is divided into two basic sections. One is the market for replacing hair lost to a natural process of balding, or to illness or cancer treatments. This is an older, more-traditional business, which grows in accordance with population growth or because of trends and changes in medical therapies. At the beginning of this century a market for hair as a fashion accessory opened up. Growing numbers of consumers have begun to think of an extension or "ready to wear" hairpiece as a new option in beauty and fashion, in a category with hairstyling and coloring or clothing accessories.

According to one estimate nearly 30 percent of the entire hair market is now taken up in supplying hair for fashion accessories. That market is worth $400 million per year, and is hotly competitive, with no firm occupying more than 10 or 12 percent of the market. "Three years ago, the idea of selling hair to a teenager, or a 20 or 30 year old, was an unheard of thing," a hair industry executive said in 2001. "Today, we sell more than 100,000 little hair accessories every month; things like ponytail wraps and other small items made of hair, to 13-year-old, 23-year-old, and 33-year-old people who would never have thought of wearing a wig, but are now wearing alternative hair as a fashion accessory." Hair extensions, strands of hair woven semi-permanently into existing hair, represent another rapidly growing market for human hair.[53]

Italy has traditionally been thought of as the central source for high-quality hair. In recent years, however, "harvesters" have turned to scouring small Russian villages for women and girls anxious to make a little extra money by selling their hair. This hair is often sent to Italy and processed and sold as European hair. Most hair from India and China, two other major sources, is processed in Korea, where it is run through acid baths to clean it and remove the cuticle, the rough outermost layer. It may then be colored, and silicon is applied to make it shiny. Then the hair is made into toupees, wigs, "add-on" pieces, or hair extensions. A major source for extensions, which require long strands, is something called the "temple" market in India. Before marrying, some traditional Indian women go to the temple and sacrifice their beauty, in the form of their long flowing hair. This hair is later sold at auction. The Sri Venkateswara temple has become the richest temple in India due to its hair sales. Women come to the temple to have their heads shaved in order to make a sacrifice. Some 25,000 heads are shaved every day. The hair is bundled up and brokered through middlemen to hair factories. Workers in these factories, some as young as 11, sort and clean the hair. They get as little as a dollar a day for a ten-hour shift. The hair brokers, on the other hand, are in a profitable enterprise worth $50 million a year. Strands of hair from such factories sell for anywhere from $10 to $100.[54]

The United States imports a considerable quantity of human hair—1.6 million pounds between January and October 1999, according to the *New York Times*. Most of the hair enters the country at Los Angeles and is marketed by Koreans who have displaced established merchants. Most of the New York hair enterprises obtain their hair from China and Indonesia. In China thousands of buyers scour the countryside collecting hair in bags and sell it to a market in southern China for 20 cents a kilogram. There the hair is turned into weaves and various other hair pieces.[55]

There are three basic types of human hair on the market, with prices to match. At the bottom of the price range is "regular Indian or Chinese human hair, chemically treated and colored to match a sample of the buyer's hair," priced in 2001 at $499 per unit. (Certain hair dealers claim this hair is often taken from dead bodies, although there is no proof of this.) Second is Bohyme Remy Human Hair, a kind of Indian hair that has been treated to look like European hair. This hair is supposed to be soft and have a smooth, fine feel to it so that it can blend with a person's own hair. It is considered to be a good, middle-of-the-road hair product, and sells for $649 per unit. The ultimate in hair is true Russian European hair—fine European hair, untreated, the best in the world—$999 per unit.

The Sky

Americans have always been bent upon exploring new frontiers. Fueled by Manifest Destiny, they pushed westward in the nineteenth century with the secure belief—until quite recently, seldom questioned—that land and resources were there only to be settled and exploited. During the twentieth century they pushed their frontiers abroad, initially to create global markets for surplus farm products, and eventually to freely access the world's petroleum and other resources and to make markets for goods and services. At mid-century, with the Soviet Union's launch of Sputnik and the advent of President Kennedy's ambitious space program, Americans began to view space as a new frontier—in the popular phrase, indeed, the final frontier. But the highly publicized space missions are just a minute part of the process which, over the last 50 years, has led to the industrialization and commodification of our skies—of the air we breathe. Together air and water are the ultimate commodities.

The steady increase in space exploration is dwarfed by the exponential growth in everyday air travel, as airplanes have grown larger, faster, and far more numerous. Farther from the earth's surface, the skies are filled with an ever-increasing number of communications satellites for military and civilian use. And most of all, our atmosphere has been slowly turned into a huge waste dump for all kinds of refuse from the industrial age.

What we call the sky or the atmosphere is an intricately layered protective blanket that wraps around the earth. It stretches up from the ground about 400 miles and, together with electrical and magnetic forces, protects us from the frigid vacuum of space and the sizzling rays of the sun. It supports life on earth, providing the environment for biological activity and influencing ocean and lake environments. It absorbs the sun's energy, recycles water and chemicals, and shelters us from radiation and the forces of space.

There are four distinct layers of the earth's atmosphere. The troposphere goes up from 5 to 9 miles from the ground. The higher one goes, the colder it gets, reaching $-52°$ C. Above the troposphere there is a tropopause of ozone. This region also reaches into the stratosphere which extends up to around 30 miles, followed by the mesosphere, reaching 50 miles. Finally comes the thermosphere, reaching up 300 miles above the earth.[1]

These endless wastes of atmosphere have come to be seen as a dump for trash from the earth—a sink which only grows in size as our technological capabilities enable us to reach into more and more distant layers. The skies have been viewed just as waterways were in the industrial era. Then, the tried and true method for getting rid of wastes was to dump them in a fast-flowing stream or river, where it was assumed—incorrectly as it turned out—that wastes would be diluted and rendered harmless. All the dilution theory accomplished was to postpone the need to confront the effects of this waste until water pollution became impossible to ignore—and to turn what rightly should have been a problem of private industries into a public controversy.

The same thinking has been applied to the skies, with, inevitably, the same result. For much of the industrial age, the practice of spewing wastes into the air was never even questioned; not only was the sky apparently limitless, but it was no one's property, and therefore no one's responsibility. Looked at this way, industry staked out the sky and, under the rubric of exploration, persuaded the public to pay the price for using it as a dump. Piercing the ozone layer of the sky promised to exact the terrible price of threatening the atmosphere and life itself on earth. From an industrial point of view, the sky is a bonanza for business since there are no national laws to worry about. There is no sovereignty, and any regulation depends on complex international treaties. In the case of greenhouse gases, the United States, for one, tends to ignore the agreements and proceeds to make use of the atmosphere at its own pace and for its own interests.

The gaseous wastes that are the byproducts of numerous industries and, most ubiquitously, the burning of fossil fuels are expensive and complicated to treat; it is simpler and cheaper just to release them, untreated, into the air. Today we face numerous examples of the dangers wrought by this approach. Acid rain is a proven example of the consequences that result from using the atmosphere as a waste sink. Acid rain in the United States is caused by sulfur emissions from Midwestern coal-fired power plants. When the coal is burned to create electricity, it emits bits of sulfur into the air. These float eastward on the air currents, turning into sulfuric acid as they mix with water vapor and falling as rain in the Northeast and eastern Canada—a rain that effectively kills forests and lakes.

Acid rain illustrates another aspect of the industrial sky: it knows no national boundaries. In the sky the fact that our modern concept of sovereignty can have little meaning confounds regulatory efforts. It is difficult enough to regulate air pollution within more or less known boundaries in the United States, but attempting to place rules in an atmosphere that crosses national boundaries is especially difficult.

Other pollutants do not yield such dramatic visible results as the specter of dead trees and poisoned fish, but they are no less dangerous. Many scientists believe so-called greenhouse gases are a dire threat to the planet and to human health. In the United States, according to the EPA, each person emits 6.6 tons of greenhouse gases every year—more per capita than any other country. And these emissions have grown 3.4 percent between 1990 and 1997. About 82 percent are carbon dioxide from burning fossil fuels to generate electricity and to power motor vehicles. The rest are in the form of methane deriving from several different sources: wastes from landfills, livestock, natural gas pipelines, coal, and industrial chemicals.[2]

Carbon dioxide is in fact the largest waste product of the industrial world's economy. In the past there was not enough carbon dioxide in the air to throw the atmosphere out of balance. But more and more cars, along with heavy reliance on carbon-bearing coal to create electricity, have led to critical mass.

The poisonous greenhouse gases pile up at the top of the atmosphere all along the layer of ozone that separates the troposphere and stratosphere. Ozone shields us from the fierce rays of the sun. If the ozone layer is punctured or otherwise harmed, life on earth is threatened. Tearing the ozone layer, making holes in it, creates the so-called greenhouse effect, warming the earth, and little by little changing its weather: Winter starts later and is shorter in duration. The earth warms, and icebergs around the North and South Poles begin to melt. The oceans and seas of the earth gradually rise, washing over barrier reefs and threatening low-lying coastal cities. The changing oceans are death to the coral reefs, where a multitude of species spawn. Low-lying islands in the Pacific sink slowly into the sea. Already such trends have had deadly effects. Over the last 30 years, Bangladesh has lost 600,000 people to cyclones and other storms.[3]

Changing climate patterns that affect the already strained supply of fresh water may lead to more massive dislocations of the world's populations than we have ever experienced before. By one estimate, 25 million environmental refugees are afoot in the world already. By 2010 their numbers are expected to double. At highest risk are people in sub-Saharan Africa, the Indian sub-continent, China, and Mexico and Central America. For example, changes in the patterns of Indian monsoons, which provide 70 percent of the rainfall on the subcontinent, could dislocate 1.1 million people. An increasing number of people cutting down forests for basic fuel could even further reduce the planet's ability to absorb carbon dioxide, which would in turn accelerate the pace of warming. This might lead to outbreaks of new diseases.[4]

The industrialization and contamination of our skies can also largely be attributed to the dramatic increase in air traffic, which has turned the lower atmosphere into something like an interstate roadway map, crisscrossed by airline routes. An estimated 1.5 billion people annually travel by air. In the United States alone, there are about 6,000 commercial planes that make 29,000 flights a day. At 9 A.M. on September 11, 2001, there were 2,500 planes in the air over the United States. Adding in general aviation, there are 200,000 flights through U.S. skies. And this does not include warplanes and missiles. In the future there is the prospect of more and more space travel and tourism, a phenomenon inaugurated at the start of this century with two wealthy businessmen each paying the Russians $20 million for their respective trips into space. Promoters are anxious to set up space tours—with stops at hotels and sports stadiums—for $10,000 a shot. In 2002 U.S. airlines began offering promotional awards with names like "Space Adventures," giving customers a chance to redeem frequent flyer miles for anywhere from one "Zero Gravity" flight for 250,000 miles plus $2,005; to a flight called "One Edge of Space Award" aboard a MIG 25 Foxbat jet fighter for 275,000 miles and $8,000; and ultimately to a suborbital space flight for 10 million miles traveled.[5]

Planes burn large amounts of fuel, and their emissions are accounting for a larger and larger segment of all pollutants coming from transportation. These emissions also have a far-reaching effect on the atmosphere and climate. Aircraft engines spew out water vapor, carbon dioxide, small amounts of nitrogen oxides, hydrocarbons, carbon monoxide, sulfur gases, soot, and metal particles, all of which are formed by combustion of jet fuel at high temperatures. These emissions are visible as contrails, the line-shaped clouds or condensation trails composed of particles visible behind jet aircraft engines. Contrails increase the cloudiness of the atmosphere, and persistent contrails often evolve and spread into extensive cirrus cloud cover that is indistinguishable from naturally occurring cloudiness. The EPA points out that changes in cloudiness are important, because clouds help control the temperature of the earth's atmosphere. (The interiors of airplanes are often toxic as well. In December 2001 the National Research Council reported that air inside planes sometimes failed to meet existing federal health standards. Planes flying at high altitudes can import ozone into their cabins, which can be a hazard to some people. In addition there is concern that the air inside the plane cabin may be a breeding ground for infectious diseases and pesticide contamination on some international flights.)

In addition to the map of plane routes, higher up, the sky accommodates an intricate complex communications system made up of satellites. At the beginning of the twenty-first century, 2,500 satellites were stationed across the atmosphere to transmit information of one sort or another back to earth. Some satellites hovering in geosynchronous orbit are for television and audio communications. Weather satellites can track hurricanes and other major disturbances and are an aid in weather forecasting. Another group of satellites map the locations of minerals, water, and vegetation, providing aid in pinpointing mineral deposits.[6]

The military makes great use of the atmosphere to gather intelligence (as in the Afghan and Iraq wars, when satellites were used to locate caves and track enemy movements). In the future the military hopes to conduct more and more warfare by remote means using sensors to operate vehicles, planes, and weapons. "Already, autonomous sentinels on the ground, in the air and in orbit are probing the battlefield with heat detectors, radar, camera, microphones and other devices. Some can reveal decoys and pierce camouflage, darkness and bad weather," reports the *New York Times*. The idea is to integrate data from high-flying drones or satellites.[7]

There are science fiction type fears that the Pentagon will one day send up weapons that can beam death back on earth. In 2001 there was even a Space

Preservation Act introduced in Congress to prohibit the use of "psycho-tronic" devices aimed back at earth and "directed at individual persons or targeted populations for the purpose of . . . mood management, or mind control."[8]

Another group of satellites looks out into space; the best known is the Hubble Space Telescope, which can be reached via the space shuttle so that its instrumentation can be checked and changed around when needed. There are satellites for navigation that make it possible for people to figure out exactly where they are—anywhere on the globe. The Global Positioning System, a small device that connects to several satellites, allows users to triangulate—and thereby determine—their position. American and Russian networks of these satellites are spread around the earth.

There are other objects orbiting the earth in the form of orbital debris, such as nose cone shrouds, lenses, hatch covers, rocket bodies, payloads that have disintegrated or exploded, and even objects that "escape" from manned spacecraft during flight. NASA issued a warning in late January 2002 to watch out for an out-of-control satellite weighing 3.5 tons originally sent aloft in June 1992 to study ultraviolet light. Most of the disintegrating satellite burned up as it descended, but 100-pound objects could land on earth as the satellite spread debris over 625 miles.[9] Thus this use of the atmosphere, too, leaves behind large amounts of waste products. Russia, with 1,336, has more satellites spinning around space than any other nation. The United States is second. Government and business put up 878 satellites. When space probes, decayed satellites, and other debris are added up, there is a total of 9,028 such objects in space. Russia and the United States together account for three quarters of this total.[10]

In addition to serving as a communications hub, a transportation grid, and a waste heap, the sky also holds out a distant potential as an industrial base for alternative energy systems driven by the wind and the sun. Aus-tralia, for example, has set off on a project aimed at harnessing Antarctic gales for full-scale electricity production. At its Mawson Station in eastern Antarctica high towers are to be built that can absorb sustained winds up to 130 kilometers an hour and gusts up to 300 kilometers an hour. These gales are thought to be the most intense of any place on earth. Hence the Austra-lian experiment has the potential to transform wind power into a major energy source.[11]

There is the distant potential for turning the sky into a staging area for solar power. Research and development is underway on an apparatus that could beam solar energy back to earth. Such energy could replace current fossil fuels—oil, gas, and coal. This reality is some ways off, but if and when it occurs, it will change politics and economics on earth as few things in human history have.

As the various players stake out their positions, carving up the dumping ground and stationing the foundations of new industry, the sky becomes ever more valuable. What we take for granted as free and common to all becomes more and more like private property; what seemed limitless becomes a finite commodity. Peter Barnes in *Who Owns the Sky?* writes, "As happened with once common (or public) land, atmospheric property rights will be established, prices will be charged, and money will change hands— lots of money. Because of global warming, the creation of these property rights will occur soon. Then, it's off to the races. Owners of sky will collect sky rent, and that rent will flow back into the economy just as land rent now does. The battle that's looming is over who'll collect the sky rent." Barnes, seeing such developments as inevitable, proposes that "it should go to all of us equally: one citizen, one share. The mechanism for doing this should be a trust."[12]

Barnes may turn out to be unduly optimistic, since the first "property rights" of a sort already exist in the form of pollution credits, which allow electric utilities in the United States to trade rights to pollute a set amount of space back and forth. Critics contend pollution credits make regulation more difficult and that they do not abate pollution, just shift it from one part of the atmosphere to another.

The sky presents a tricky challenge in how to regulate a seemingly unregulatable international commodity and, like water, one necessary to human survival.

The Oceans

It seems natural enough to think of the oceans of the world as a commons, owned by and for the benefit of everyone. In fact these bodies of water, which cover more than 70 percent of the earth's surface, have been dominated for hundreds of years by empires with maritime interests. Today they are fast taking on the characteristics of private property, with nations vying for control, if not outright ownership, of the most valuable parts of watery areas.

The ocean is divided into four major sections: Atlantic, Pacific, Indian, and Arctic. For the most part the commercial wealth lies along the continental shelves that border the continents. These shallow waters are parceled out for fishing rights and minerals, and have recently been cut up into farms for aquaculture. Coastal tourism is a booming industry worth an estimated $161 billion in 1995. With the world running out of garbage dumps, the oceans, like the sky, are of increasing value as a free dump.

PRIVATIZING THE OCEANS is reminiscent of the enclosure movement in Great Britain that took place over three centuries and accompanied the industrialization of the British economy. Starting in the sixteenth century, rural landowners, eager to profit from the burgeoning textile industry, were permitted by the government to fence their lands for sheep, throwing off the peasants who had rented for generations and forcing them into the industrial labor force in the cities.

When it comes to the oceans, the enclosure proceeds slowly, with nation states extending their control of underwater territory out to the edge of the continental shelf. The water, all that lives in it, and the land beneath it are treated as an addition to the public domain—in the case of the United States, an important part of the public domain, for most of the nation's oil and gas deposits now lie under the water on the shelf.

American law permits the states to lease this public domain out to the three-mile limit, with the federal government administering leases beyond that to where the shelf drops into the ocean deeps. In this way to all intents and purposes the waters are privatized, as neither the state nor federal government exercise any serious control over the territory, but lease it to entities that effectively determine the amount of money paid and the uses to which it is put. Ever since oil and gas were discovered on the continental shelf after the Second World War, reformers have sought to bring the administration of these offshore lands under strict federal regulation. But these attempts generally have failed.

One little-noticed aspect of the commercialization of the oceans is the role of the military in protecting these areas. The military has its own interests in the oceans. The Pentagon sees the oceans not as a mythic commons, but as a battleground for future wars. Its interests range far beyond the outer continental shelf to include such things as trade routes and missile ranges. If anything, the war on terror has made these interests more acute than before, and the Bush administration's unilateral strike doctrine lends even more weight to the Pentagon's concerns for protecting routes and bases and, as the Middle East has proven, energy and other natural resources. All in the interests of national security.[1]

In the later stages of the cold war U.S. control over the world's main water supply routes occupied a central position in President Reagan's rollback strategy against the Soviet Union. As a practical matter, that entailed protecting routes through which oil and other vital resources were transported. Much of America's oil imports come by ship. All grain is transported by ships. The United States has often exerted a claim of national security when it comes to the access routes to and from the Panama Canal, around the Cape of Good Hope in Africa, and throughout the Persian Gulf. In recent years it has taken a greater interest in protecting the Strait of Malacca, through which Middle Eastern oil is shipped to China and Japan. To maintain military influence in these faraway places, America maintains military bases at such strategic points as Diego Garcia in the Indian Ocean and Singapore.

The United States already depends on the ocean for national security in other ways. The huge missile test range extending from Vandenberg Air Force base in California to the Kwajalein atoll catch basin in the Marshall Islands creates an umbrella over vast stretches of the Pacific Ocean that are treated as American territory for national security reasons. The Aleutian island chain extending out from Alaska, and marking the boundary of the Barents Sea with the Pacific Ocean, has been used as a military garbage dump for nerve gas and a site for underground testing of hydrogen bombs. The radioactivity from one such blast has leaked out into the Pacific.

During the cold war, a good deal of the nation's scientific knowledge of oceans was financed from Navy budgets (including such schemes as attempting to harness dolphins as soldiers by carrying explosives into Cam Ranh Bay during the Vietnam War). Rear Admiral Paul Gaffney, the former head of the Office of Naval Research at the end of the twentieth century, told the writer David Helvarg, "We spent a lot of time looking at the deep ocean because that's where the major threat was." Gaffney said, "Now with the increase in mine warfare and diesel subs, smaller quieter subs that can be obtained by Third World countries or any number of nations, you get into the shallows and it's a more complex environment. On the deep ocean bottom, on the abyssal plain, processes tend to be very gradual. The shallows change quickly. You can see differences taking place a meter apart, and to try and predict them is very difficult."[2]

What this means is more military research into maritime environments— "reefs, sea grasses, barrier islands, mangroves," stated Gaffney. "We want to understand the processes taking place in these different near-shore environments so if we're going to war somewhere, and if there is not a comprehensive oceanographic survey that's been done [of that location], we'll still be able to see what's going on there, we'll have a reliable model of what takes place in that environment. That's our goal."[3]

In addition the military eyed the oceans as the arena for a new sort of guerilla warfare. Pirates have always been a problem. But there are new threats in the form of rebels seizing tankers and transforming them into massive torpedoes just as commercial airliners were turned into missiles on

September 11. The War on Terror has made us aware of the ocean for other reasons: for example, identifying and blocking off routes being used by refugees to escape the violence in Afghanistan and elsewhere in the Middle East and South Asia. In the South Pacific Australia intercepts refugee vessels and sends them to island prison fortresses in Nauru and Papua, New Guinea.

There are other ways the oceans will affect the military. Because of climate warming the actual contours of the world are gradually but profoundly changing. During the winter of 2002 news reports said a huge block of ice split off from Antarctica, which was reckoned to be yet another sign that the polar icecaps are melting at an unexpectedly rapid rate—so fast that the famed Northwest Passage will be open to commercial shipping within a decade, creating new problems for the U.S. military. When this happens, there will not only be a boom in shipping, because the passage cuts by one-third the distance from Europe to East Asia, but commercial fishing boats will be able to get at vast schools of fish hitherto unreachable because of the ice. The world's stock of fish already has long been shown to be declining due to overharvesting. At the same time an open Northwest Passage will make accessible yet another wild frontier in the far north, with nations fighting each other over fishing boundaries—not to mention environmentalists trying to save the poles from marine pollution, and pirates skulking behind ice floes to prey on unarmed passing ships. Both Russia and Canada consider their northern sea routes as national territory, but the United States views them as international waterways. In anticipation of trouble in the Arctic the U.S. Navy organized a top-level inquiry into protecting the North Pole from unwelcome incursions. The Office of Naval Research's study points out that policing the North Pole will be difficult because there are no good communications satellites in orbit that cover it.

The area of the Arctic pack ice is diminishing at the rate of 3 to 4 percent every 10 years, according to Peter Wadhams, professor of ocean physics at the Scott Polar Research Institute at Cambridge University. Submarine data show that the Arctic ice thickness in the central Arctic and Eurasian Basin in summer has diminished by a staggering 40 percent in the past 30 years. Some scientists expect that winter ice will be gone from the Barents Sea by 2030 to 2050 and summer ice from the entire Arctic by the 2080s.[4]

If the military has been or will be a prime cause of turning oceans into past and future battlegrounds, urban development is making seacoasts more and more commercialized. Today all our major population centers border the oceans. One statistic has the average American spending ten days a year at the beach. Half the American population lives along the coasts, and two-thirds of the world's cities are also along the coasts.[5]

This leads to pollution. Most of it comes from pollution-choked rivers flowing out to sea, pesticide-laced agricultural runoff, and chemical pollutants carried by air from petrochemical works and power plants. Heavy metals such as mercury poison the ocean. This has led to an increase in algae blooms, which, because of runoff from farmlands are more and more common, spreading across the oceans, killing living things that get in their way by soaking up oxygen and suffocating marine life. The situation is particularly pronounced in the Atlantic, Adriatic, Baltic, and Black seas and the Gulf of Mexico, closing beaches and leading to fish kills.

Most of the commercial gains to be had from the oceans are centered along the coasts and are related to recreation. There the water is polluted with sewage as well as chemical runoff. In a 1999 Worldwatch Institute paper, Anne Platt McGinn states, "Activities on land, such as municipal sewage, agricultural runoff and industrial waste account for 75 percent of marine pollution and are the main cause of damage to marine habitat."[6]

More than half of America's oil production now comes from the ocean, with individual states controlling oil and gas from the shore out to 3 miles. From there to 12 miles out is part of the formal public domain, under jurisdiction of the Interior Department, which leases out tracts for oil and gas exploration, development, and production. During the 1970s most of the nations of the world agreed by treaty to a 200-mile limit. At first the United States did not sign the treaty, but eventually, during the Clinton administration, became a signatory, but the Senate has never approved it. The United States, by and large, follows the treaty, however.[7]

Oceans remain the roadways for the still extensive shipping business. Industrial shipping remains an extensive business (5 billion tons of oil, dry goods, and other cargo were carried in 1995). There are 29,000 oceangoing vessels, each holding more than 1,000 tons. The trade benefits the industrial world: 50 percent of all the cargo is loaded in industrial countries. Three-fourths of that was unloaded in industrial countries. Shipping is the single biggest pollution source in the oceans, with vessels dumping 20 million tons of oil every year, according to one estimate. Fifty percent of the total comes from tankers. As they reach port, ships pump out ballast water all along the coasts, creating a sort of biological attack with one or another of the millions of species festering in the ballast tanks set loose and killing native marine life, as jelly fish have killed fish in the Black Sea. The Asian Long Horn beetle, which was seen for the first time in North America during the late 1990s, is thought to have hitchhiked its way aboard a ship, perhaps stowed away in cargo crating. The beetle threatens to wipe out North America's maple trees.

Commercialization of the oceans creeps out into the depths. Fishing now, for example, can actually involve ploughing the ocean deeps. Ocean water can be run through desalinization plants to become drinking water, a process that is done extensively in the Persian Gulf. With the sources of clean water drying up, there even has been talk of cutting off hunks of icebergs at the North and South poles and towing them to urban centers. A more likely scheme envisions great plastic bubble barges filled with clean water from the poles plying the coasts and oceans.

The ocean may well be used for electric power production. Advocates of alternative energy have long pushed for development of technology that can successfully harness the tides and turn the ocean winds into power. There have been proposals for anchoring fossil fuel plants offshore. We know little about all the different forms of life in the ocean, and much of the ocean floor is yet to be mapped. But much life begins in the ocean. For example a group of microbes called Archaea have become important in medical research, with one enzyme being crucial to DNA. In her 1999 paper cited above, McGinn runs down a list of therapeutic compounds from marine species: a sponge that helps alleviates herpes; the shells of shrimp, lobsters, and crabs used against fungus infections; algae that attacks hookworm; corals and algae used in food modifiers; and oils of the cod, sharks, menhaden, and barnacles for treating postmenopaulsal rthjerosclerosis and as an adhesive for tooth fillings.

It is by now commonly agreed that the burning of fossil fuels over the last 150 years—since the onset of the Industrial Revolution—has slowly changed the earth's prevailing weather. As a result the sea level around the world has risen 4 to 6 inches over the last 100 years, and is expected to rise another half a foot to three feet by the year 2100. In the United States the East Coast sea level has risen approximately 12 inches in the last 100 years. Matters will only get worse: temperatures are also on the rise, expected to rise anywhere from 1.8 to 6.3 degrees Fahrenheit by 2100. This will cause oceans to expand, as glaciers and ice sheets melt at a faster rate than they have in the past.

The springboard for the U.S. economy has always been its coastal cities. And as waters rise, they face an expensive and possibly debilitating future. New York City is especially susceptible, as the December 1992 storm of the century amply demonstrated. It sent surf pounding through the seawall at Coney Island, washing away large portions of the beach, and pouring water into downtown Manhattan, inundating parts of Wall Street and the FDR drive which runs along the East Side.

The key to the future viability of coastal cities is the insurance industry—consisting of thousands of companies that issue insurance and a smaller number that reinsures the insurers. It really determines whether and where houses and factories get built. Insurance companies decide whether a homeowner, say, can build on an exposed coastline or whether a shopping mall can go into a flood plain. They also have considerable sway in determining the types of energy that are used in residential and industrial development.

From the late 1980s through the mid-1990s the industry lost tens of billions of dollars because of hurricanes, cyclones, and other natural disasters. Eight storms in Europe in 1990 cost the industry some $13 billion. Hurricane Andrew in Florida and Cyclone Iniki in Hawaii drove companies out of business. As the losses mounted, many of the syndicates that stand behind Lloyds have dropped out of the business. Reinsurance rates during the 1990s rose by 400 percent in the United States, 600 percent in Great Britain, and 1,000 percent in Japan. As rates rose large reinsurers—the companies that back up the insurance companies in Europe—began to back out of the business altogether, citing global warming as the reason. In addition those that remained began to reexamine policies that permitted insuring buildings along high-risk coastlines.[8]

Biodiversity

The trajectory toward commodification of life itself has as its source the discovery in 1953 by Watson and Crick of the structure of DNA molecules, one of the most significant moments in twentieth-century science. It was the jumping-off point for new fields of research, including the Human Genome Project, which succeeded in 2000 in mapping the billions of DNA pairs that comprise the hundreds of thousands of genes on the human chromosomes. It was also the starting point for new fields of business, culminating in the private ownership of things previously considered impossible to own: the commodification of the underlying building blocks and processes of life.

The key to this type of ownership lies not in simply understanding the genetic blueprint of a particular plant or animal, but in changing it. So-called genetic engineering gives scientists the tools to change small elements in the DNA structure of a living thing in order to create, in effect, a new living thing. This relatively new science has genetic engineers around the world busily combining genes, inserting genes across species, or even among plants, animals, and humans. And the entities for which these scientists work—governments, universities, or, most often, private corporations—are claiming proprietary rights not only over the processes of genetic manipulation, but over the newly created organisms themselves. This is clearly a phenomenon with important ethical implications but with business potential as well.[1]

As is often the case with such scientific breakthroughs, business has sped ahead to take advantage of this potential, while academic and government leaders have just begun to waffle over the ethics. The vision of human clones or genetically engineered human beings tends to give most people pause, but hundreds of other plant and animal species have had their DNA rearranged with relatively little discussion or regulation of how such processes are carried out, by whom, for what purpose, and to whose profit.

Much of the activity has been concentrated in agricultural and pharmaceutical industries, to create, for example, higher-yield or disease-resistant crops, or new and improved drugs. Beyond any of the practical benefits, there is an obvious business reason for a company to undertake such genetic engineering. A naturally occurring type of living thing cannot really be owned. While it has always been possible to own, for example, an individual corn plant, or thousands of acres of corn plants, it has not been possible to claim ownership to all corn plants of a particular variety—to the unique combination of DNA molecules that produces the unique living thing that is that plant. Genetic engineering makes such ownership possible. It introduces a proprietary element to a particular slice of life on our planet. The company that has developed a new type of corn plant may claim that plant as its own product, its own intellectual property—and thus make a case that it should be compensated in some way for every plant of this type that is grown, every ear of corn from that plant that is sold.

It is difficult, of course, to enforce intellectual property rights of this kind. A company may sell the seed or seedlings for a new genetically engineered crop—but like all plants, that crop will in turn produce its own seed. And controlling how these seeds are used would seem as hopeless an effort to protect intellectual property as controlling when a book is photocopied or when a CD is copied. But corporations are becoming amazingly resourceful at meeting such challenges, finding ways to protect their investments and ensure their profits—again, with relatively little scrutiny and virtually no regulation.

Beginning in the 1980s the biotech industry took steps to give corporations the ability to patent all biological products and processes. Through such instruments as bilateral treaties and the World Trade Organization, the United States has sought to impose its own approach on other countries.

Traditionally, patents have been the primary means of protecting intellectual property—of ensuring a company's right to profit exclusively from a new product it has created. But the very idea of applying patent laws in a new and relatively untested arena, where various corporations are slugging it out, can turn out to be more trouble than it is worth. To begin with patents are time consuming and expensive for companies to obtain, and they have only become more and more complex along with the technologies they seek to commodify—it took 400,000 pages to get a patent on one biotech product. They often need to be repeatedly defended over the years, at additional expense. If a patent is challenged in court, it can easily cost a company $1 million or more to defend its rights—and the courts are jammed with more and more legal patent disputes. A 2001 communiqué from ETC Group states:

> Twelve of every one hundred biotech patents end up in court. Forty-six percent of all U.S. biotech patents that are challenged in court are over-turned and some legal experts suggest that a still larger percentage would be rejected if they were challenged. The outcome of patent litigation can literally make or break a biotech business. CellPro Inc. lost 50 percent of its stock market value in a single day after a federal court ruled the company infringed a competitor's patent. When Visx lost a patent dispute its stock plunged 40 percent within one hour. Even the larger patent-holders are vulnerable, however. If an enterprise surfaces with a "submarine" patent, for example, it could hold competitors ransom at the point of commercialization. For the biotech industry, these uncertainties are becoming more and more unacceptable. Even if it secures and successfully defends a patent, a company must constantly be on alert for infringements of its "intellectual property." And although the time period they cover is substantial—generally twenty years—it is finite.[2]

In addition, patents have come under attack from another direction. They are a major target of both free-trade and antiglobalization groups whose arguments seem to be gaining broader public sympathy in the wake of such high-profile events as the fight over AIDS drugs for the developing world. As has been the case with these drugs, there is also the real possibility that in exigent situations, some countries may simply choose to defy the power of patents, the consequences be damned.

A specially charged issue is the fact that these patents most often end up being granted to corporations, when in fact the research and development was done by other individuals or nonprofit organizations. Many have charged that products funded by governments should be open to the public. The entire issue also has become tricky on political grounds. In Europe groups challenged the unchecked march of patent control over human life. And the United Nations formally warned against the trend. Its 1999 Human Development Report states that "the relentless march of intellectual property rights needs to be stopped and questioned." In August 2000 the UN Sub-Commission for the Protection of Human Rights recognized that the World Trade Organization's Trade-Related Intellectual Property Agreement could infringe on the rights of poor people and their access to both seeds and pharmaceuticals.[3]

In the face of such developments, companies are coming up with new ways to enforce their intellectual property rights. One challenge to companies' proprietary control of new, genetically modified crops has been the age-old agricultural practice of using seed from one season's harvest to plant the next season's crops. Two technologies, menacingly named Terminator and Traitor, have been developed to counter this practice. If a farmer tries to save seed from one season to plant the next, Terminator springs into action, setting off a chemical trigger that renders the saved seeds useless for growing new crops. The idea is to put farmers in the position of having to buy seed every year, thereby increasing the biotech firm's own profitability. And it can influence what crops are grown and how much of any crop. These technologies allow companies to go well beyond the patent limitations. Unrestricted by any exemptions, the companies' control is guaranteed the for the foreseeable future. Similar safeguards are being developed for livestock. One firm plans to breed a transgenic chicken, which the company hopes will grow faster and be disease-resistant. It can control its chickens by inserting a DNA copyright tag into the chicken's genes. In addition genetic encryption devices would prevent anyone from trying to break into, say, a type of seed and steal the formula for making it.

The U.S. government, through NASA, pioneered remote sensing techniques through satellites, and these technologies have now been been applied to private, corporate-owned satellites. This type of remote-sensing satellite allows governments, private companies, or individual farmers to monitor farm operations on different continents, and there are gadgets developed by the U.S. Department of Agriculture that sense data—temperature, whether a crop has been watered recently, and several other markers—and relay the information over a few miles or a few thousand miles. This allows a farmer to send a signal to start or stop an irrigation pump. It also opens up the possibility for corporations that run farms in different countries to not only monitor what their farms are doing, but also gather information on other crops grown by competitors, and to arrange rotation of crops and organize their crops in relation to what others are growing. It is a management and planning device that knows no national borders. Yet another technological invention takes advantage of the satellites' global positioning system (GPS) to precisely pinpoint the location of a herd of cattle or wandering sheep. A tiny electronic device implanted in an animal's ear allows the satellite to find it, and can even be used to send a jolt to the animal to make it move in another direction.

One problem is bioprospecting—the search for valuable biological compounds that can be utilized in drugs. Businesses, universities, research, indigenous communities, and national governments all have an interest here. Their desires to have the biological valuables can lead to the new crime of biopiracy—in which a company sneaks in, steals biologicals, and leaves without thinking of preserving biodiversity, let alone compensating the local community. The great spawning grounds for all kinds of life are the rain forests around the equator. The biopirates more often than not make a beeline for the equator.

A systematic plan to prevent biopiracy was still being worked out at the end of the twentieth century. It consisted of a mix of both national laws and international treaties, along with professional self-regulation. The 1993 Convention on Biological Diversity is one important part of this system. It recognizes a nation's sovereign rights to biological resources in exchange for opening the door to regulated exploitation of its genetic resources. The nation gets certain benefits, including access to biotechnology. Access to biological resources in all cases depends on "informed consent," under which the owners will be told what the resources will be used for and what benefits are to be shared. The benefits can include fees paid before operations begin, royalties, and other less-tangible things such as research and conservation support, contributions of equipment and materials, and help for local communities.

To make this work, nations began to set up regulations governing biological poaching—the gathering and export of resources without permission. If an organization or individual fails to abide by the new rules, patents can be attacked, and the wronged nation can go into a U.S. court and seek to recover lost profits. Those who do not follow the rules cannot get clear title, which reduces the value and makes difficult any future dealings.

NOTES

INTRODUCTION

1 *Making a Killing*, by the International Consortium of Investigative Journalists, Center for Public Integrity (Washington), 28 Oct. 2002, at www.publicintegrity.org.
2 Ibid.

FRESH WATER

1 Two recent, excellent reports on the earth's dire water crisis are Barlow and Clarke, *Blue Gold: The Fight to Stop the Corporate Theft of the World's Water*, 3–50, and Postel, *Last Oasis*, 27–37.
2 Ridgeway, *The Politics of Ecology*, 18.
3 World Resources Institute, *Pilot Analysis of Global Ecosystems* (Washington, Oct. 2000).
4 Sampat, *Deep Trouble*, 154. This Worldwatch paper provides a valuable detailed discussion of pollution of groundwater.
5 U.S. National Research Council, as quoted in Sampat, *Deep Trouble*, 18; Kolpin et al., "Pharmaceuticals, Hormones, and Other Organic Wastewater Contaminants in U.S. Streams, 1999–2000," 1202-11.
6 Sampat, *Deep Trouble*, 32.
7 Phillips and Project Censored, *Censored 2001*, 39–44.
8 "Water Investment Bill Wrongly Promotes Privatization of Critical Public Resource"

(Washington: Public Citizen, 28 Feb. 2002 press release). The bill was bottled up in a House committee as of spring 2004.

9   Barlow and Clarke, *Blue Gold*, 107.

10   Barlow, *Blue Gold: The Global Water Crisis and the Commodification of the World's Water Supply*, 16.

11   See ibid., Barlow, *Blue Gold*, 101, and chap. 5, and Barlow and Clarke, *Blue Gold*.

12   "Water Investment Bill," Public Citizen, 28 Feb. 2002 press release.

FUELS

1   These figures come from the U.S. Department of Energy, courtesy of Richard Bon-skowski, analyst at the Energy Information Administration (EIA). See also the administration's website at EIA.doe.gov and the World Watch Institute's *Vital Signs 2002*, 38.

2   Averitt, "Coal Resources of the United States," U.S. Geological Survey *Bulletin*, 1412 (1 Jan. 1974).

3   Bethell, "Conspiracy in Coal."

4   Ibid.

5   RWE Group Annual Reports available at www.rwe.com/en/; Barlow and Clarke, *Blue Gold*, 121.

6   Moody, *Great Leaders in Business and Politics. Part 1: The Masters of Capital*, 52. For the history and development of Standard Oil, see Tarbell, *The History of the Standard Oil Company*, esp. chap. 2.

7   Churchill, *The World Crisis, 1911–1915*, excerpted in Ridgeway, *Powering Civilization*, 20–25.

8   For a closer look at Iran and the rise of Khomeni, see Bill, *The Eagle and the Lion*; Halliday, *Iran*; Sick, *All Fall Down*; Keddie and Hooglund, *The Iranian Revolution and the Islamic Republic*; and Roosevelt, *Counter Coup*.

9   Manning, *The Asian Energy Factor*, 85, and chap. 11.

10   Ibid., 41. See also Rashid, *Taliban*, 143–83 and chaps. 11–13. For a concise rundown on oil and American security concerns, especially in the Caspian area, see Grau, "Hydro-carbons and a New Strategic Region."

11   Hall, *The Fourth World*, 194.

12   James F. Smith, "High Oil Prices Present Tough Choice to Mexico," *New York Times*, 30 Jan. 2000.

13   Deffeyes, *Hubbert's Peak*, 127.

14   For Shell's vision of the industry's future, see the letter of its Chairman of the Committee of Managing Directors, Sir Philip Watts, to stakeholders, on Shell's web-site (www.shell.com). For slightly skeptical but generally upbeat discussions of what the energy future holds see Easterbrook, *A Moment on the Earth*, 334–68, and Lom-borg, *The Skeptical Environmentalist*, 118.

15   As with oil, a reliable and detailed source of information on natural gas is available on the U.S. Department of Energy website (www.dea.gov). A good book on the prospects for synthetic gas is Welles, *The Elusive Bonanza*.

16 The saga of just how the dire scarcity of natural gas was transformed into a surplus is recounted in several different books and investigations. See Barnet, *The Lean Years*, 68–71; Ridgeway, "Out of Gas"; Sherrill, *The Oil Follies of 1970–1980*, 320–27; Weidner, "What Natural Gas Shortage?" 19. See also the U.S. Comptroller General's 1979 report to Congress, *Oil and Gas Royalty Collection* , reprint. in *Royalty Accounting System within the U.S. Geological Survey*, Oversight Hearings, Subcommittee on Mines and Mining and Oversight and Investigations Committee on Interior and Insular Affairs, U.S. House of Representatives, 23 Sept. and 6 Oct. 1981 (Serial No. 97–19), 321–354; and " 'Behind-the-Pipe' Natural Gas Reserves," 22, 23 Feb. 1977 Hearings on Allegations of the Withholding of "Behind-the-Pipe" Natural Gas Reserves, 95th Congress, 1st Session (Serial No. 95–16).

17 The story of Algeria's role in the development of LNG is based on contemporary interviews by the author with Algerian diplomats during the late 1970s. For El Paso and Algeria, see California Energy Commission, *Liquefied Natural Gas in California: History, Risks, and Siting.* Staff White Paper, 17 July 2003 (http://www.energy.ca.gov/reports/2003-07-17_700-03-005.pdf), 7.

18 EIA interview, December 2003.

19 See "Petroleum and Natural Gas Forecasts," Dept. of Energy, Energy Information Administration, *Annual Energy Outlook 2003.*

20 Wayne Arnold, "A Gas Pipeline to World Outside," *New York Times*, 26 Oct. 2001.

21 EIA interview, December 2003.

22 Keith Bradsher, "China Called Close to Deal to Import Natural Gas," *New York Times*, 22 May 2002, and "Energy Concerns Said to be near China Pipeline Pact," *New York Times*, 3 July 2002.

23 "Phillips and El Paso Plan to Deliver Australian LNG to California and Mexico in 2005," Phillips Petroleum Company news release, 8 March 2001, www.phillips66.com/newsroom/newreleases/re1319.html.

24 "The Electric Revolution," *The Economist* (U.S.), 5 August 2000.

25 James Ridgeway, "Mondo Washington" column, *The Village Voice*, 13 Feb. 2001; Peter Navarro, "Commentary: Plug Electric Cord into a Grassy Knoll," *Los Angeles Times*, 26 Jan. 2001.

26 Seth Rosenfeld, "S.F. Sues 13 Major Power Producers," *San Francisco Chronicle*, 19 Jan. 2001; Public Citizen press release, "The Facts are in: Electricity Demand in California was Lower in Four of Past Six Months than in 1999," 19 Jan. 2001. Public Citizen released its conclusions, based on the group's analysis of systems' hourly load data. The release was not associated with a specific published report.

27 Public Citizen press release, "Memo Shows Enron Division Headed by Army Secretary Thomas White Manipulated California Electricity Market," 8 May 2002. See www.ferc.gov.

28 Public Citizen press release, 8 May 2002.

29 "Remarks by the President at Energy Policy Meeting," and "Remarks by the President in Question and Answer Session with the Press," both 29 Jan. 2001, White House Office of the Press Secretary, transcript.

30 Lowell Bergman and Jeff Gerth, "Power Trader Tied to Bush Finds Washington All Ears," *New York Times*, 25 May 25 2001.

31 For a thoroughgoing history of the birth of the industry and its complex relations with the U.S. government, see Pringle and Spigelman, *The Nuclear Barons*.

32 World Nuclear Association, London (www.world-nuclear.org); see also www.antenna .nl/wise/uranium/index.html.

33 Uranium Information Center, Ltd., Melbourne, Australia (www.uic.com.au/nip41 .htm)

34 See the company's website at www.cogema.ca.

35 See www.cameco.com.

36 See the firms' websites at www.energyres.com.au and www.riotinto.com.

37 Alison Mitchell and Matthew L. Wald, "Senators Declare Support for Waste Site," *New York Times*, 9 July 2002.

38 Howard W. French, "Japanese Shipment of Nuclear Fuel Raises Security Fears," *New York Times*, 5 July 2002.

39 "Dirty Bombs: Assessing the Threat," *Washington Post*, 2 July 2002.

METALS

1 For a comprehensive history of the copper industry, see Prain, *Copper*.

2 The U.S. Geological Survey provides good basic information on copper industry resources and developments at http://minerals.usgs.gov/minerals/pubs/commodity/copper/.

3 Wright, "Tin," 56.1–56.11.

4 Carlin, "Tin," U.S. Geological Survey, *Minerals Yearbook*, 78.1–78.7. See also Carlin, "Tin," U.S. Geological Survey, *Mineral Commodity Summaries*, 176–77.

5 For basic information on zinc see www.mbendi.co.za/indy/ming/ldzc/p0005.htm. Mbendi Information Services (Pty) Ltd., based at Capetown, South Africa, is an Internet service with news and basic data on subjects involving mining, energy, and international trade.

6 See http://minerals.usgs.gov/minerals/pubs/commodity/lead/.

7 I am especially indebted to Moody, *The Masters of Capital*, which deepened my understanding of the origins of Wall Street and the steel industry. For a wider historical setting, see Hobsbawm, *Industry and Empire*. On the role of the railroad in American economic expansion, see Shannon, *The Farmer's Last Frontier*, esp. chap. 3, "Disposing of the Public Domain."

8 Weiss, *Manganese*. See also www.mbendi.co.za/indy/ming/p0005.htm.

9 See www.mips1.net/422567D90030EAB4/UNID/DMKY-4PEK2F?OpenDocument.

10 For basic information on nickel, see the U.S. Geological Survey site at http://minerals.usgs.gov/minerals/pubs/commodity/nickel. For New Caldonia, see www .cia.gov/cia/publications/factbook/geos/nc.html.

11 For basic information on cobalt see the U.S. Geological Survey's periodic reports and updates at http://minerals.usgs.gov/minerals/pubs/commodity/cobalt/210302.pdf.

12 For basic information on bauxite see the U.S. Geological Survey site: http://minerals
.usgs.gov/minerals/pubs/commodity/bauxite/090302.pdf. See also www.mbendi.com.

13 See http://minerals.usgs.gov/minerals/pubs/commodity/magnesium/401302.pdf.

14 See www.amm.com/ref/magnes.HTM.

15 See www.nrcan.gc.ca/mms/cmy/content/2000/36.pdf.

16 See www.roskill.co.uk/titmet.html.

17 See www.mbendi.co.za/indy/ming/hvym/p0005.htm.

18 See http://minerals.usgs.gov/minerals/pubs/commodity/titanium/stat/.

19 See www.silverinstitute.org. See also www.goldandsilvermines.com/abtsilver.htm.

20 See www.nrcan.gc.ca/mms/efab/mmsd/minerals/silver.htm.

21 For the basic facts on and history of gold see www.goldinstitute.org and Sutherland,
Gold.

22 See http://minerals.usgs.gov/minerals/pubs/commodity/gold/.

23 See www.moles.org/ProjectUnderground/reports/goldpack/fools_gold.html.

24 See Geoffrey S. Plumlee, Pat Edelmann, and Robert C. Bigelow, "The Summitville
Mine and Its Downstream Effects. An Online Update, Open File Report 95-23"
(http://pubs.usgs.gov/of/1995/ofr-95-0023/summit.htm).

25 U.S. Geological Survey, "Mineral Commodity Summaries," Jan. 2002, at http://
minerals.usgs.gov/minerals/pubs/commodity/gold/300302.pdf.

26 See www.moles.org/ProjectUnderground/reports/goldpack/fools_gold.html.

27 Babbit quote at "American Barrick Resources," www.endgame.org/dtc/a.html.

28 Moskowitz, *The Global Marketplace*, gives Anglo's history and basic information. See
also Wheatcroft, *The Randlords*.

29 Ridgeway and St. Clair, *A Pocket Guide to Environmental Bad Guys*, 62–64.

30 See http://minerals.er.usgs.gov/minerals/pubs/commodity/platinum/.

31 Mitchell, "Platinum Group Metals," at www.amm.com/ref/platgrp.htm. American
Metal Market LLC is a division of Metal Bulletin PLC.

32 Douglas Farah, "Easy Money from Gems is Making the Rebels Reluctant to Disarm,"
Washington Post, 17 April 2000. See also World Bank, press briefing on the report,
"Economic Causes of Civil Conflict and Their Implications for Policy," 15 June 2000,
Washington.

33 UN, *Report of the Panel of Experts on Violations of Security Council Sanctions against
UNITA*, 28 Feb. 2000 (www.un.org/News/dh/latest/angolareport_eng.htm).

34 Global Witness, "Conflict Diamonds, Possibilities for the Identification, Certifica-
tion and Control of Diamonds. A Briefing Document" (June 2000).

35 UN, *Report of the Panel of Experts*, 28 Feb. 2000.

36 Ibid., chap. 3, "How UNITA Exchanges Diamonds for Commodities or Cash."

37 Ibid., chap. 4, "Where UNITA Goes to Sell its Diamonds."

38 Ibid., chap 7, "Diamonds as a Tool for Buying Friends and Suppliers."

39 Gary Ralfe, press conference in Russia, Oct. 1997, as quoted in Global Witness,
"Conflict Diamonds."

40 *Observer* (London), 20 June 1999 and *South African Mail & Guardian* (Johannesburg), 17 March 2000, as quoted in Global Witness, "Conflict Diamonds."

41 UN, *Report of the Panel of Experts*, 28 Feb. 2000, 97.

42 Alan Cowell, "Bumpy Start for DeBeers's Retail Diamond Venture," *New York Times*, 21 Nov. 2002.

FORESTS

1 Much of my basic outline of the growth, decline, and renewal of forests relies on Williams's excellent *Americans and Their Forests*. See chap. 4, esp. 82–94.

2 Jensen and Draffan, *Railroads and Clearcuts*, 7, offers a detailed view of the impact of railroads on forests and the timber industry in Western history.

3 Ibid., 39. A satellite photo on 41 presents a clear picture of the effect of overcutting.

4 Williams, *Americans and Their Forests*, 3–4.

5 Hays, *Conservation and the Gospel of Efficiency*, esp. 261–76.

6 Worldwatch Institute, *Vital Signs 2002*, 104.

7 See Howard, *U.S. Timber Production, Trade, Consumption, and Price Statistics*.

8 I am indebted to George Draffan's website, www.endgame.org, itself a project of the Public Information Network, for current data on the business activities of the different lumber companies. His website is chock full of details culled from companies' annual reports, filings before the Securities and Exchange Commission, and statistics compiled by the federal government.

9 "Weyerhaeuser: The Tree Cutting Company," Aug. 2003 (www.endgame.org).

10 Weyerhaeuser annual report, FY 2002 (www.weyerhaeuser.com).

11 See www.internationalpaper.com.

12 See ibid., www.endgame.org, and www.gp.com.

13 See www.rma.org/about_rma/rubber_faqs/.

14 Borkin, *The Crime and Punishment of I.G. Farben*, 76–94.

15 The International Natural Rubber Organization's website (http://www3.jaring.my/ inro/contents.htm) provides useful information on the natural rubber industry.

16 See *Rubber and Plastics News*, 9 July 2001.

17 See www.rma.org/about_rma/rubber_faqs/.

FIBERS

1 For the historical background to the cotton industry, see Cash, *The Mind of the South*, and Hobsbawm, *Industry and Empire*.

2 Braudel, *Capitalism and Material Life*, 237–38. See also www.nps.gov/colo/Jthanout/ SilkProd.html.

3 See www.insects.org/ced1/seric.html.

4 Ibid.

FERTILIZERS

1 For BASF, see the corporate profiles compiled by George Draffan at www.endgame .org/dtc/b.html. Borkin's *The Crime and Punishment of I.G. Farben* excellently de-

scribes just how German scientists struggled to manufacture synthetic nitrates and synthesize coal into oil.

2 See "Phosphate Mining Moving South: Addressing Commonly Asked Questions," at the website of the Florida Institute of Phosphate Research (www.fipr.state.fl.us/Southintro.htm), and "Phosphate Rock" at http://minerals.usgs.gov/minerals/pubs/commodity/phosphate_rock/54 0302.pdf.

3 Waldo Proffitt, "Phosphate's Boom is Ending," *Sarasota-Herald Tribune* (Fla.), 3 Nov. 2002; "Bowling Green Commission Backs Phosphate Industry," *Tampa Tribune* (Fla.), 6 Nov. 2002.

4 "HM Treasury Acts against Money Laundering Risks in Nauru," *Hermes Database*, 14 Dec. 2001; Mark Forbes, "Falling off the Map," *The Age* (Melbourne), 17 Aug. 2002; Moira O'Neill, "How to Pick a Safe Harbor for Your Treasure," *Manchester Guardian Weekly*, 6 Nov. 2002; Russell Robinson, "From Riches to Ruin," *Herald Sun* (Melbourne), 17 Nov. 2002.

FOODS

1 Institute of Medicine, *Emerging Infections*, 64.

2 Institute for Food and Development Policy, *Food First Resource Guide*, 20. For a succinct, critical history of the farm in the West, see Shannon, *Farmer's Last Frontier*.

3 Krebs, *The Corporate Reapers*; Williams, *The Tragedy of American Diplomacy*.

4 Krebs, *The Corporate Reapers*, 362.

5 See the National Cattleman's Beef Association website, www.Beef.org, and "Industry Statistics and Beef," www.foodservice.com, Aug. 2003.

6 "Consumer Appetite for Beef Prevails," Fact Sheet, Nov. 2001, National Cattlemen's Beef Association website.

7 Singer, *Animal Liberation*, 96–112.

8 Schlosser, "The Chain Never Stops."

9 Bill Graveland, "Electronics May Track Future Cattle Disease Outbreaks," CANOE CNEWS (www.cnews.canoe.ca), 16 Aug. 2003.

10 General Accounting Office, *Mad Cow Disease*, 14.

11 "The Return of Mad Cow," at www.Counterpunch.org.

12 General Accounting Office, *Mad Cow Disease*, 37.

13 James Ridgeway, "Slaughterhouse Politics: Ranchers Fought Rules that Might Have Prevented Mad Cow," "Mondo Washington" column *Village Voice*, 31 Dec. 2003–6 Jan. 2004.

14 Institute of Medicine, *Emerging Infections*.

15 Economic Research Service, "U.S. Agricultural Trade Update," 2002, USDA; ERS briefing room, "U.S. Agricultural Trade"; and USDA "Foreign Agricultural Trade in the United States" (FATUS), database, 2000.

16 Figures from Mary Hendrickson and William Heffernan, "Concentration of Agricultural Markets," 2002, for the National Farmers Union.

17 Marvin Hayenga, "Cargill's Acquisition of Continental Grain's Grain Merchandizing Business," AGDM Newsletter (March 1999).

18 See www.Forbes.com, Nov. 2002.

19 Nathan Childs, senior rice analyst at the Economic Research Service, USDA, Aug. 2003.

20 Payer, ed., *Commodity Trade of the Third World*, 106–07. See also Braudel, *Capitalism and Material Life*, 156–58.

21 Smith, *An Inquiry into the Nature and Causes of the Wealth of Nations*, Bk. 1, chap. 11, pt. 1.

22 Payer, ed., *Commodity Trade of the Third World*, 108.

23 Ibid., 111.

24 Dinham and Hines, *Agribusiness in Africa*, 75.

25 John Dorschner, "White Gold: Big Sugar, Florida's Second Most Destructive Industry," *Tropic Magazine* of the *Miami Herald*, 28 Jan. 1990; Roberts, "The Sweethereafter."

26 The Sweetener Users Association is headquartered at One Massachusetts Ave., NW, Washington, D.C.

27 Roberts, "The Sweethereafter."

28 For details on the Fanjul family's sugar operations in Florida, see the Center for Responsive Politics, *The Politics of Sugar*, 41; Roberts, "The Sweethereafter," 54; and Dorschner, "White Gold."

29 For a description of this labor system in action, see Wilkinson, *Big Sugar*.

30 Center for Responsive Politics, *The Politics of Sugar*, 47–50.

31 Ibid., 13–18.

32 Ibid., 48.

33 Ibid., 9.

34 Dorschner, "White Gold."

35 See the fact sheet on the Vanilla.COMpany's website at www.vanilla.com/html/facts-faq.html.

36 See www.michiganfarmbureau.com/press/2002/20020808.php.

37 See "The History of Vanilla" on the website of Nielsen-Massey Vanillas, Inc., at www.nielsenmassey.com/historyofvanilla.htm.

38 See "Cinnamon (Cinnamomum zeylanicum) and CASSIA (Cinnamomum cassia)" at www.hungrymonster.com/FoodFacts/Food_Facts.cfm?Phrase_vch=Spices&fid=5596.

39 See "Mustard and Mustard Seeds at http://homecooking.about.com/library/weekly/aa010101a.htm.

40 See http://batavia.rug.ac.be/.

41 See www.hungrymonster.com/FoodFacts/Food_Facts.cfm?Phrase_vch=Spices&fid=6024.

42 Information on cloves can be found on Gernot Katzer's "Spice Pages" at www-ang.kfunigraz.ac.at/7Ekatzer/engl/generic_frame.html?Syzy_aro.html.

43 Ibid.

44 See "Pepper: The King of Spices" in the *Encyclopedia of Spices* at the Epicenter's website, www.theepicentre.com/Spices/king.html.

45 Ibid.

46 See "Pepper" in Food Product Design's *Spice Rack* (July 2000) at www
    .foodproductdesign.com/archive/2000/0700sr.html.

47 See "Salt: Statistics and Information" on the U.S. Geological Survey's website at
    http://minerals.usgs.gov/minerals/pubs/commodity/salt/. For basic data from the
    industry's point of view, see the Salt Institute's website at http://www.saltinstitute
    .org/. See also the website (http://www.roskill.com/reports/salt) of Rosalie Consult-
    ing Group, Ltd., a British TD UK firm that provides the industry with detailed reports
    on minerals and metals.

48 A 1984 study by the United Nations Conference on Trade and Development (UNCTAD)
    estimated that in 1978 four transnational corporations accounted for one-third of the
    world market for roasted and ground coffee. These same companies controlled four-
    fifths of the market for instant coffee, which represents 20 percent of all coffee sold.

49 Maizels et al., *Commodity Supply Management by Producing Countries*, 30.

50 Two excellent books provide the basics on the history, politics, and economics of
    growing coffee: Dicum and Luttinger, *The Coffee Book*, and Pendergast, *Uncommon
    Grounds*.

51 Payer, ed., *Commodity Trade of the Third World*, 155.

52 Ibid.

53 Maizels et al., *Commodity Supply Management by Producing Countries*, 34.

54 See www.rimag.com/014/400seg.html#coffee.

55 Saritha Rai, "India to Ease Limits on Foreign Ownership of Media and Tea," *New York
    Times*, 26 June 2002.

56 Braudel, *Capitalism and Material Life, 1400–1800* (1972), 179–81.

57 See www.unilever.com/brands/food/lipton.asp?ComponentID=9077&SourcePage
    ID=9451#1.

58 See www.nestle.com/.

59 See www.tata.com/tata_tea/index.htm and www.tatatea.com/tetley_group.htm.

60 The *World Coffee and Tea* magazine is published monthly in Rockville, Maryland. See
    also F.O Licht's *World Tea Markets Monthly*, 4 (July 2002), 1–5.

61 Terrio, *Crafting the Culture and History of French Chocolate*, 10, 246. See also 245–48
    on the exoticism of chocolate. For basic facts regarding cocoa, see the London-
    based International Cocoa Organization's website at www.icco.org. Another useful
    source is www.raise.org; the group is an offshoot of the U.S. government's AID pro-
    gram. Also informative are Morton and Morton, *Chocolate*, and Young, *The Choco-
    late Tree*.

62 Maizels et al., *Commodity Supply Management by Producing Countries*, 25.

63 Norimitsu Onishi, "The Bondage of Poverty that Produces Chocolate," *New York
    Times*, 29 July 2001.

64 Maizels et al., *Commodity Supply Management by Producing Countries*, 28.

65 "America's Private Giants," *Forbes*, 25 Nov. 2002, 174.

66 See www.mars.com.

67 See Reuters, www.planetark.com/dailynewsstory.cfm/newsid/22871/story.htm.

68 Terrio, *Crafting the Culture and History of French Chocolate*, 247.

69 For an overview of the international fishing industry see FAO Fisheries Department,

The State of World Fisheries and Aquaculture, 2000; see also *The Economist*, 19 March 1994, 13.

70 Buck, *Overcapitalization in the U.S. Commercial Fishing Industry.*

71 See Lovitt, "Boats and Banks," 109–16.

72 Helvarg, *Blue Frontier*, 172, 175.

73 Watson and Pauly, "Systematic Distortions in World Fisheries Catch Trends."

74 FAO reports, 1990–1993.

75 Myers and Worm, "Rapid Worldwide Depletion of Predatory Fish Communities"; Seaweb.org press release, 14 May 2003.

76 Watson and Pauly, "Systematic Distortions in World Fisheries Catch Trends."

77 Ibid.

FLOWERS

1 Mackay, *Extraordinary Popular Delusions and the Madness of Crowds*; Dash, *Tulipomania*. The weight of a *last* varied, but was often equal to 4,000 pounds. A *tun* could refer to either a large cask in general or a measure equal to 252 gallons.

2 There are several good sources on the organization and operation of the modern day flower industry. See the International Labor Organization, Sectoral Activities Programme, Industrial Activities Branch, "The World Cut Flower Industry: Trends and Prospects" (working paper, SAP2.80/WP.139). In addition, see *Migration News* (Oct. 1998), from which all statistics in the text derive. One of the best articles is Vivienne, "Flower Trade: San Francisco's Flower Market" in April 2001's *National Geographic Magazine*. An excellent recent research effort was conducted by Cynthia Mellon under the pseudonym "Milagros Campos": *Deceptive Beauty: A Look at the Global Flower Industry*. For a more extensive treatment of the flower industry in Colombia from labor's point of view, see Mellon, "International Codes of Corporate Conduct and the Colombian Export Flower Industry."

3 Andrew Hamer, Director of Operations for Floramor, which is part of Floramex, one of the largest cut-flower traders in the world, quoted in *Floraculture International* (March 1998), 24.

4 Alan Cowell, "Kenya Lets 100 Flowers Bloom," *New York Times*, 23 May 2003.

5 See Mellon, *Deceptive Beauty.*

DRUGS

1 UN Office of Drugs and Crime, spokesperson, Aug. 2003.

2 Collis, *Foreign Mud*, 12–18, provides an overview; see also 74–93. McCoy, *Politics of Heroin*, contains an extensive and excellent account of the drug business from its origins to the end of the Vietnam War.

3 Alfred W. McCoy, "Opium: Opium History, Basic Terms," at http://opioids.com/opium/.

4 See "Breaking Heroin Sources of Supply," fact sheet of the Office of National

Drug Control Policy, at www.whitehousedrugpolicy.gov/publications/international/factsht/heroin.html.

5   UN Office on Drugs and Crime, *World Drug Report 2000*, 37 (www.unodc.org/unodc/world_drug_report.html). See also the Drug Enforcement Administration's June 1996 "The South American Cocaine Trade: An 'Industry' in Transition" at www.usdoj.gov/dea/pubs/intel/cocaine.htm.

6   See Scott Wilson, "Colombia: Cocaine Trade Causes Rifts in Colombian War," *Washington Post*, 16 Sept. 2002.

7   Sibylla Brodzinsky, "Coca Cycle: From Leaf to Market: Following the Trail from the Jungles of Putumayo," MSNBC, 15 Feb. 2001 (http://msnbc.msn.com:80/id/3071728/).

8   Andrew Selsky, "Colombian Official Warns of Risks to U.S. Pilots in Drug War," 14 March 2001, at www.foxnews.com.

9   See "Coca and Colombian Environment (COLCOCA Case)" at the Schaffer Library of Drug Policy (www.druglibrary.org/schaffer/cocaine/cocaenv.htm.

10 Salamonde interview with the *Village Voice*.

11 Larry Rohter, "To Colombians, Drug War Is a Toxic Foe," *New York Times*, 1 May 2000.

12 Ibid.

13 See www.wola.org/publications/publications.htm#DrugPolicy.

14 See James Ridgeway, "Agent Orange, All over Again," *Village Voice*, 1 Aug. 2001. See also Congresswoman Schakowsky's website at www.house.gov/schakowsky.

15 See www.usdoj.gov/dea/concern/#6.

16 See the DEA's drug intelligence brief "The Cannabis Situation in the United States—December 1999" at www.usdoj.gov/dea/pubs/intel/99028/99028.html.

17 See www.usdoj.gov/dea/concern/#7.

18 World Health Organization, "Tobacco Health Facts," fact sheet, April 1999. See also Worldwatch Institute, "Vital Signs Face of the Week," 28 May 2003.

19 Mackay and Eriksen, *The Tobacco Atlas*.

20 BAT *Annual Report*, 2002.

21 See www.gallaher-group.com.

22 See www.rjrt.com/home.asp.

23 Another useful source of information on tobacco and the tobacco industry is David Moyer, *The Tobacco Reference Guide* (2000) on UICC GLOBALink's website at www.globalink.org/tobacco/trg/.

24 See the website of the Nutrition Business Journal at www.nutritionbusiness.com/.

25 McCaleb et al., *Encyclopedia of Popular Herbs*.

26 For the best source of information on pregnant mares and their offspring, see the "Anti-Premarin Campaign" of the United Animal Nations on its website at www.uan.org/premarin/index.html. For a contemporary report, see Nicholas Read, "Thousands of Foals Slaughtered for Popular Drug," *Vancouver Sun*, 8 Sept. 2001.

HUMAN BEINGS

1   Jacobs, "Slavery Worldwide Evil."

2 "Human Trafficking and Migrant Smuggling" 7 Oct. 2002, on Canada's Dept. of Foreign Affairs and International Trade's website, www.dfait-maeci.gc.ca/inter nationalcrime/human_trafficking-en.asp.

3 Several reports give the full dimensions of the slave trade: U.S. Dept. of State, "Victims of Trafficking and Violence Protection Act of 2000: Trafficking in Persons Report" (June 2003), www.state.gov/g/tip/rls/tiprpt/2003/; Human Rights Watch, "Owed Justice: Thai Women Trafficked into Debt Bondage in Japan" (New York, Sept. 2000), www.hrw.org/reports/2000/japan/; and "World Report" (2003), www .hrw.org/wr2k3/. See also "Office to Monitor and Combat Trafficking in Persons" on the State Dept.'s website, http://state.gov/g/tip/.

4 Advocates for Free the Children, "Sexual Exploitation" (Aug. 2003).

5 Advocates for Free the Children, "Child Labor: Research Material" (20 Aug. 2001); American Anti-Slavery Group, "Human Collateral: The Institution of Debt Bondage," www.anti-slavery-org/global/india/debt-html. See also Cockburn, "21st Century Slaves."

6 William Booth, "A High Seas Mystery of Mutiny," *Washington Post*, 14 April 2002.

7 Larry Rohter, "Brazil's Prized Exports Rely on Slaves and Scorched Land," *New York Times*, 25 March 2002.

8 Antony Barnett and Solomon Hughes, "British Firm Accused in U.S. 'Sex Scandal,' " *Observer*, 29 July 2001.

9 "Macedonian Village is Center of Europe Web in Sex Trade," *New York Times*, 28 July 2001.

10 Ian Fisher, "Account of Punjab Rape Tells of a Brutal Society," *New York Times*, 17 July 2002.

11 Human Rights Watch, "U.S. State Department Trafficking Report a 'Mixed Bag,' " press release, 12 July 2001, www.hrw.org/press/2001/07/traffick-0712.htm.

12 Human Rights Watch, "Owed Justice: Thai Women Trafficked into Debt Bondage in Japan" (New York, Sept. 2000), www.hrw.org/reports/2000/japan/.

13 Amnesty International, "SAARC Leader: Make Child Rights a Priority," press release, 28 July 1998.

14 Human Rights Watch, "Owed Justice: Thai Women Trafficked into Debt Bondage in Japan" (New York, Sept. 2000), www.hrw.org/reports/2000/japan/.

15 "Affordable, Expertly Guided Asian Sex Tours for Singles and Couples" at www.love-tours.com. The website bears the disclaimer: "Our tours are for grown men who like grown women. Please DO NOT EVEN ASK us about pictures or tours involving children."

16 Office of Congresswoman Carolyn Maloney, "Maloney Targets Child Sex Predators," press release, 16 May 2001, www.house.gov/Maloney.

17 The American Anti-Slavery Group, "Chattel Slavery in Mauritania," www.anti-slavery .org/global/chattel.html.

18 Charles Jacobs and Mohamed Athie, "Bought and Sold," *New York Times*, 13 July 1994; Amnesty International press release "Stolen Children's Stolen Lives," 11 Sept. 1997.

19 Human Rights Watch Campaign, "Sierra Leone: A Call for Justice" (2000), www .hrw.org/campaigns/sleone/.

20 Humphrey Hawksley, "Ghana's Trapped Slaves," BBC News, 8 Feb. 2001.

21 "Diplomats in Canada 'Abuse' Children," BBC News, 9 Feb. 2001.

22 Ruben Castenada, "Couple Sentenced for Enslaving Illegal Immigrants," *Washington Post*, 28 March 2002.

23 Barry Bearak, "Children as Barter in a Famished Land," *New York Times*, 8 March 2002.

24 James Ridgeway, "Riding for Their Lives," "Mondo Washington" column, *Village Voice*, 6–12 March 2002.

25 UNICEF, "Profiting From Abuse" (2000), www.unicef.org.

26 Ruchira Gupta, journalist and filmmaker, works at UNIFEM as Information and Communications Specialist. Producer, *The Selling of Innocents*, CBC, Associated Producers, Inc., 1996.

27 Council of Europe Parliamentary Assembly, Recommendation 1545 (2002).

28 Ori Twersky, "Renegade Researchers Tell Committee They Will Defy Any U.S. Ban on Human Cloning," *Reuters Health*, 7 Aug. 2001.

29 Quoted in James Ridgeway, "Stem Cell Research 101," *Village Voice*, 1–7 Aug. 2001.

30 Ibid.

31 Ibid.

32 Marina Jimenez and Stewart Bell, with Jim Ritter contributing, "Americans Buying Kidneys in Manila," *National Post*, reprinted in *Chicago Sun-Times*, 22 July 2001.

33 Erik Baard and Rebecca Cooney. "China's Execution, Inc.," *Village Voice*, 2–8 May 2001.

34 Ibid.

35 Craig S. Smith, "In Shift Chinese Carry out Executions by Lethal Injection," *New York Times*, 28 December 2001.

36 Steven Mufson, "Chinese Doctor Tells of Organ Removals after Execution," *Washington Post*, 27 June 2001.

37 "Milburn Condemns Body Parts Trade," BBC, 26 Jan. 2001.

38 Scheper-Hughes, "Truth and Rumour on the Organs Trail," 2–10.

39 Ibid.

40 Ibid.

41 Martha Frase-Blunt, "Ova-Compensating? Women who Donate Eggs to Infertile Couples Earn a Reward but Pay a Price," *Washington Post*, 4 Dec. 2001.

42 Sandra Blakeslee, John M. Broder, Charlie LeDuff, and Andrew Pollack, "In Science's Name, Lucrative Trade in Body Parts," *New York Times*, 12 March 2004.

43 Starr, *Blood*, is an excellent history of blood. For a detailed investigation and chronicle of the modern blood business, see Canada's *Commission of Inquiry on the Blood System in Canada: Final Report* (*Krever Commission Report*).

44 Starr, *Blood*, 46.

45 Henderson quote in Suzi Parker, "Blood Money," *Salon*, 24 Dec. 1998. For the Arkansas State Police investigation of HMA in 1986 see CID (Criminal Investigation Division), ASP-3-A CID ASP investigation of HMA. Dictated by Inv. Anderson; Witness: Dr. Francis M. Henderson. File number: 55-964-86 58-382-86.

46 The CBC aired *Fifth Estate's* "Bad Blood" episode on 6 Jan. 1999.

47   *Krever Commision Report.*

48   CBC, *Fifth Estate,* "Bad Blood," 6 Jan. 1999.

49   Maria L. Henson, "Governor responds to Glover; Clinton not Seeking Lockhart Resignation," *Arkansas Democrat-Gazette,* 8 Aug. 1986.

50   Poor Law Commission, "Inquiry into the Sanitary Conditions of the Labouring Population of Great Britain, 1839, in Ridgeway, *The Politics of Ecology,* 18-39.

51   Ridgeway, *The Politics of Ecology*; Bo Ling is an associate professor of environmental health and engineering at the Chinese Academy of Preventive Medicine, Beijing; *BioCycle* (Jan. 1995); Reuters, Beijing, 24 Dec. 2000.

52   Sam Olukoya, "Nigeria's Dirty Business," BBC, 4 Jan. 2001.

53   Anita Wadhwani, "From India to Nashville: The Human Hair Trade Links People a World Apart," Parts 1–3, *The Tennesseean,* 9–11 March 2003.

54   Ibid.

55   Jen McCaffery, "Rapunzel's Offspring Are Cashing In," *New York Times,* 20 Feb. 2000.

THE SKY

1   See "Earth's Atmosphere" on NASA's website at http://liftoff.msfc.nasa.gov/academy/space/atmosphere.html.

2   EPA spokesperson, phone interview, Aug. 2003.

3   Gelbspan, *The Heat is On,* 160.

4   Myers and Kent, *Environmental Exodus.* See also the website of the Climate Institute, Washington (www.climate.org/).

5   See www.usairways.com/dividendmiles/redeemingmiles/space.htm.

6   Goddard Space Center, "Satellite Situation Report," (Greenbelt, Md., Sept, 1997), http://liftoff.msfc.nasa.gov/academy/rocket_sci/satellites/ssr.htm l; FAA spokesperson, Aug.2003; www.spacetoday.org/Astronauts/SpaceTourists.html.

7   James Dao and Andrew C. Revin, "Revolution in Warfare," *New York Times*; *Science Times,* 16 April 2002.

8   Federation of American Scientists, Project on Government Secrecy, *Secrecy News,* 10 Jan. 2002 (www.fas.org/sgp/news/secrecy/2002/01/011002.html).

9   CNN, 30 Jan. 2002.

10   Environmental Protection Agency, "Aircraft Contrails Factsheet" (Washington, Sept. 2000), www.epa.gov/otaq/regs/nonroad/aviation/contrails.pdf.

11   Environmental News Service, Canberra, Australia, 22 Aug. 2001.

12   Barnes, *Who Owns the Sky?,* 30.

THE OCEANS

1   See World Watch, *A Worldwatch Addendum* (May/June 2001); www.hfac.uh.edu/gl/glossary.htm, and https://www.mises.org/easier/E.asp.

2   Helvarg, *Blue Frontier,* 63.

3   Ibid.

4   Office of Naval Research, Naval Ice Center, Oceanographer of the Navy and the Arctic

Research Commission. *Final Report.* Naval Operations in an Ice-Free Arctic Symposium, 17–18 April 2001; James Ridgeway, "Controversy Boils: New Poles Hint of Doom," "Mondo Washington" column, *Village Voice*, 27 March 2002.

5 James Ridgeway, "Barbarians at the Flood Gates," *Village Voice*, 25 Feb. 1997.

6 McGinn, "Safeguarding the Health of Oceans," Worldwatch Institute Paper #145 (March 1999), www.worldwatch.org/pubs/paper/145/.

7 Stanislav Patin, "Environmental Impact of the Offshore Oil and Gas Industry," transl. by Elena Cascio, at www.offshore_environment.com.

8 Coral reefs, which protect shorelines from storms, are also breeding places for fish, especially in the southern developing countries. They have been damaged by pollution from passing ships, draining rivers, and blast fishing, which removes reef fish for food and aquariums. Blast fishing is bad enough, but some fishers in the Philippines inject cyanide into the reefs to get at the fish. Indonesia's reefs have been especially hurt.

BIODIVERSITY

1 Cummins and Lilliston, *Genetically Engineered Food.* See also Dawkins, *Gene Wars.*

2 "New Enclosures: Alternative Mechanisms to Enhance Corporate Monopoly and BioSerfdom in the 21st Century," Action Group on Erosion, Technology, and Concentration, *Communiqué*, 73 (Nov./Dec. 2001), www.etcgroup.org/documents/NewEnclosuresFinal.pdf.

3 United Nations, *Globalization with a Human Face, Human Development Report 1999* (New York, 1999), http://hdr.undp.org/reports/global/1999/en/.

BIBLIOGRAPHY

Abramowitz, Janet N. *Imperiled Waters, Impoverished Future: The Decline of Freshwater Ecosystems*. Washington: World Watch Institute, 1996.

Adams, Walter. *The Structure of American Industry*. New York: Macmillan, 1977.

Averitt, Paul. *Coal Resources of the United States, January 1, 1974*. U.S. Geological Survey *Bulletin* 1412 (Washington: U.S. Government Printing Office, 1974).

Aykroyd, Wallace R. *The Story of Sugar*. Chicago: Quadrangle Books, 1967.

Bari, Judi. *Timber Wars*. Monroe, Maine: Common Courage Press, 1994.

Barlow, Maude. *Blue Gold: The Global Water Crisis and the Commodification of the World's Water Supply*. San Francisco: International Forum on Globalization, June 1999.

———— and Tony Clarke. *Blue Gold: The Fight to Stop the Corporate Theft of the World's Water*. New York: New Press, 2002.

Barnes, Peter. *Who Owns the Sky?* Washington: Island Press, 2001.

Barnet, Richard J. *The Lean Years: Politics in the Age of Scarcity*. New York: Simon and Schuster, 1980.

Bates, Robert H. *Open-Economy Politics: The Political Economy of the World Coffee Trade*. Princeton: Princeton University Press, 1997.

Bethell, Thomas N. "Conspiracy in Coal." *Washington Monthly* (March 1969).

Bill, James A. *The Eagle and the Lion: The Tragedy of American-Iranian Relations*. New Haven: Yale University Press, 1988.

Blair, John. *The Control of Oil*. New York: Pantheon, 1976.

Borkin, Joseph. *The Crime and Punishment of I. G. Farben*. New York: Free Press, 1978.

Braudel, Fernand. *Capitalism and Material Life, 1400–1800. Translated from the French by Miriam Kochan*. New York: Harper and Row, 1973.

———. *The Mediterranean and the Mediterranean World in the Age of Philip II. Translated from French by Siân Reynolds*. 2 vols. New York: Harper and Row, 1972-73.

Bryce, Robert. *Pipe Dreams: Greed, Ego, and the Death of Enron*. New York: Public Affairs, 2002.

Buck, Eugene H. *Overcapitalization in the U.S. Commercial Fishing Industry*. Washington: Congressional Research Service, 2001.

Burbach, Roger and Patricia Flynn. *Agribusiness in the Americas*. New York: Monthly Review Press, 1980.

Butts, Allison, ed. *Silver: Economics, Metallurgy, and Use*. New York: D. Van Nostrand, 1967.

Canada. *Commission of Inquiry on the Blood System in Canada: Final Report* [Krever Commission]. Ottawa: Canadian Government Publishing, 1997.

Carlin, James F., Jr. "Tin," U.S. Geological Survey, *Mineral Commodity Summaries* (February 2000). http://minerals.usgs.gov/minerals/pubs/commodity/tin/index.html.

———. "Tin," U.S. Geological Survey *Minerals Yearbook* (1999): 78.1–78.7.

Cash, Wilbur J. *The Mind of the South*. New York: Knopf, 1950.

Center for Responsive Politics. *The Politics of Sugar*. Washington, 7 May 1995. www.opensecrets.org/pubs/cashingin_sugar/sugaroo.html.

Churchill, Winston S. *The World Crisis, 1911–1915*. New York: Scribners, 1931.

Clawson, Marion. *The Federal Lands since 1956*. Washington: Resources for the Future, 1965.

Cockburn, Andrew. "21st Century Slaves," *National Geographic* (Sept. 2003).

Cohn, David L. *The Life and Times of King Cotton*. New York: Oxford University Press, 1973.

Collis, Maurice. *Foreign Mud*. London: Faber and Faber 1946.

Commoner, Barry. *The Poverty of Power: Energy and the Economic Crisis*. New York: Knopf, 1976.

Cummins, Ronnie and Ben Lilliston. *Genetically Engineered Food: A Self Defense Guide for Consumers*. New York: Marlowe and Company, 2000.

Dash, Mike. *Tulipomania: The Story of the World's Most Coveted Flower and the Extraordinary Passions It Aroused*. London: Victor Gollancz, 1999.

Dawkins, Kristen. *Gene Wars: The Politics of Biotechnology*. New York: Seven Stories Press, 1997.

Deffeyes, Kenneth S. *Hubbert's Peak: The Impending World Oil Shortage*. Princeton: Princeton University Press, 2001.

Dicum, Gregory and Nona Luttinger. *The Coffee Book: Anatomy of an Industry from Crop to the Last Drop*. New York: New Press, 1999.

Dinham, Barbara and Colin Hines. *Agribusiness in Africa*. Trenton, N.J.: Africa World Press of the Africa Research and Publications Project, 1984.

Dowie, Mark. *Losing Ground: American Environmentalism at the Close of the Twentieth Century*. Cambridge, Mass: MIT Press, 1995.

Easterbrook, Gregg. *A Moment on the Earth: The Coming Age of Environmental Optimism*. New York: Viking, 1995.

Engler, Robert, ed. *America's Energy: Reports from the Nation on 100 years of Struggles for the Democratic Control of Our Energy Resources*. New York: Pantheon, 1980.

Fisher, Douglas Alan. *The Epic of Steel*. New York: Harper and Row, 1963.

Gatt-Fly. *Sugar and Sugarworkers: Popular Report of the International Sugar Workers Conference*. Toronto: Gatt-Fly, 1978.

Gelbspan, Ross. *The Heat is On: The High Stakes Battle over Earth's Threatened Climate*. Reading, Mass.: Addison-Wesley Publishing Company, 1997.

Girvan, Norman. *Corporate Imperialism: Conflict and Expropriation*. New York: Monthly Review Press. 1976.

Grau, Lester W. "Hydrocarbons and a New Strategic Region: The Caspian Sea and Central Asia," *Military Review* (May-June 2001).

Hall, Sam. *The Fourth World: The Heritage of the Arctic and Its Destruction*. New York: Vintage, 1988.

Halliday, Fred. *Iran: Dictatorship and Development*. New York: Penguin, 1979.

Hamilton, Martha M. *The Great American Grain Robbery and Other Stories*. Washington: Agribusiness Accountability Project Study, 1972.

Hays, Samuel P. *Conservation and the Gospel of Efficiency*. Cambridge, Mass.: Harvard University Press, 1959.

Helvarg, David. *Blue Frontier: Saving America's Living Seas*. New York: W. H. Freeman, 2001.

Hertsgaard, Mark. *Nuclear Inc.: The Men and Money behind Nuclear Energy*. New York: Pantheon, 1983.

Hobsbawm, E. J. *Industry and Empire*. New York: Penguin, 1969.

Howard, James L. *U.S. Timber Production, Trade, Consumption, and Price Statistics 1965–1999*. Research Paper FPL-RP-595. Madison, Wisc.: U.S. Dept. of Agriculture, Forest Service, Forest Products Laboratory, April 2001.

Institute for Food and Development Policy. *Food First Resource Guide: Documentation on the Roots of World Hunger and Rural Poverty*. San Francisco: Institute for Food and Development Policy, 1979.

Institute of Medicine. *Emerging Infections: Microbial Threats to Health in the United States*. Washington: National Academy Press, 1992.

International Consortium of Investigative Journalists, Center for Public Integrity. *Making a Killing: The Business of War* (Washington, 28 October 2002). www.publicintegrity.org.

Jacobs, Charles. "Slavery Worldwide Evil," *World and I Magazine* (April 1996).

Jensen, Derrick and George Draffan. *Railroads and Clearcuts*. Spokane, Wash.: Inland Empire Public Lands Council, 1995.

Josephson, Hannah G. *The Golden Threads: New England's Mill Girls and Magnates*. New York: Duell, Sloane, and Pearce, 1949.

Kahn, Ely Jacques. *The Staffs of Life*. Boston: Little, Brown, 1985.

Keddie, Nikki R. and Eric Hooglund. *The Iranian Revolution and the Islamic Republic*. Syracuse, N.Y.: Syracuse University Press, 1986.

Kimball, Lee A. *International Ocean Governance*. Gland, Switzerland: World Conservation Union, 2001.

Klare, Michael T. *Resource Wars: The New Landscape of Global Conflict*. New York: Henry Holt and Company, 2001.

Kluger, Richard. *Ashes to Ashes: America's Hundred Year Cigarette War, the Public Health, and the Unabashed Triumph of Philip Morris*. New York: Knopf, 1996.

Kolpin, Dana W., Edward T. Furlong, Michael T. Meyer, E. Michael Thurman, Steven D. Zaugg, Larry B. Barber, and Herbert T. Buxton. "Pharmaceuticals, Hormones, and Other Organic Wastewater Contaminants in U.S. Streams, 1999–2000: A National Reconnaissance." *Environmental Science and Technology* 36 (March 2002): 1202-11.

Krebs, A. V. *The Corporate Reapers: The Book of Agribusiness*. Washington: Essential Books, 1992.

Ladurie, Emmanuel Le Roy. *Times of Feast, Times of Famine: A History of Climate Change since the Year 1000*. New York: Farrar, Straus and Giroux, 1971.

Lappé, Frances Moore and Joseph Collins, with Cary Fowler. *Food First: Beyond the Myth of Scarcity*. Boston: Houghton Mifflin, 1977.

Lash, Jonathan. *A Season of Spoils. The Story of the Reagan Administration's Attack on the Environment*. New York: Pantheon, 1984.

Lomborg, Bjørn. *The Skeptical Environmentalist: Measuring the Real State of the World*. Cambridge: Cambridge University Press, 2001.

Lovitt, Robb. "Boats and Banks: How Foreign Banks Floated America's Factory Trawler Fleet," *Seafood Leader* (Nov.–Dec. 1994), 109–16.

Mackay, Charles. *Extraordinary Popular Delusions and the Madness of Crowds*. London: Richard Bentley, 1841; reprint. New York: Crown, 1980.

Mackay, Judith and Michael Eriksen, *The Tobacco Atlas*. Geneva: World Health Organization, 2002. www.who.int/tobacco/statistics/tobacco_atlas/en/.

Maizels, Alfred, Robert Bacon, and George Mavrotas. *Commodity Supply Management by Producing Countries: A Case Study of the Tropical Beverage Crops*. Oxford: Oxford University Press, 1997.

Makhijani, Arjun. *Radioactive Heaven and Earth: The Health and Environmental Effects of Nuclear Weapons Testing in, on, and above the Earth*. New York: Council on International and Public Affairs, 1991.

———and Scott Saleska. *High Level Dollars, Low Level Sense: A Report of the Institute for Energy and Environmental Research*. New York: Council on International and Public Affairs. 1992.

Manning, Robert A. *The Asian Energy Factor: Myths and Dilemmas of Energy, Security, and the Pacific Future*. New York: Palgrave. 2000.

Mayer, Carl J. and George A. Riley. *Public Domain. Private Dominion*. San Francisco: Sierra Club Books, 1985.

McCaleb, Robert S., Evelyn Leigh, and Krista Morien. *The Encyclopedia of Popular Herbs: Your Complete Guide to the Leading Medicinal Plants*. Roseville, Calf.: Prima, 2000.

McCoy, Alfred W. *The Politics of Heroin:* CIA Complicity in the Global Drug Trade. New York: Lawrence Hill, 1991.

McDonald, Donald. *A History of Platinum*. London: Johnson, Mathey and Company, 1960.

McGinn, Anne Platt. "Safeguarding the Health of Oceans." Worldwatch Institute Paper #145 (March 1999). www.worldwatch.org/pubs/paper/145/.

Mellon, Cynthia [pseudonym "Milagros Campos"]. *Deceptive Beauty: A Look at the Global Flower Industry*. Vol. 1, Issue 5 in *Global Citizens for a Global Era Series*. Victoria, B.C.: VIDEA, 2002.

———. "International Codes of Corporate Conduct and the Colombian Export Flower Industry: A Look at the Model from a Labor Rights Perspective." M.A. thesis, International Institute for the Sociology of Law, Oñati, Spain, March 2003.

Metcalf, Lee and Vic Reinemer. *Overcharge: How Electric Utilities Exploit and Mislead the Public and What You Can Do about It*. New York: David McKay Company, 1967.

Mining Journal. Annual Review. London, 1978.

Mitchell, Broadus. *The Rise of Cotton Mills in the South*. New York: DeCapo Press, 1968.

Mohide, Thomas Patrick. *Platinum Group Metals—Ontario and the World*. Mineral Policy Background Paper #7. Toronto: Ontario Ministry of Natural Resources, 1979.

Moody, John. *Great Leaders in Business and Politics*. Part 1: *The Masters of Capital*. New Haven: Yale University Press, 1919.

Morgan, Dan. *Merchants of Grain*. New York: Viking Press, 1979.

Morton, Marcia and Frederic Morton. *Chocolate: An Illustrated History*. New York: Crown, 1986.

Moskowitz, Milton. *The Global Marketplace: 102 of the Most Influential Companies outside America*. New York: Macmillan, 1987.

Murray, Roger et al. *The Role of Foreign Firms in Namibia: Studies on External Investment and Black Workers' Conditions*. London: Africa Publications Trust, 1974.

Myers Norman and Jennifer Kent. *Environmental Exodus: An Emergent Crisis in the Global Arena*. Washington: Climate Institute, 1995.

Myers, Ransom and Boris Worm. "Rapid Worldwide Depletion of Predatory Fish Communities," *Nature* (15 May 2003).

North American Congress on Latin America and Empire. *Report: Bolivia, the War Goes On*. 1974.

———. *Report: Steelyard Blues, New Structures in Steel*. New York, January–February 1979.

———. *Report on the Americas: Caribbean Conflict, Jamaica and the U.S.* May–June 1978.

Pacific Studies Center. *Rubber in the World Economy*. Mountain View, Calif, 1977.

Payer, Cheryl, ed. *Commodity Trade of the Third World*. New York: John Wiley and Sons, 1975.

Pendergast, Mark. *Common Grounds: The History of Coffee and How It Transformed Our World*. New York: Basic Books, 1999.

Phillips, Peter and Project Censored. *Censored 2001: 25 Years of Censored News and the Top Censored Stories of the Year*. New York: Seven Stories Press. 2001.

Pope, Liston. *Millhands and Preachers: A Study of Gastonia*. New Haven: Yale University Press, 1942.

Postel, Sandra. *Last Oasis: Facing Water Scarcity*. New York: Norton, 1992.

————. *Pillar of Sand: Can the Irrigation Miracle Last?* New York: Norton, 1999.

Prain, Ronald. *Copper: The Anatomy of an Industry*. London: Mining Journal Books, 1975.

Pratt, Larry. *The Tar Sands: Syncrude and the Politics of Oil*. Edmonton: Hurtig, 1976.

Pringle, Peter and James Spigelman. *The Nuclear Barons*. New York: Holt, Rinehart and Winston, 1981.

Rashid, Ahmed. *Taliban: Militant Islam, Oil, and Fundamentalism in Central Asia*. New Haven: Yale University Press, 2001.

Rich, Bruce. *Mortgaging the Earth: The World Bank, Environmental Impoverishment, and the Crisis of Development*. Boston: Beacon, 1994.

Ridgeway, James. "Out of Gas: Notes on the Energy Crisis." *Ramparts* (Oct. 1973).

————. *The Politics of Ecology*. New York: Dutton, 1970.

————. *Powering Civilization: The Complete Energy Reader*. New York: Pantheon Books, 1982.

————and Bettina Conner. *New Energy: Understanding the Crisis and a Guide to an Alternative Energy System*. Boston: Beacon Press, 1975.

————and Jeffrey St. Clair. *A Pocket Guide to Environmental Bad Guys*. New York: Thunder's Mouth Press, 1998.

Roberts, Paul. "The Sweethereafter: Florida's Everglades Endangered by Sugar Industry." *Harper's Magazine* (1 November 1999).

Roosevelt, Kermit. *Counter Coup: The Struggle for the Control of Iran*. New York: McGraw-Hill, 1979.

Rose, John Holland, Arthur P. Newton, Ernest A. Benians, and Henry Dodwell, eds. *The Cambridge History of the British Empire*. 8 volumes. Cambridge: University of Cambridge Press, 1929–.

Rudolph, Richard and Ridley Scott. *Power Struggle: The Hundred Year War over Electricity*. New York: Harper and Row, 1986.

Sampat, Payal. *Deep Trouble: The Hidden Threat of Groundwater Pollution*. Washington: World Watch Institute, December 2000.

Sampson, Anthony. *The Seven Sisters: The Great Oil Companies and the World They Shaped*. New York: Viking Press, 1975.

Sandberg, Lars G. *Lancashire in Decline: A Study in Entrepreneurship, Technology, and International Trade*. Columbus: Ohio State University Press, 1974.

Scheper-Hughes, Nancy. "Truth and Rumour on the Organs Trail." *Natural History Magazine* (Oct. 1998): 2–10.

Schlosser, Eric. "The Chain Never Stops." *Mother Jones* (July/August 2001).

Shannon, Fred A. *The Farmer's Last Frontier: Agriculture 1860–1897. The Economic History of the United States*, Volume 5. New York: Holt, Rinehart and Winston, 1945.

Sherrill, Robert. *The Oil Follies of 1970–1980: How the Petroleum Industry Stole the Show (And Much More Besides)*. New York, 1983.

Shiva, Vandana. *Water Wars: Privatization, Pollution, and Profit*. Cambridge, Mass.: South End Press, 2002.

Sick, Gary. *All Fall Down: America's Tragic Encounter with Iran*. New York: Random House, 1985.

Singer, Peter. *Animal Liberation: A New Ethics for our Treatment of Animals*. New York: Avon Books, 1975.

Singh, Shansher et al. *Coffee, Tea and Cocoa: Market Prospects and Development Lending*. Washington: World Bank, 1977.

Smith, Adam. *An Inquiry into the Nature and Causes of the Wealth of Nations*. 4 volumes. Edinburgh, 1776; reprint. London: Adam Smith Institute, 2001.

Splitz, Peter H. *Petrochemicals: The Rise of an Industry*. New York: John Wiley and Sons, 1988.

Starr, Douglas. *Blood: An Epic History of Medicine and Commerce*. New York: Knopf, 1999.

Stegner, Wallace. *Beyond the Hundredth Meridian: John Wesley Powell and the Second Opening of the West*. Lincoln: University of Nebraska Press, 1982.

Sternglass, Ernest J. *Low-Level Radiation*. New York: Ballantine, 1972.

Sutherland, Carol H. V. *Gold: Its Beauty, Power and Allure*. New York: McGraw Hill, 1969.

Tarbell, Ida M. *The History of the Standard Oil Company*. New York: Macmillan, 1904.

Terrio, Susan J. *Crafting the Culture and History of French Chocolate*. Berkeley: University of California Press, 2000.

Turner, Frederick Jackson. *Rise of the New West, 1819–1829*. Volume 14, *The American Nation: A History Series*. New York and London: Harper and Brothers, 1906; reprint. Gloucester, Mass.: Peter Smith, 1961.

United Nations. *Report of the Panel of Experts on Violations of Security Council Sanctions against UNITA*. Letter dated 28 February 2000 from the Chairman of the Panel of Experts established by the Security Council pursuant to resolution 1237 (1999) addressed to the Chairman of the Security Council Committee established pursuant to resolution 864 (1993) concerning the situation in Angola. www.un.org/News/dh/latest/angolareport_eng.htm.

———. Conference on Trade and Development. *Marketing and Distribution of Tobacco*. New York, 1978.

———. Food and Agriculture Organization, Fisheries Department. *The State of World Fisheries and Aquaculture, 2000*. Rome, 2000.

United States. Department of Energy, Energy Information Administration. *Annual Energy Outlook 2003*. www.eia.doe.gov/oiaf/aeo/gas.html.

———. Department of Health, Education, and Welfare. *Smoking and Health: A Report of the Surgeon General*. Washington: Government Printing Office, 1979.

———. Department of Interior, Bureau of Mines. *Mineral Facts and Problems*. Bulletin 667. Washington: Government Printing Office, 1975.

———. General Accounting Office. *Oil and Gas Royalty Collections: Serious Financial Management Problems Need Congressional Attention. Report to the Congress by the Comptroller General of the United States*. Washington: U.S. General Accounting Office, 1979.

————. General Accounting Office. *Mad Cow Disease: Improvements in the Animal Feed Ban and other Regulatory Areas Would Strengthen U.S. Prevention Efforts*. Washington: Government Printing Office, January 2002.

Vivienne, Walt. "Flower Trade: San Francisco's Flower Market," *National Geographic Magazine* (April 2001).

Ware, Caroline F. *The Early New England Cotton Manufacture: A Study in Industrial Beginnings*. Boston: Houghton Mifflin, 1931.

Watson, Reg and Daniel Pauly. "Systematic Distortions in World Fisheries Catch Trends." *Nature Journal* (29 Nov. 2001).

Weidner, Bethany. "What Natural Gas Shortage?" *The Progressive* (April 1977).

Weiss, Stanley A. *Manganese: The Other Uses*. London: Metal Bulletin Books, Ltd., 1977.

Welles, Chris. *The Elusive Bonanza: The Story of Oil Shale—America's Richest and Most Neglected Natural Resource*. New York: Dutton, 1970.

Wheatcroft, Geoffrey. *The Randlords*. London: Weidenfeld and Nicolson, 1985.

Wiley, Peter and Robert Gottlieb. *Empires in the Sun. The Rise of the New American West*. New York: G. P. Putnam, 1982.

Wilkinson, Alec. *Big Sugar: Seasons in the Cane Fields of Florida*. New York: Knopf, 1989.

Williams, Michael. *Americans and their Forests*. Cambridge: Cambridge University Press, 1989.

Williams, William Appleman. *The Tragedy of American Diplomacy*. Cleveland, Ohio: World Publishing Company, 1959.

Wilson, Edward O. *The Future of Life*. New York: Knopf, 2002.

World Resources Institute. *Pilot Analysis of Global Ecosystems*. Washington, October 2000.

Worldwatch Institute. *Vital Signs 2002*. New York: Norton, 2002.

Wright, Philip. "Tin," *Canadian Minerals Yearbook*. Ottawa: Energy, Mines and Resources Canada, Minerals, 1997: 56.1–56.11.

Young, Allen M. *The Chocolate Tree: A Natural History of Cacao*. Washington: Smithsonian Institution Press, 1994.

INDEX

American Home Products, 164
American Tobacco, 163
American Water Works Company, 6, 12
Amnesty International, 170, 172
Amsterdam, 146
Anaconda, 62
Anaconda copper mine, 42
Anatolian Plateau, 149
Andean Trade Preferences Act, 148
Anglian Water, 6
Anglo American Corporation, 74
Anglo American Corporation of South
    Africa, 55
Anglo American PLC, 70–71
Anglo-Belgian India Rubber Company, 87
AngloGold, 71
Anglo-Iranian Oil Company, 16
Anglo-Persian Oil Company, 14
Angola, 125; use of diamonds in warfare,
    73, 75–76, 78–80
Animal rights activists, 166
Antarctica, 201
Anti-globalization groups, 207
Antwerp, 74, 76–77
Aquaculture, 140–41
Aquifers. See Groundwater
Arabia, 67
Arabian Sea, 22
Arab traders (historic), 41, 117
Arch Coal, Inc., 12
Archer Daniels Midland (ADM), 111, 136
Arctic, 22, 201
Arctic National Wildlife Refuge, 35
Argentina, 71, 110, 112–13, 139
Argyle, ownership of, 74
Arkansas, 60, 114, 184–85
Arkwright spinning frame, 90
Armenia, 65
Armour (company), 183
Arms, xi, 73, 75–78
Asarco, 72
Ashton Minerals, 74
Asia, 3, 9, 49, 63, 117, 125, 129; aquaculture
    in, 138, 141; as cocoa producer, 136; cot-
ton trade and, 89, 93; eastern, 128; as log
importer, 83–84; medicinal herbs in,
164; Minor, 65; and Pacific region, 160;
rice trade and, 113–15; sex trade in, 174–
75; southwest, 159; as synthetic rubber
producer, 88; as tea producer, 132; use of
human excrement in, 187. *See also*
Southeast Asia *and names of individual
countries*
Assmang, Ltd., 55
Atlanta, 5
Atlantic ocean, 138, 140, 202
Atmosphere. *See* Sky
Atomic Energy Commission, 36
AUP, 111
Auschwitz, 87
Australia, 2, 17, 50, 55, 57, 64, 67, 80, 120,
    177, 187; alternative energy project of,
    196; as bauxite producer, 62–63; as coal
    producer, 9, 13; as copper and tin pro-
    ducer, 46–47; as diamond producer, 73–
    74; gold industry in, 68–69, 71; as lead
    producer, 49; and liquefied gas, 19, 30–
    31; timber industry in, 85; as titanium
    producer, 65; as uranium producer, 37;
    wheat trade and, 110, 112; as zinc pro-
    ducer, 48
Austria, 84, 180
Automobile industry, 48, 57, 63–64, 87
Azerbaijan, 20–21
Azores, 118
Aztecs, 134

Babbitt, Bruce, 70
Bahamas, 158
Baja peninsula, 32
Balkans, 169
Baltic Sea, 202
Baltic States, 152
Bandua, Jacinto (General), 76
Bangkok, 175
Bangladesh, 3, 141, 168, 175, 194
Barents Sea, 201
Bari, Judy, 86

Canada (*continued*)

114–15; as source of gas, 29–30; timber industry in, 81, 83, 85–86; as uranium producer, 36–38; as zinc producer, 48. *See also names of individual provinces*

Canadian Cattle Identification Agency, 107

Canary islands, 118

Candy industry, 121, 124, 136–37

Canning industry, 47–48

Cape of Good Hope, 199

Cape Verde islands, 118

Capon, Tim, 78

Cappadocia, 65

Caquetá River basin, 155

Cargill, 110–11, 136

Caribbean nations, 93–94, 114, 121–22, 124; bauxite industry in, 59–62. *See also names of individual countries*

Carnegie, Andrew, 51–52

Carter, Jimmy, 28

Carter Holt Harvey, 85

Carthaginians, 66

Caspian sea, 19, 20–21, 29

Castro, Fidel, 122

Catholic Church, 134

Cenex Harvest States, 111

Center for Responsive Politics, 123

Central African Empire, 79

Central America, 29, 114, 125, 130, 194. *See also names of individual countries*

Central Asia, 18, 37, 94, 149, 153

Central Intelligence Agency (CIA), 16, 151–52

Central Selling Organization, 74

Chadwick, Sir Edwin, 186

Chemical industry, 55, 58, 98, 101, 127

Chevron, 21

Chile, 43–46, 71, 97–98, 140

China: x, 3, 42, 46–49, 67, 75, 86, 98–99, 124–26, 145, 164–65, 189, 194; body-organ industry in, 178–79; Caspian play and, 21–22; as coal producer, 9, 13; cotton-textile industry in, 90–91, 93–94; as energy consumer, 18–19; fishing industry of, 140–42; gas pipeline projects of, 29–32; grain trade and, 109, 112–114; human excrement in, 187; as magnesium producer, 63–64; opium business in, 150–52; as silk producer, 94–96; slavery and, 168–70; steel trade and, 54; tea trade and, 132, 134; tobacco trade and, 160–61; 200-mile territorial limit and, 20

China National Petroleum Corporation, 31

Chinese National Tobacco Corporation, 161

Chinese traders (historic), ix

Chocolate. *See* Cocoa and chocolate

Chocolate Manufacturers Association, 137

Chrome, 55–56

Churchill, Winston, xiv, 9, 15

Cia de Minas Buenaventura, 67

Cigarettes. *See* Tobacco

Cities Service, 45

Clinton, Bill, 86, 123, 184–85

CNOOC Limited, 31

Coal, 22, 31, 38, 53, 82–83; industry, 10–13; resources, 9

Coarse Grains, 111–12

Cobalt, 53, 58–59

Coca-Cola, 7, 124, 131

Cocaine and coca, 153–57

Cochin, 132

Cocoa and chocolate, 134–37

Coffee, 129–31, 133, 153

COGEMA Resources, Inc., 37–38

Cold War, 199–200

Colombia, 13, 72, 80, 133, 152, 158; cocaine trade and, 153–57; as coffee producer, 129–30; flower industry in, 145–46, 148

Colombo, 132

Colonialism, 46, 72–73, 130, 146; agriculture and, 102–3; aluminum industry and, 59; quest for resources and, ix–x, xii, xiv; railroads and, 50–51; tea trade and, 132; timber industry and, 81. *See also* Belgium, empire of; Great Britain, empire of; Netherlands: empire of; Spain: empire of

Drugs (illicit), xvi, 149. *See also* Cocaine and coca; Marijuana and cannabis products; Medicinal herbs; Opium and heroin; Tobacco

Dunkin' Donuts, 131

DuPont, 12, 65, 96

Dutch East India Company, 126

Dutch traders, 103, 132

Echo Bay Mines, Ltd., 71

Economist, 33

Ecuador, 145–46, 155

Edinburgh, 186

Egypt, 50, 94, 117; in ancient times, 68, 125

Eisenhower, Dwight D., 16, 37

Electrical and electronics industry, 42, 46, 48, 59, 67

Electricity, 61, 103; coal-fired, 10–11; Enron scandal and, 34–35; natural gas and, 29–30, 32–33; nuclear energy and, 38–39

El Paso Natural Gas Company, 27–28, 32

El Salvador, 130

Energy crisis (2000), 33–35

Energy Industry, 17

Energy Resources of Australia, Ltd., 37–38

Energy Task Force, 36

England. *See* Great Britain

Enron-Azurix, 6

Enron Company, 12–13, 34–36

Environmental movement, 12, 28, 53–54, 86, 123

Environmental Protection Agency (U.S.), 156, 193

ETC Group, 207

Ethiopia, 130

Europe, 2–3, 50, 58, 65, 67, 95, 100, 103, 109, 115, 118, 126, 165, 185, 204; aluminum industry and, 60, 62; coal trade and, 9–13; as cocoa consumer, 134–36; as coffee consumer, 129–30; cotton trade and, 90–91; eastern, 132, 160; flower trade and, 144, 146, 148; hashish trade in, 159; mad cow disease in, 107; market for gas in, 26–27, 29; opium trade and, 150, 152–53; spices and, 126, 128; western, 86, 99, 175. *See also* European Union; *and names of individual countries*

European Union, 120–21, 134, 139; grains trade and, 112–14; lead banned by, 47, 49; as raw iron and steel producer, 54; tobacco trade and, 160, 162

Everglades, 123

Exxon, 11–12

Exxon Mobil, 14, 31, 156

Eyadema, Gnassingbe, 77

Falconbridge Mining Company, 57

Fanjul family, 122–23

Farm Credit System, 139

Farms and farming. *See* Agriculture

Federal Power Commission, 25–26

Federal Trade Commission, 182

Feed Grains, 111–12

Fernando Po, 134

Fertilizers, chemical, 3, 121, 187–88; Nitrogen, 97–98; Phosphate, 97–98; Potash, 99

Fibers. *See names of specific types*

Finland, 56, 72, 84

Fishery Products International, 139

Fishing industry, 2, 137–39, 201, 203, 225 n.8; and overfishing, 139–41

Floramerica, 147

Florida, 5, 98, 163, 158; as sugar cane producer, 121–22

Flo-Sun Group, 122

Flowers, cut, 143–48

Foal meat market, 166

Food and Agricultural Organization, 140–41

Food and Drug Administration (U.S.), 7, 107–8, 184

Food for Peace program, xiii, 115

Foods, 100–42. *See also* Agriculture; *and names of specific foods*

Foot-and-mouth disease, 105–6

Ford, 64

Forests and forest-products industry, 81–87

Fort Union formation, 11

France, 60, 85, 91, 95, 151, 177, 120, 126; banking of gold in, 68; cocoa trade and, 134–35; colonial agriculture of, 103, 131; nuclear power and, 38, 40; water privatization in, 5

Freeport McMoRan Copper & Gold, Inc., 71

Free trade and markets, xii, 105–7, 110; NAFTA and, 5, 22–23, 86

Frei regime, 44

Frick, Henry, 51–52

Fuels, 9–40. *See also names of specific fuels*

Fulbright, William, 114

Gabon, 55

Gaffney, Paul (Rear Admiral), 200

Galen (physician), 150

Gallagher Group, PLC, 162

Gambia, 103

Gazprom, 29, 31

Gems and jewels, 80. *See also* Diamonds

General Electric, 74

General Mills, 111

General Nutrition Centers, Inc., 164

Genetic Engineering, 205–6

Georges Bank, 140

Georgia (former Soviet republic), 55

Georgia (U.S.), 63, 93

Georgia Pacific, 84–86

Germany, 38, 60, 84, 91, 97, 134, 136, 161, 177, 180, 187; coal industry in, 13; as cut-flower consumer, 146; market for body parts in, 180; as salt producer, 128; silk trade and, 96

Geron Corporation, 177

Ghana, 79, 103, 133, 136; slavery in, 172–73

Gillespie, Ed, 35

Globalization, xii, xvi, 58, 145, 147, 160, 176

Global Positioning System, 196, 209

Global warming, 193–94, 201, 203–4

Gold, 67–71; 82

Goodyear, 88

Grains, xiii–xiv, 103, 109–11. *See also names of specific types*

Grant, Ulysses S., 82

Great Britain, 22, 27, 38, 67–69, 86, 95, 121, 124, 132, 152, 166, 177, 204; blood centers in, 182; body parts trade in, 179; as cocoa consumer, 136; copper industry in, 42; cotton industry in, 89–92; foot-and-mouth disease in, 105–6; Middle Eastern oil interests of, 14–15; modern sanitation and, 185–86; nuclear development and, 38, 40; steel industry in, 50; water privatization in, 5–6. *See also* Great Britain, empire of

Great Britain, empire of, x, 72–73, 81, 131, 158; colonial agriculture of, 103; cotton industry of, 89–91; grain trade and, 109–10; Jamaican trade and, 61; oil and, xiv–xv, 14–15; opium trade and, 150–51; sugar and slave trades and, 118–20; tea trade and, 132; tin industry and, 46–47. *See also* British Commonwealth

Great Lakes: untapped oil in, 24. *See also names of individual Lakes*

Great Plains, 110, 112

Great Salt Lake, 64

Greece, 49, 65–66, 90, 109, 162, 170

Greenhouse gases, 192–93, 195, 203

Greger, Dr. Michael, 107

Groningen gas field, 27

Groundwater, 2–4

Grupo Mexico, 67

Guangdong Province, 31

Guatemala, 57, 130, 187

Guinea: as bauxite producer, 59, 62–63; diamonds in economy of, 74; independence of, from De Beers, 79

Guinn, Kenny, 39

Gulf of 'Aqaba, 41

Gulf of Guinea, 18

Gulf of Mexico, 24, 26, 32, 140, 202

Gulf War (1991), xv

Guyana, 60–63, 90

Iron ore, 51, 53–54. *See also* Steel and steel industry
Israel, 75, 79, 170, 180
Italy, 91, 95, 109, 158, 166, 189; Iranian oil and, 16
Ivory Coast, 129, 136

Jamaica, 60–63, 122, 124, 158
Japan, 13, 46, 54, 56, 83–84, 91, 95–96, 104, 121, 134, 146, 166, 177, 185, 204; copper and, 42, 45; fishery industry in, 138, 140; grains trade and, 112–15; and liquefied gas, 28; nuclear power and, 38, 40; as platinum consumer, 71–72; tobacco trade and, 161–62; trafficking of women in, 170–71
Japan Tobacco (JT Group), 163
Java, 103
Jego-Quere, 139
Jewelry, 67, 69–71
Johannesburg, 175
John Hopkins University, 177
John Paul II (Pope), 176
J. P. Stevens, 93
Justinian I (Emperor), 95

Kaiser Aluminum & Chemical Corp., 60, 62
Kano, Nigeria, 187–88
Kansas, 112
Kansas City, Mo., 183
Kazakhstan, 37–38, 55–56, 65; oil interests in, 20–21
Kazatomprom Company, 37
Kelda Group, 6
Kelly, William, 50
Kennecott Energy Company, 12
Kennecott Minerals Company, 72
Kentucky, 10, 113, 158, 161
Kenya, 80, 129, 132; cut-flower industry in, 145–46, 148
Kimberley, South Africa, 68
Kimberly-Clark, 86
Kinshasha, Zaire, 58

Korea, 83, 95, 189
Kraft Foods, Inc., 124, 162
Kuala Lumpur, 175
Kumtor gold mine, 38
Kyrgyzstan, 153

Laos, 125, 149, 151
Labor: 10–11, 92–93, 123, 148; in bauxite industry, 60; in coal industry, 10–11; in cotton textile industry, 91–93; in cut-flower industry, 147–48; in meatpacking industry, 105; in steel industry, 53; in sugar industry, 122–24
Latin America, 3, 154, 158; cut-flower labor in, 146–47; decline of cocoa farming in, 135–36. *See also names of individual countries*
Laurium silver-lead mines, 49, 65–66
Lavazza, 131
Law of the Sea Treaty, 20
Lay, Ken, 35
Lead, 47–50, 67
League of Nations, 150
Lebanon, 159, 170
Leiner Health Products, 164
Le Nickel, 56
Leopold II, 87
Lewis, John L., 10–11
Liberia, 18, 73, 75, 77
Liggett Group, 163
Lincoln, Abraham, 82
Lipton, 133
Liquefied Natural Gas (LNG), 19, 27–28, 30–32
Livestock, 103–7
Lockhart, Art, 185
Loews Corporation, 163
London, 42, 77, 132, 175; gold trade in, 68–69
Lonrho, 124
Lorillard Tobacco, 163
Los Angeles, 146
Louisiana, 114, 121
Love, George, 11

Prague, 175
Pratt and Whitney group, 59
Precious Metals, 71. *See also* Gold; Silver
Premarin, 165–66
Proctor and Gamble, 87, 131
Public Citizen, 34
Puerto Rico, 103, 115
Puget Sound, 82
Punjab, 117, 169
Putumayo, 153, 156–57

Qatar, 29, 31, 174, 178
Queensland, 64
Quinn Gillespie and Associates, 35

RAG American Coal Holding, Inc., 13
Railroads, 10, 12, 50, 82, 109–10
Ralfe, Gary, 78
Ranger mine, 38
Reagan, Ronald, 28, 199
Recycling, 47, 49, 56
Red Cross, 182–83
Reeve, Christopher, 176
Renewable energy, 24
Revere, 62
Revolutionary United Front (RUF), 77
Rexall Sundown, 164
Reynolds Metals Company, 60–62
Rhodes, Sir Cecil, 70
Rice, 103, 113–14
Rio Tinto Group, 38, 74
Rio Tinto Zinc Company, 71
R. J. Reynolds Tobacco Holdings, Inc., 163
Rockefeller, John D., xiv, 13–14, 51
Rocky Mountains, 28
Romania, 170
Romans, 41, 66, 90, 125
Rome, 109
Roosevelt, Theodore, 83
Rössing Uranium Mine, 37
RoundUp (herbicide), 155–57
Rubber, 87–88
Russia, 10, 13, 42, 109, 113, 120–21, 134, 158, 161, 194, 201; as diamond producer, 73–

74; as metals producer, 54–55, 57–58, 64–65, 68–69, 71–72; nuclear power and, 27–38; oil and gas industry in, 18, 21, 28; opium trafficking and, 152; as potash producer, 99; satellites and, 196; as source of human hair, 189–90; timber industry and, 83–85
Russian Federation, 140
Rustenberg Platinum Mines, Ltd., 72
Rwanda, 75–76, 130
RWE Group, 12–13
RWE-Thames Water, 6
Rykiel, Sonia, 137

Sable Island, 29
Sahara Desert, 98
Saldamando, Alberto, 155
Salem, 127
Salt Lake City, 30
Samancor, Ltd., 55
San Francisco, 146, 175
Sara Lee, 129, 131
Saskatchewan, 38, 99
Satellites, 195–96
Saudi Arabia, 17–19, 29, 170, 178
Savimbi, Jonas, 76–77
Scandinavia, 56. *See also names of individual countries*
Schakowsky, Jan, 156–57
Scheper-Hughes, Nancy, 180
Second World War, 87
Secretan, Pierre, 42–43
Senate (U.S.), 39. *See also* Congress (U.S.)
September 11, 2001, 152–53
Seven Sisters cartel, xv
Severn Trent, 6
Shaba province, 79
Shanghai, 31, 88
Shanghai Tire and Rubber, 88
Shell, 15, 31
Shenzhen, 31
Shipbuilding industry, 50–51, 64
Shipping industry, 201–2
Sibeka, 75

Tajikstan, 153
Taliban, 22, 152–53
Tanzania, 71, 80, 129
Tata tea, 133
Tate and Lyle, 124
Taylor, Charles, 77
Tea, xvi, 132–33
Tel Aviv, 175
Tengiz oil field, 21
Tennessee Valley Authority, 11, 61
Terminator technology, 208
Tetley Tea, 133
Texas, 10, 30, 93, 121, 128, 163; as producer of grains, 112, 114
Texas Company, 14
Texas Railroad Commission, 15
Textiles. *See* Cotton and cotton textiles; Silk
Thailand, 19, 29, 47, 75, 88, 133; as exporter of rice, 113–14; illicit drugs trade and, 151, 158; slavery and, 168, 170–71, 175
Tian Shan Mountains, 144
Timber, 81–87
Tim Hortons, 131
Tin, 46–48
Titanium, 64
Tobacco, xvi, 103, 159–64
Tobago, 30
Tongass forests, 86
Trade Routes: for body parts, 180; historic, ix, 66, 118, 150–51; for human beings, 169–70, 173–75; for illicit drugs, 152, 158–59; "strategic," x, 18–20, 199–201. *See also* Pipelines
Traitor technology, 208
Transport industry, 88
Transvaal, 72
Trinidad, 30
Tulips, 144
Tulsa, 30
Tunisia, 187
Turkey, 50, 56, 64, 86, 94, 144; Caspian oil and, 21; illicit drugs trade and, 151–52, 159; tobacco trade and, 161–62

Turkmenistan, 20, 21, 134
Tyson Foods, 139

Udachny diamond mine, 74
Uganda, 129–30, 172
Ukraine, 54–55, 64–65
Unilever, 132–33, 136
Union Camp, 85
Union Carbide, 56
UNITA, 75–78
United Animals Nations, 166
United Arab Emirates, 75, 79, 174
United Kingdom. *See* Great Britain
United Mine Workers, 10
United Nations, xi, 20; on biotech patents, 208; on diamonds and arms in Africa, 75–78; and illicit drugs, 151, 154
United Nations Commission on Sustainable Development, 8
United Nations Subcommission for the Protection of Human Rights (2000), 208
United States: aluminum/light metals and, 59–64; biotech industry in, 206, 208; blood banking in, 182–83; body-organs market in, 178, 180; cattle and meat-packing in, 103–9; chocolate business in, 134, 136–37; coal industry in, 9–13; coffee industry in, 129–31; cotton and textiles industry in, 90–94; cut-flower market in, 146, 148; diamond trade and, 73, 75, 79; fishing industry of, 138–40; fresh water in, 1–3, 5–8; grain industry in, 109–16; hair market in, 189; human excrement in, 187–88; illicit drugs market in, 150–53, 157–58; industrialization of farming in, 100–103; industrialization of skies and, 191–97; iron and steel in, 50–59; market for silk in, 96; medicinal herbs in, 164–66; natural gas and, 24–32; nuclear industry in, 36–40, 45–46; oceans and, 199–202, 204; oil industry of, 13–24; older metals and, 43–44, 46–50; as phosphate producer, 99; precious metals and, 66, 68–72; as pro-

James Ridgeway is the Washington correspondent
for the *Village Voice*. He is the author of 16 books,
including *The Ku Klux Klan, Aryan Nations, Nazi
Skinheads, and the Rise of the New White Culture*
(Thunder's Mouth Press, 1990); (with Sylvia Plachy),
Inside the Sex Industry (Powerhouse Books, 1996);
and (with Jasminka Udovicki) *Burn this House: The
Making and Unmaking of Yugoslavia* (Duke University
Press, 1997).

Library of Congress Cataloging-in-Publication Data
Ridgeway, James
It's all for sale : the control of global resources / James Ridgeway.
p. cm.   Includes bibliographical references and index.
ISBN 0-8223-3426-7 (cloth : alk. paper)
ISBN 0-8223-3374-0 (pbk. : alk. paper)
1. Natural resources. 2. Commodity control. 3. Raw materials—
Political aspects. 4. Primary commodities. 5. Strategic materials.
I. Title.
HC85.R533 2004   333.7—dc22   2004009139